POPULAR
Poultry Breeds

TABLE POULTRY FARMING

FANCY POULTRY
YOKOHAMAS OR COCHINS WOULD SUPPLY ALL THE COLOUR AND FEATHER REQUIRED BY THE ARTISTIC TEMPERAMENT OF THE GENTLEMEN FANCIER.

EGG FARMING.
WHITE LEGHORNS & WHITE WYANDOTTES OF GOOD LAYING STRAINS WILL KEEP THE EGG BASKET WELL FILLED

DORKINGS AND INDIAN GAME ARE ESSENTIALLY HIGH CLASS TABLE BREEDS.

BACKYARD FANCIER
BLACK MINORCAS & WHITE ORPINGTONS WILL KEEP THE FAMILY SUPPLIED WITH EGGS ALSO A NICE MEAL WHEN KILLED

CHICKEN FARMING.
WHITE WYANDOTTE WHITE LEGHORN & RHODE ISLAND RED CHICKS ARE THREE OF THE BEST SELLING BREEDS TO HATCH OUT.

SMALLHOLDING AND ALLOTMENT
WHITE WYANDOTTES & ANCONAS WILL TURN ALL WASTE PRODUCE INTO EGGS.

EGGS & TABLE POULTRY FARMING.
LIGHT SUSSEX AND RHODE ISLAND REDS ARE EXCELLENT DUAL BREEDS

POPULAR
Poultry Breeds
DAVID SCRIVENER

THE CROWOOD PRESS

First published in 2009 by
The Crowood Press Ltd
Ramsbury, Marlborough
Wiltshire SN8 2HR

www.crowood.com

British Library Cataloguing-in-Publication Data
A catalogue record for this book is available from the British Library.

ISBN 978 1 84797 103 6

Acknowledgements
Thanks to Mrs Joyce Tarren for allowing me to buy her late husband's collection of photographs, over 180 of which are reproduced in this book; and to Fred Hams and Andrew Sheppy for help with details of some breed histories.

Typeset by Bookcraft, Stroud, Gloucestershire

Printed and bound in Malaysia by Times Offset (M) Sdn Bhd

Contents

'Bantams'. Like many of the illustrations in this book, this picture comes from a print that was originally a free gift with a magazine, in this case Feathered World *magazine, 2 March 1928. Artist: A.J. Simpson*

Introduction

This is intended to be a companion volume to *Rare Poultry Breeds*, which should explain any apparent omissions or inconsistencies in the breeds covered. There are references to some 'rare breeds' where they were involved in the development of 'popular breeds', mainly some now extinct American breeds, which had to be mentioned again in the histories of Plymouth Rocks, Rhode Island Reds and Wyandottes.

Fortunately a lot of detailed information was documented, during the nineteenth and early twentieth centuries, on the origins of the breeds covered in this book. In most cases it has been possible to give names and details of key individuals. In the case of some very ancient breeds, Dorkings for example, although their early history was never recorded, changes made to them in the Victorian era are known. Poultry shows, and the publication of detailed breed standards for show judges to go with them, stimulated most breeders to selectively breed for specific plumage patterns, comb shapes and so on, more than they had before.

In addition to the historical content, there are also some details of the main difficulties in breeding perfect specimens, and how to overcome them. Another of the author's books, *Exhibition Poultry Keeping* (also published by the Crowood Press) covers breeding and showing techniques, including 'double mating' in much greater detail. It did not seem sensible to duplicate too much.

Most of the breeds included in *Popular Poultry Breeds* are also kept by many hundreds, in some cases thousands, of hobbyists all over the world. In some cases their breed standards are noticeably different from one country to another. These differences have been fully covered, and it is hoped that breeders in one country will be interested by the fact that their champion birds would not even be recognized by breeders and judges elsewhere.

Anconas. Originally a free gift with Poultry *magazine, circa 1912. Artist: J.W. Ludlow*

CHAPTER 1

Ancona

Ancona is a city on the east coast of Italy, from which the first recorded shipments of chickens arrived in England in about 1850. Among the first importers and subsequent exhibitors were Mr Simons and Mr John Taylor. The latter, who lived at Cressy House, Shepherd's Bush, London, was also a leading early breeder of Andalusians. For most of the century-and-a-half since then, Anconas have been universally recognized as a single plumage colour breed, black with small white tipping. This was not the case in the first few decades of the changes from simply being local laying hens to being an internationally recognized 'proper' breed. Readers should be aware that in the 1850s, although some birds had already been taken from the west-coast port of Livorno to the USA, the Leghorn breed had not yet been properly established. In addition to the expected ancestors of the present Ancona breed (birds with variations of black-and-white mottling from neat spotting to random markings like the later Exchequer Leghorns), there were also Black-Red/Partridge and Cuckoo barred 'Anconas'. The then local name for black-and-white plumaged birds was 'Marchegiana', the name of a nearby district. However, even these varied, some coloured as Spangled OEG or a white-spotted variation of Duckwing Game.

Although they were good layers, their varied appearance led many authorities in the world of poultry keepers to write them off as mongrels for many years. This attitude started to change when Mr A.W. Geffcken of Southampton obtained a fresh importation of more uniformly coloured Anconas in 1886. These were all black with white spots, although the white markings were not yet as neat and tidy as they would become. They also had the present shank/foot colour of yellow with black spots. Over the following decade Mr Geffcken, and subsequently his customers, spread them around the country. Mrs Constance Bourley of Frankley Rectory near Birmingham was a particularly enthusiastic Ancona breeder of this period, who was quoted in the livestock *Journal Almanack* of 1895 and in *Wright's Book of Poultry* praising their hardiness, activity and laying ability on her wet, windswept hilltop farm. She said most other breeds she had tried had sickened and died there, with the survivors laying very few eggs. In contrast, Anconas kept themselves warm by foraging around the fields, even when there was snow on the ground. No doubt she would have been one of the founder members when the Ancona Club was formed in 1898. Some Ancona Club members concentrated on tidying up their plumage markings, in response to the very generous show prize money and high sale prices of potential winners then. However, Ancona Club members were aware of the dangers of separate exhibition and utility types developing, as happened with some other breeds. The Club agreed a joint breed standard with the National Utility Poultry Society in 1926 to avoid this.

Mrs Bourley's praises of Anconas as active layers in free range conditions were confirmed by hundreds of other small scale poultry keepers through to the 1950s, but they were also rather wild and nervous. These were valuable survival instincts in free range flocks, which could get safely up a tree when foxes were on the prowl, but less welcome with larger scale commercial egg producers. Several such producers gave up Anconas during the 1920s because they could not be tamed when kept in laying flocks of 100 to 1000 in deep litter houses, with or without outside runs (normal commercial conditions then), without birds being lost by panicking. A Mr Messenger reported in 1921 that fifteen glass windows were smashed by a flock of 150 Anconas over a three-week period, despite their attendant being a quiet and elderly man with a lifetime of chicken-keeping experience.

Most Anconas have always been single-combed, but a rose-combed variety was bred by crossing with Hamburghs and Wyandottes, the latter type predominating. These first appeared about 1902–5. Eventually, say by 1930, the only difference was the comb; but up to about 1920 rose-combed Anconas were noticeably heavier and more docile than single-combed Anconas. They were made to cope with cold climates, as large single-combed chickens can suffer from frostbite. There was a separate Rosecomb Ancona Club in the UK, 1923–26.

Francis A. Mortimer of Pottsville, Pennsylvania, was the first to import Anconas to America from England in 1888. He bred and sold several batches before his death a few years later. One buyer was Mr H.J. Branthoover of Pittsburgh, Pennsylvania, who was so impressed that he arranged further importations from Mrs Bourley. Mr Branthoover promoted them, becoming President of the Ancona Club of America, formed in 1903. The club grew from thirteen founders to over 400 members by 1912, but then declined as White Leghorns became the only breed used in America for commercial egg production.

Ancona Bantam

Mr Endson exhibited a team of Ancona Bantams at the 1912 Dairy and Crystal Palace shows, the first mention of them found by the author. Another leading breeder of them was Robert W. Tunstall of Leyburn, Yorkshire. He claimed to have made them from successive generations of ever smaller undersized large Anconas, without crossing with other bantam breeds. However, photos of Ancona Bantams in the 1920s show muscular birds with rather small tails, indicating some breeders had tried crosses with Spangled Old English Game Bantams. Mr D. Dennison was showing rose-combed Ancona Bantams in 1929.

During the 1930s the largest displays of Ancona Bantams, even at major shows, were about twenty birds, Mr Tunstall usually taking most of the prizes. They became more popular after the war, as indicated by an entry of twelve males and twenty-five females at the 1954 National Show at the Olympia exhibition hall, London. The 1962 event in the same hall had an impressive display of sixty-nine Ancona Bantams in six classes (cock, hen, cockerel, pullet, novice male, novice female). Entries at major UK shows in recent years (2000–2007) have been typically about fifty birds.

Mr W.L. Marr of Narembum, New South Wales established Ancona Bantams in Australia. He imported some hatching eggs from Gerald Gill of Kent, England in 1946, just before the Australian government banned all importations of livestock and hatching eggs. Unfortunately only one cockerel was successfully reared from these eggs, but another Australian fancier, Joe Saul, had already started to make a strain by selecting from the smallest available large Anconas. Thus Ancona Bantams were established in Australia from the imported cockerel and 'half size' pullets from Mr Saul. Mr Marr noted (in the 1980 *Bantam Club of N.M. Yearbook*) that other Australian fanciers had also tried crossing with Spangled OEG Bantams, resulting (as in the UK) in Ancona Bantams with rather small tails, some of which (unusually for Mediterranean light breeds) went broody.

ANCONA DESCRIPTION

For full details consult *British Poultry Standards*, the *American Standard of Perfection* or their equivalents in other countries. General

Ancona, large male. Photo: John Tarren

Ancona, large rose-combed female. Photo: John Tarren

body shape is similar to other Mediterranean breeds, perhaps more compact and meatier in body and a little shorter in leg and neck than their relations. Large fowl weights range from 2kg (4½lb) pullets up to 3kg (6½lb) adult cocks. The equivalent bantam weights are 510g (18oz) and 680g (24oz). Most specimens appear to be of approximately correct weight.

Single combs should be of medium size, upright on males, flopping over on females. Some females have rather small, straight combs, which could be helped by keeping pullets in warm houses for a few weeks before showing. The opposite problem is often seen on the rarer rose-combed variety; they often have rather coarse, poorly shaped combs. A neat rose comb, of Wyandotte type with the leader close to the skull, is the ideal. Cool conditions, with access to outside runs, help to limit comb growth. Remember that combs are heat-losing organs. Ear lobes should be medium sized, oval and white. Anconas allowed out on grass sometimes have a yellowish tinge, which is not considered a major fault by most judges, unlike partly red lobes, which are more serious. Eyes are orange-red. The beak should be yellow with black or horn shadings, to match their shanks and feet, which are yellow with black spots.

Ancona, bantam female. Note rather small tail, a legacy from the Spangled OEG Bantams used to make Ancona bantam strains circa 1920. Photo: John Tarren

Plumage is glossy greenish-black with neat white, V-shaped tips on enough of them to give the impression of even markings. A white tip on every feather would be too much. The white tips get larger and more numerous with each moult after they reach maturity. Novice Ancona breeders should be aware that their juvenile plumage is nothing like the adult pattern; instead they have a penguin-like arrangement of white breast and black back and wings. Very few Anconas are still showable by the time they are three years old, although some that were almost completely black in their first year, might come into their prime. The black pigment should extend down to the skin, some faulty specimens having a light undercolour. Excessive white in plumage is most likely to be seen in main wing and tail feathers. A new Blue-Mottled variety has, so far (2008) only been seen in Germany and the Netherlands.

Araucanas. Artist: Cornelis S. Th. van Gink

Rumpless Araucanas. Artist: R. Hoffmann

CHAPTER 2

Araucana, British, Rumpless and Ameraucana

As far as the scientific community was concerned, South American blue-egg laying chickens were first discovered by Prof. Salvadore Castello in 1914, which he made known to the general public in 1921 at the first World Poultry Congress at Den Haag (The Hague), the Netherlands. In fact, European explorers had recorded blue chicken eggs in South America as early as 1520.

Despite being four centuries behind their real initial European discovery, Prof. Castello's rediscovery is a significant part of the history of Araucana chickens, so is as good a start to this chapter as any.

Prof. Castello was Director of the Royal Spanish Poultry School, Arenys De Mar, Barcelona. His duties included advising and lecturing on poultry farming in several Spanish-speaking South American countries. On one such trip, on 6 August 1914, he noticed a lot of blue eggs for sale in the market of Punta Arenas, a city at the southern end of Chile. He also saw the chickens who laid them, which were rumpless, had small single combs, many of them being white or pile in plumage colour. He was told they were called 'Colloncas', and that local people had a vocabulary of poultry-keeping words, completely different from equivalent Spanish terms. Thus there were three unusual features: blue eggs, rumplessness and local linguistics, all suggesting they might have existed in South America for a very long time.

Although nominally a Chilean breed, Araucanas were found in many parts of South America. Ferdinand Magellan's expedition across the Pacific from the Philippines recorded them on the west coast (now Chile) in 1520, but so did Sebastian Cabot, who found blue-egg laying chickens on the east coast (now Brazil), on his expedition which had started from Bristol.

Moving on a few centuries, one wonders why British poultry experts in the nineteenth century had not investigated the matter, as they are clearly described in Bonington Moubray's book *A Practical Treatise on Breeding, Rearing and Fattening all kinds of Domestic Poultry* (various editions, 1815–1842). 'In addition, there is a South American variety, either from Brazil or Buenos Aires, which will roost in trees. They are very beautiful, partridge-spotted and streaked; the eggs small and coloured like those of the pheasant; both the flesh and eggs are fine flavoured and delicate.' ('Buenos Aires' because the state of Argentina did not exist then.)

The chickens were named after the Araucano tribe of Native South Americans, one of the few on the continent who were warlike enough to survive in large numbers as Spanish immigration increased over the centuries.

When the scientific community was made aware of the sixteenth-century references to them being bred in large numbers in many parts of South America, clearly having been there long before Christopher Columbus arrived in 1492, they were faced with a mystery. Domestic chickens were known to be mainly descended from Red Jungle Fowl, with some contributions from the other three species of Jungle Fowl, all of which live in south and east Asia. It was then also thought that all Native Americans came across from northern Asia, Siberia to Alaska (to use current place names) when they were connected, before chickens were domesticated. There have been many suggestions of answers to this riddle, including the domestication of now extinct wild South American species, as none of the living Galliformes, Curassows and Guans are likely candidates.

Recent discoveries have confirmed one of the other suggestions made since the 1920s, that chickens were brought across the Pacific, island by island, by another group of early Native Americans, Polynesians, in ancient times. Chicken bones have been found in South America by palaeontologists which have been dated to a century before Christopher Columbus arrived. There will no doubt be more such discoveries, which will be found to be older.

Rapanui (also known as Olmec) fowl also lay blue eggs, and are found on Easter Island (called Rapu Island locally), Pitcairn and other Polynesian islands. As these are more remote than most places on earth, these are likely to be as near to the ancient ancestors of Araucanas as it will be possible to find.

As blue-egg laying chickens were found in many parts of South America, and were 'just chickens' to the people who kept them, it is not surprising that they vary in appearance. Since 1921 there has been quite a lot of argument among American and European poultry experts on the question of what 'a true Araucana' should look like. The matter was confused by Prof. Castello who, to be fair to him, was misled about the origin of the birds he first obtained. These laid blue eggs, were rumpless, pea-combed, and had very unusual tufts of feathers growing out from near their ears, which soon became popularly known as

'ear rings'. This type, which was said to be known locally as 'Collonca de Artez', eventually became the standard type of rumpless exhibition Araucanas around the poultry-showing world.

They had been supplied to Prof. Castello by Dr Reuben Bustos of Santiago University, who confessed to Prof. Castello after the 1921 World Poultry Congress that they were the result of crossing two different breeds Dr Bustos had discovered many years earlier. Prof. Castello explained the mistake at the next World Poultry Congress in 1924, but it was too late; poultry enthusiasts had taken to the 1921 description of Araucanas, and they still choose not to change the standard to avoid its inherent problems. Embryos with two ear-tuft genes never hatch, and some of those with only one ear-tuft gene have head deformities.

Dr Bustos found his two original breeds when in the Chilean Army in 1881. The Colloncas, the blue-egg laying rumpless type, were in the village of the Araucano chieftain Quineoa. Being rumpless was considered an advantage, as predators had difficulty catching them. The other type, called 'Quetros' locally, were found in another village, the chief of which was Michinues-Toro-Mellin. These birds were tailed, had ear rings, and laid brown eggs. They were popular with the villagers because the cocks had a peculiar crow, possibly a result of the ear-tuft gene affecting their larynx. 'Quetros' apparently translates as 'laughing hens', the sound they made said to resemble human laughter.

Many of the originals had single combs and beards, both now counted as show disqualifications. It was later found that pea comb is associated with blue eggs, both being close together on the same chromosome. Some Colloncas already had pea combs, but as many of the birds made available to American and European fanciers came from Dr Bustos' stock, they nearly all had pea combs. A few single-combed, and a lot of bearded, rumpless Araucanas still appear. There are also a lot without ear tufts, which will always be the case because of its semi-lethal nature. If

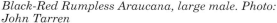
Black-Red Rumpless Araucana, large male. Photo: John Tarren

White Rumpless Araucana, large female. Photo: John Tarren

show birds, with good ear tufts on both sides, are mated together, few chicks will hatch, but birds with no/only one/small ear tufts can be bred with winners for best possible results.

Dr Bustos crossed the two breeds simply because he was intrigued by the two unusual characteristics of ear tufts and rumplessness, and (unfortunately, as it turned out) decided to try to combine both on one bird. Surprisingly, he thought blue eggs were only 'quite interesting', and he never really concentrated on preserving this characteristic. Despite trying for over thirty years (1881–1914) he had not stabilized 'Collonca de Artez' as he imagined them.

There were few shipments of Araucanas from Chile to the USA over the following years, and they were featured by John Robinson in his book *Popular Breeds of Domestic Poultry*, which, as it was published in 1924, must be the first widely available (apart from scientific

works) poultry book to include Araucanas, although Mr Robinson had described them in the November 1923 issue of *Reliable Poultry Journal* (the magazine also published the book). The book has three photos of Araucanas; one shows a pair with single combs, no ear tufts and coloured 'same as Brown Leghorns'. The other two photos show a young Pile cockerel and a White pullet, both with well formed ear tufts. They seem to have small single combs, but as they are both immature, they could have been pea combs. Other Americans imported tailed blue-egg layers, and there were many arguments between groups of fanciers, spanning several decades, which greatly delayed Araucanas being standardized in the USA.

The poultry fancy in the USA has two governing bodies, the American Poultry Association and the American Bantam Association, which say in public that they work in harmony, although this may not have always been true. The ABA first standard-ized Araucanas in 1965, recognizing tailed and rumpless types, with or without ear tufts, perhaps in an attempt to satisfy rival breed-ers. These standards were, of course, only for bantams. The APA called interested parties to their APA Convention, at Pomona, California in 1975 to clarify matters. The APA decided to only recognize the pea-combed, ear-tufted, non-bearded, rumpless type in 1976. The ABA decided to cut down to just this type in 1983, when they were trying to harmonize with APA standards.

However, all was not lost for tailed Araucanas; they were to be standardized under a new name, the Ameraucana. These more convential looking chickens, along with the broadly similar British type Araucana (see below), are both reasonably representative of blue-egg laying chickens as they had been bred for centuries all over the rest of South America. Rumpless 'Colloncas' were probably a speciality of southern Chile.

AMERAUCANA

Harry Cook of New Jersey is mentioned by the Ameraucana Breeders Club as a pioneer breeder of bearded and tailed Araucanas since before 1960, although he was not alone, as there was a short-lived American Araucana Breeders Association which tried to support tailed Araucanas after the APA's decision in 1976. Don Cable of Orangevale, California, Mike Gilbert (Iowa in 1977, later Holmen, Wisconsin) and Jerry Segler, Illinois took up the cause of tailed Araucanas, forming a pro-visional (then unnamed) club in 1978 with eleven scattered founder members, includ-ing Dorian Roxburgh, then Secretary of the British Araucana Club.

The name Ameraucana was preferred by the majority of the founder members over the other proposed alternative: American Araucana. A provisional standard, initially just for bantams, was written in 1979, when the new club had twenty-eight members. Only bantams were standardized initially because

the ABA was usually more willing to accept new breeds than the APA. Ameraucana Bantams were presented at the ABA at Pleasanton, California in November 1979, and were recognized by the ABA in May 1980. The APA accepted large Ameraucanas in 1984, requiring a name change, from Ameraucana Bantam Club to Ameraucana Breeders Club.

BRITISH ARAUCANA

Araucanas seem to have been first brought to the UK in enough numbers for many people to notice in 1930, no doubt including a fair number brought for the World Poultry Congress at the Crystal Palace that July. There were certainly some here earlier, however, including some bought by Ian Kay's father in about 1920 from someone who brought some eggs back from Peru. These were Black-Red Partridge, and the strain was kept going by Ian until about 1970.

Mr F.C. Branwhite, of Often Belchamp Hall, Clare, Suffolk, wrote an article about them in the 1932 *Feathered World Yearbook*. As well as an early UK Araucana breeder, he was also one of the last known people with Yorkshire Hornets. His Araucanas were imported from the USA, and were Black-Reds, with pea combs and green shanks and feet. The article has photos of a male and a female, taken by Arthur Rice. Mr Branwhite preferred red ear lobes, but the cockerel photographed had white lobes. His males weighed 2.7kg (6lb), females 2.5kg (5½lb).

The 1935 *Feathered World Yearbook* had an article on Araucanas by Miss V. Barker Mill, with photos of birds owned by Mrs Whiteway, of Exmouth, Devon, 'who has kept Araucanas for some time'. These birds were similar to Mr Branwhite's.

Another early breeder of Araucanas obtained indirectly from the USA was Mr Ernest Wilford Smith of Great Glen, near Leicester, who bought Black-Reds with single combs from George Beaver, a salesman who had been to America. Mr Smith still had Araucanas

Lavender British type Araucana, bantam female.
Photo: John Tarren

Duckwing British type Araucana, large female.
Photo: John Tarren

when he died, aged 89, in May 1994, that were latterly cared for by a neighbour, Richard Billson, Rare Poultry Society Secretary for many years, then President.

Apart from American stocks, much of the stock which eventually became British type Araucanas (tailed, bearded, crested, and often with Lavender plumage) came to the north of Scotland and the Hebrides. A Chilean nitrate (fertilizer made from dried seabird droppings) ship foundered on the coast somewhere in this area during the thirties, and Araucanas on board became established in the Hebrides from then on. More blue eggs, some of which were incubated, were brought to Scotland from South America in the early years of the Second World War. A club, the Araucana Society of Great Britain, was formed in 1956. Its secretary was Mrs Main, of Turriff, Aberdeenshire, who bred a great many birds (by hobbyist standards), and must be remembered for keeping them going when Araucanas almost died out about 1945. She and the other members, who despite the 'Great Britain' title were almost

all in the north of Scotland and the Scottish islands, adopted beards and crests as their ideal because many of the original birds had them, so it was assumed these features must be correct. Unfortunately, for reasons which are not entirely clear, the ASGB chose not to become involved when English breeders tried to get Araucanas standardized by the PCGB in the 1960s. The ASGB existed until 1985, but never affiliated to the PCGB. This situation could not continue, so English Araucana breeders joined the Rare Poultry Society when it was formed in 1969 (many also had other rare breeds, so were members anyway) as a first step, before they formed a new British Araucana Club, covering the whole of the UK, in 1972.

One long-time Scottish Araucana breeder deserves special mention: George Malcolm, of East Lothian. He started to make Araucana Bantams about 1945, using Belgian Bantams to cross with undersized large Araucanas. Some of the Belgians must have carried the Lavender gene, although it is not known whether they were Lavender Quail, Barbu d'Anvers or Porcelain Barbu d'Uccles. The result was the Lavender British type Araucana, which has remained the most popular variety of the breed ever since. Large Lavenders were made much later by a Mr Edwards, address unknown, who crossed Crested Legbars with other colours, also unknown, of large Araucanas, possibly Blacks.

The British Araucana Club also supports Rumpless Araucanas, but there have never been many breeders of them in the UK. British type Araucanas have been bred in much greater numbers than the number seen at shows would suggest; however, a lot of regular exhibitors keep some for showing their eggs. Here are a few examples of entries at British Araucana Club Annual Shows, which illustrate the gradual increase in the colour varieties kept:

1978 National Show: 15 large (mostly Lavenders), 18 Lavender bts, 5 AOC bts, 9 Rumpless
1990 National Show: 13 large Lavender, 14 large AOC, 0 Rumpless, 28 Lavender bts, 9 Black bts, 6 AOC bts
2004 National Show: Large: 15 Lavender, 9 Black-Red, 15 Black, 15 AOC, 14 AC youngstock. Bantam: 17 Lavender, 5 Black-Red, 11 Black, 18 AOC, 15 AC youngstock. Rumpless: 8 large, 8 bantam.

(Rumpless Araucana Bantams were a recent arrival in the UK then, *see* below for details.)

RUMPLESS ARAUCANA DESCRIPTION

For many years there was only one size of Rumpless Araucanas, a smallish large fowl, but now we have a bantam version; which will no doubt encourage breeders to try to increase the size of their large birds. The British Araucana Club Rumpless standard weights have been 2.7kg (6lb) males, 2.25kg (5lb) females for a long time, although it is highly unlikely that any have ever appeared at a UK

show up to these weights. Weights given in the Netherlands' standards are much more realistic for the majority of Rumpless Araucanas bred worldwide over the last fifty years or so: 1.8–2kg (4–4½lb) males, 1.4–1.6kg (3–3½lb) females. German standard weights represent an achievable target: 2–2.5kg (4½–5½lb) males, 1.6–2kg (3½–4½lb) females.

Rumpless Araucana Bantams were made by two German fanciers, Friedrich Proebsting, of St Augustin–Meindorf, and Hubert Voßhenrich, of Schloss Holter, *circa* 1965–75. They were made by crossing smallish large Rumpless Araucanas, Dutch Bantams and Zwerg-Kaulhuhn (German Rumpless Bantams, similar to UK Rumpless Game Bantams but less 'gamey'). Standard weights are 750g (26oz) males, 650g (23oz) females. Most are bigger and heavier than this, nearer 900g (31oz) and 800g (28oz).

Rumpless standards in all countries require pea combs, ideally small and compact, although many have rather high and floppy combs. Fanciers have to cope with the genetic problems of ear tufts as best they can. Laws have been passed in some countries prohibiting the breeding of livestock with harmful characteristics, which may affect Araucana breeders in future. Such laws, however well intentioned, may unfortunately cause the extinction of some historic breeds of livestock, but as Rumpless-Tufted Araucanas seem to have been a mistake in the first place, it is not a great concern. Beards on Rumpless Araucanas are required in some countries (such as the UK), a disqualification in others (such as the USA), and tolerated in the rest.

The main colour varieties seen around the world are variations of Black-Red, with Partridge, Wheaten or 'in-between' females. The standards in some countries only allow one type of female plumage, but evidence suggests some latitude would be more historically correct. Blue-Reds and Duckwings are also seen, again with historical evidence suggesting a range of female colours should be allowed. There are also Blacks, Blues, Cuckoos and Whites. Piles are not included in the standards of Rumpless Araucanas in many countries, but have been known since the 1920s, so perhaps some of the breed clubs should review this variety.

BRITISH ARAUCANA DESCRIPTION

While still a light breed, these are a good sized utility breed. There are some undersized birds around, but many are well up to standard weights of 2.7–3.2kg (6–7lb) males, 2.25–2.7kg (5–6lb) females. Bantam standard weights are 740–850g (25–30oz) males, 680–790g (24–28oz) females. As is often the case, quite a lot of bantams are above these weights, but over-sized bantam pullets are still very saleable as pet blue-egg layers.

General body shape is similar to many light-to-medium type breeds, as can be seen in the photos. Their most characteristic features are on their heads: a pea comb, compact crest, and beard. Walnut combs have been common over the years, but are a show disqualification.

The most popular colour variety is the Lavender. Good females are not too difficult to breed, but many males have yellow (or 'straw') neck and saddle hackles. Bright sunlight worsens this fault, so runs under the shade of trees are ideal for show birds. Other self colours are Blacks, Blues and Whites. There are also Cuckoo British type Araucanas.

Black-Reds, Blue-Reds, Gold-Duckwings, Silver-Duckwings, Creles, Piles and Spangles are all standardized, in all cases with the relevant Partridge-based female colour pattern. This is no doubt why some Club members have been reluctant to accept wheaten females on Rumpless Araucanas: they have not fully understood the differences in origins of the two types.

Blue-Red large Araucana male. Photo: John Tarren

AMERAUCANA DESCRIPTION

General body shape and type is similar to British type Araucanas, with slightly lower standard weights. The most noticeable difference is that Ameraucanas do not have a crest.

Standardized self-colour varieties are Black, Blue, Buff and White. There are no Lavender Ameraucanas. The patterns are a rather difficult to understand list: Black-Red/Wheaten, Blue-Red/Blue-Wheaten, Brown-Red, Silver Duckwing. The last named apparently with salmon-breasted (that is, a silver version of partridge pattern) females. Considering the other varieties, one would have expected Silver-Wheaten (as Salmon Faverolles) females.

Large Araucana Pile cock. Photo: John Tarren

Asil. Artist: F.W. Perzlmeyer

CHAPTER 3

Asil (formerly Aseel)

The name Asil is derived from an Arabic word meaning pure, or of long pedigree. Similar birds were described in Indian documents written over 3000 years ago, which probably makes Asil the most ancient poultry breed. The name has been applied to fighting cocks across much of Asia. Some regional types, especially in the north-western part of this range, were somewhat larger birds, which have now been standardized for showing in the UK as 'Kulang' or 'Kulang Asil'. They are rare here, and are a recent addition to UK poultry shows, so have not been considered in this book. The smaller type of Asil has never been popular in the UK, but there has been a steady succession of enthusiasts since the first specimens were brought to England in the seventeenth century. They have been shown here, in modest numbers, since Victorian times.

Although there is some variation in size and shape between the larger Kulang type and the smaller versions of Asil, they have enough common features to support their relationship. All have hard, scanty plumage, usually showing bare red skin along the breastbone, on their wing joints and around the vent. Tail feathers are almost straight on males, and carried at or below the horizontal. All types have a powerful skull and beak, a long, very muscular neck, minimal wattles and a small pea or walnut comb. These features have been developed to suit them for their original purpose, 'naked-heel' cockfighting. This is the type of cockfighting where artificial steel or silver spurs are not used, instead the cocks are left to fight with

the tools nature, and a lot of selective breeding, has provided. Cockfights with artificial spurs were sometimes over in under a minute, but naked-heel fights could last an hour or more. Naked-heel fights did not always end in the death of the loser, as one bird might 'run'. Naked-heel cockfighting enthusiasts have long said, with some justification, that unlike the quarry animals in all forms of hunting (including fishing), game cocks fight because they want to. They may be in an enclosure ('pit'), but if one cock ran, that was it, end of contest. Within the social context and mores of those times, all forms of cockfighting were bound by strict rules and conventions, so were not the scenes of bloodlust most people imagine.

The type of Asil mainly bred and exhibited in the UK and elsewhere since the 1860s were based on the type bred in the Mughal kingdom of Oude (or Awadh) in northern India, around Lucknow, *circa* 1670 to 1870. This region was a 'puppet' kingdom for many years under British colonial rule. Some other regional types, such as those traditionally bred around Calcutta, were not too different, and were no doubt added to the stocks brought to England by British army officers and colonial civil servants when they came back on leave or at the end of their time in India. Captain Spencer Astley was one such, employing a dozen Indian servants to look after his Asil until he retired to England in 1898. Another was Charles F. Montresor, who was given a Black Asil hen by the (then) ex-king of Oude. Another was Herbert Atkinson, a wealthy artist who spent summers at his home in Oxfordshire, and winters in India until his death in 1936. An Asil Club briefly existed during the 1890s, and he was its secretary. Robert de Courcy Peele, of Ludlow, Shropshire, was secretary of the Aseel Club (the spelling used then), when it was re-activated for a few more years, *circa* 1909–22.

All of the above had seen Asil in India, so were occasionally upset by some of the birds bred and given prizes by fanciers and judges at British shows by those who were not so well travelled. It was suspected that some had been crossed with Indian Game/Cornish, as they had puffy cheeks and were too meaty, especially on their back (over their hip joints). The two most popular plumage colour varieties with these exhibitors and judges were Spangles and Whites. Those who had been to India had seen these colours there, but knew that Indian breeders thought they were not as good as various shades of Black-Red cocks (a few white feathers were not considered a problem) and hens which normally ranged from Black, via 'Grouse' or 'Pheasant' ('messed up' variations of the Dark Indian Game pattern), to Cinnamon and the darker shades of Wheaten (similar to Malay hens). Other colours seen since the mid-nineteenth century have included Black-Mottles, Duckwings, Greys and Piles. All are permitted, but to most Asil enthusiasts, are seldom as good as Reds. There are a number of splendid looking Spangled Asil, most of which are believed to be from German strains, seen at UK shows; but when handled, most of them have the same fleshy type (possibly part Indian Game) criticized by Atkinson in the 1920s.

ASIL BANTAM

No records have been found on the origins of the first Asil Bantams, which were popular from 1875 to 1900 but then died out. They may have been Ko-Shamo, Chibi-Shamo or Nankin-Shamo which were incorrectly identified by the fanciers who bought them, probably from ships in Falmouth or other ports in south-west England.

Black-Red Asil, male. Photo: John Tarren

Virtually nothing was seen of them, or anything like them, again in the UK until 1975–80. The birds that appeared then – probably from Germany – were very small Black-Red males and Wheaten females. They were incorrectly called Tuzo at the time. We now know Tuzo are a larger breed (halfway between large fowl and bantam size), only recognized in one colour variety, Black. A few fanciers in Belgium, Germany, the Netherlands and the UK have been working on new strains since the 1990s.

ASIL DESCRIPTION

There are full standards in American, British, Dutch and German Poultry Standards books, so this section concentrates on the key points.

The beak must be short, strong and thick. Its colour can range from ivory or yellow through to very dark horn, almost black; the darker colours are usually seen on Black, 'Grouse' and 'Pheasant' hens. Correct eye colour is considered an important breed characteristic, the ideal being yellow or white, often with some red blood vessels visible. Young birds usually have darker eye colour, which gradually lightens between 8 and 18 months of age. Asil have neat, small pea combs and no wattles at all. Instead of wattles, the skin of the throat is bright red and bare of feathers some way down the neck. The neck is of medium length and very muscular. The neck hackle feathers of males are short, not covering the shoulders.

Spangled Asil, male. Photo: John Tarren

The correct body shape is distinctive and an important breed characteristic, broad across the shoulders and shallow from the back down to the breast. Some birds seen at shows have been too deep-bodied, suggesting they were not 'the real thing'. Body plumage should be sparse and close, showing bare red skin along the breastbone, around the vent and on wing joints. The tail should be horizontal or lower, in line with the back. Male tail sickle feathers are fairly straight, sometimes described as sabre shaped. Legs are medium length, with very muscular thighs. Scales on shanks are prominent, giving a 'square' appearance. Shanks and feet are usually creamy or yellow; horn, olive or black on dark-plumaged varieties.

There are no fixed plumage colours, but most experts prefer the traditional colour varieties over new colours which might indicate dubious ancestry. Remember the name of the breed means 'of long pedigree'. Within these conventions, Asil are not judged on fine details of plumage colour. The majority of males are Black-Reds, but it does not matter if there is

some red or brown in breast or thighs, or which shade of 'red', or if there are some white feathers. Spangles are a traditional variety, as are any birds between Black-Red and Spangled. The comments made previously about some Spangled Asil being suspiciously fleshy do not mean that there are no good Spangles. The hens to go with Black-Red cocks range from 'Grouse' and 'Pheasant' to 'Cinnamon' and 'Red Wheaten'. The first two have a rich brown ground colour with black peppering (Grouse) or an irregular version of the Dark Indian Game/Cornish pattern (Pheasant). Spangled hens usually have a red wheaten ground colour with variable black-and-white spangles.

Black Asil, White Asil and Pile Asil are seen occasionally, but their plumage colour names should be regarded as a rough guide only. For example, White Asil are usually more or less 'brassy'. A snow-white Asil (as is expected with other exhibition poultry breeds) would probably be too profuse and soft in plumage to be regarded as a good specimen of this breed. Similarly, Black Asil usually have a few red or brown feathers mixed in; but if its head, body shape and other important characteristics are correct, no one cares. Duckwing and Grey Asil cocks are rarely seen, and the hens to go with them will probably be silver ground coloured versions of Grouse or Pheasant, or Silver Wheatens. Salmon-breasted Duckwing hens (as Duckwing Modern Game or OEG) would be regarded with extreme suspicion.

ASIL MANAGEMENT

Asil are usually bred in pairs, trios or (at most) quartets. Where two or three pullets are together, they will be sisters who have been reared together. When one goes broody, it is seldom possible to put them back together after they have been away sitting and chick rearing. Asil are usually kept in a range of netting-fronted, aviary-type pens. Each pen needs to be about 1.5 × 2 metres (4½ × 6ft) for a pair or group of youngsters. This makes them a very time-consuming breed. The positive side of this is that they usually become remarkably tame.

Australorps. Artist: C.S. Th. van Gink

CHAPTER 4

Australorp

William Cook's first Black Orpingtons, which he launched in 1886, were quite tight-feathered, much more like Australorps than the much more profusely-feathered Black Orpingtons which were developed by Joseph Partington a few years later, and have been the accepted type of exhibition Orpington ever since. Pictures in his book, W. Cook's *Poultry Breeder and Feeder*, clearly show the first Orpintons were like today's Australorps. Cook's type were exported to Australia as soon as 1887, with Partington's type following soon afterwards. Robert Burns, of Sladevale, Warwick, Queensland, kept both types separately for many years: Cook's for eggs, Partington's for prizes. *See* Chapter 24: Orpington for more details.

One of the key people involved in establishing Australorps as a recognized breed on its own, separate from Orpingtons, was Arthur Harwood (2 June 1887–3 October 1981). He was an Englishman who moved to Australia in July 1910, having previously worked for William Cook's daughter (after Cook's death) at St Mary Cray, Kent. He became Chief Poultry Officer at Galton (Agricultural) College, Queensland until he retired in 1938. According to some accounts he coined the name 'Australorps' (to replace the long-winded title 'Australian Utility Orpingtons') at a poultry farmers' conference at the college in 1919. The name 'Australs' was also in use at the time by several people, including George Greenwood, who was a leading breeder of both utility type and exhibition

Orpingtons in Australia. They may have argued over who invented which name, but agreed that Australian fanciers and farmers needed to be educated about the increasing differences between utility and show types. Australian poultry keepers had used *British Poultry Standards* for Orpingtons, and the British Orpington standard has never been changed to accurately describe the fluffy exhibition type. Some breeders and other experts in Australia opposed the new names, taking the attitude that the published Orpington standard still fitted the utility type. Among these was James Hadlington, New South Wales Government Poultry Expert based at Hawkesbury Agricultural College, Richmond, NSW. Like many poultry experts at the time, he supported pure breeds, even for commercial production. Many commercial breeders were already selecting stock entirely on egg numbers, not caring about plumage colour, and so on. To them a new name meant they could forget breed standards. James Hadlington did not approve, although his strains of 'Utility type Orpingtons' (his preferred name) eventually became Australorps.

Significant importations of 'Australian Black Orpingtons' to England were made in 1921, and there may have been smaller importations some years previously. The 'Austral Orpington Club' was formed in the UK in August 1921, and the name 'Australorp' was well known, if not universally used, in the UK, in 1921, with the club's name being changed to 'Australorp Club' in 1924.

Charles Arthur House, editor of *Poultry World* magazine (UK) went on a tour of Australia in 1922. In discussions with Australian breeders (who were still arguing about the name), he told them about recent developments in the UK; suggesting they had little choice but to follow suit. Australorps were eventually standardized in Australia in 1930.

British breeders started to discuss standards in 1921, but their first application for recognition by the PCGB in November 1923 was refused because the Council was concerned about the variability of imported stock: some like fluffy Orpingtons, others tighter feathered and smaller. The Australorp standard was eventually passed by the PCGB Council in 1928.

One of the first places C.A. House visited on his arrival was the Western Australia egg laying trial, where over half of the birds entered were utility Black Orpingtons/Australorps, most of the remainder being White Leghorns, very different from British tests, where Black Orpingtons were rare, Rhode Island Reds and Light Sussex being most popular. Australian breeders had certainly improved the laying performance of utility Black Orpingtons since the 1890s. One hen laid a record-breaking 339 eggs in 365 days at the 1912–22 trial at Bendigo, near Melbourne, Victoria. Another batch of six pullets laid 1760 eggs, an average of 291.4 each. A lot more birds were recorded as laying over 280 eggs, and these performances were publicized by UK importers. As soon as they had enough birds, they entered Australorps in British laying trials, with much poorer results, usually nearer 200 eggs, in our colder climate.

Despite the best efforts of the Australorp Club and a few large-scale breeders, they were never as popular in the UK itself as they were overseas, although they were bred commercially and exhibited in fair numbers, such as 81 birds at the 1934 Australorp Club Show at Olympia. Their black plumage would not have helped as cockerels were then reared for the table, and would have left black feather stubs and shanks.

This level of support for Australorps continued through to the early 1960s, after which they gradually declined until the present (2008) situation, where large Australorps are rarer in the UK than some rare breeds. Blue and White varieties have recently been added to the range, and all three varieties are still neat, tidy and attractive birds, but there are plenty of more exotic breeds for hobbyists.

AUSTRALORP BANTAM

Roy Corner of Hereford (Australorp Club Secretary 1930–35) and Jack Mann made Australorp Bantams, first showing them in 1934. No details have been found on how they made them, but we can assume it was by crossing undersized large Australorps with suitable bantams, possibly including Black Wyandottes. They do not seem to have attracted much interest from other fanciers before the war, but their practical qualities during hostilities and food rationing (which continued well into the 1950s) were clearly noticed, although not widely written about. At the 1954 National Poultry Show there was an impressive entry of 43 birds in four classes. They have continued to grow in popularity, with displays of over 100 bantams at the Australorp Club Show being not unusual. Regular exhibitors appreciate that while Black Australorp Bantams might have little appeal to the general public, they are smart little birds, easy to keep and prepare for showing.

Entirely separate strains were made by German fanciers, first exhibited in the new breeds section of the 1956 Hannover Show. More details are known of the breeds used to make them in Germany: large Australorps, Black Wyandotte Bantams, Barnevelder Bantams, Rhode Island Red Bantams and Black German Langshan Bantams. There is a noticeable difference in the back and tail profile of Australorp Bantams in the UK and Germany. In the UK the back/saddle plumage rises in an almost straight line to the tip of the tail, very similar to the top profile of German Langshans. German fanciers have avoided this similarity by selecting a flatter back with a distinct angle at the base of the tail. No

Black Australorp, bantam male. Photo: John Tarren

Blue Australorp, bantam female. Photo: John Tarren

doubt they did so to emphasize the difference between the two breeds. German Langshan Bantams have become quite popular in the UK since the 1990s, but were unknown here when Australorp Bantams became popular in the 1950s and 1960s. Photos of large Australorps through the 1920s and 1930s show enough variation to justify both types as true miniatures of the original fowl.

Blue Australorp Bantams were first made by Alan Maskrey of Sheffield, who started with a Black Australorp Bantam × Blue Orpington Bantam mating. Jack Turton of Ramsgate also started another strain on the same lines, both fanciers beginning about 1973, and having their new colour variety accepted by the Australorp Club in 1978, confirmed by the PCGB in 1979. Herbert Todtmann of Minden-Stemmer made German standard shape Blues a few years later, standardized in 1986.

White Australorp Bantams were made in Germany by Wilhelm Mayland of Wermelskirchen about 1973, with Alan Maskrey following with a British-shape version in the early 1980s. Black and Blue Australorps had followed the Orpington standard in eye, shank and foot colour, but this would have made White Australorps rather too similar to White Sussex for comfort, so White Australorps were made with dark eyes and slate shanks and feet.

AUSTRALORP DESCRIPTION

Full details are included in American, British, Dutch, German and New Zealand poultry standards books. Novice breeders should visit shows and established breeders to fully understand the details of size and shape required. Large Australorp weights range from 2.5kg (5½lb) pullets up to 4.5kg (10lb) adult cocks. The bantams have an equivalent weight range of 800 to 1000g (28–36oz), and most appear to be close to these weights.

The comb should be single, straight, not too large and nicely serrated. Eye colour should be very dark brown or black. Comb, lobes, wattles and facial skin should all be red. Many pullets either have red faces and light eyes or dark eyes and equally dark facial skin. Both are faulty, but fortunately most of the dark-faced pullets lighten to red faces in their second year.

Young Black Australorps have black shanks and feet, fading to slate on older birds, the colour required on Blue and White Australorps of all ages. All colours should have white toenails and white foot soles.

Plumage should be pure white on Whites, black with a green gloss on Blacks (blue or purple gloss a serious fault) and bluish-grey with fuzzy lacing on Blues. Blues are by far the most difficult to breed, many being too dark or an uneven mixture of shades.

'Belgian Bantams'. Originally a free gift with Feathered World *magazine, 1931. Artist: Harry Hoyle*

CHAPTER 5

Barbu d'Anvers (Antwerpse Baardkriel or Antwerp Belgian)

This true bantam is unusual among old poultry breeds in that it has been kept by many more people and in far greater numbers from the 1970s up to the present day than ever before. It was established as a breed to an agreed standard in the late nineteenth century, but what were probably its ancestors existed long before then. Some sources mention that small bearded chickens of the Quail plumage pattern (a characteristic colour variety of Barbu d'Anvers) are depicted in one or more paintings by Albert Cuyp (1620–1691), but no details of exactly which painting(s) are given.

The history of the breed really started in 1895, when fanciers in bilingual Belgium started showing Barbu d'Anvers/Antwerpse Baardkriel at Brussels (51 birds), Liège and elsewhere. A breed club, Club Avicole du Barbu Nain, was formed in 1904. Nain is French for dwarf, the general term for bantams or miniature chickens in France. There were twenty-three founder members, all still known, the most significant being René Delin (1877–1961, also a specialist poultry artist), Robert Pauwels (who made Barbu d'Grubbe and Barbu d'Everberg, rumpless versions of Barbu d'Anvers and Barbu d'Uccles, fully described in *Rare Poultry Breeds*), and L. Vander Snickt (a leading Belgian poultry expert at the time). The club published a standard which was officially recognized on 12 May 1905. There were three colour varieties, Black, Cuckoo and White at this stage. The Quail pattern was added on 18 April 1910. Their Club Show on 31 July 1910 had 465 birds entered, representing excellent progress. Het Antwerpse Baardkrielen Club was mentioned in 1916, it not being clear if this was the Flemish name for the Club Avicole du Barbu Nain or if it was a separate name for Flemish speakers.

Belgian fanciers successfully introduced their new bantams to the UK at the Crystal Palace Shows of 1911, 1912 and 1913 in London.Their displays attracted a lot of interest; however, this was mostly from casual visitors and beginners to showing rather than 'old hands'. Six Black Barbu d'Anvers had been shown by G. de la Kethulle de Ryhore at the 1901 Alexandra Palace Show, London, but not many people seem to have appreciated them. The British Belgian Bantam Club was formed in 1915, the first secretary being Robert Terrot, of Cookham, Berkshire. Mr and Mrs Terrot also promoted Malines fowl, a large Belgian heavy breed. Progress was held back by both world wars and the Great Depression, so Barbu d'Anvers did not really begin to gain popularity until after 1945. Normal life suffered even more in Belgium from 1914 to 1945, so the efforts by Belgian fanciers to popularize their breed in the UK proved vital, as British fanciers were able to help their Belgian friends restock in 1919 and 1945.

Black-Mottled Barbu d'Anvers male. One of the first seen in the UK, exhibited by Mr Jamotte at the 1912 Crystal Palace Show. Artist: A.J. Simpson

Barbu d'Anvers, Black-Mottled male and Cuckoo female. Artist: René Delin, one of the founder breeders. These show the ideal type, which clearly did not exist in 1912

Barbu d'Anvers were held back from achieving greater popularity in the UK before 1945 by the reluctance of many show organizers to provide classes for them, and older judges being less than enthusiastic about this new breed when they had to compete in mixed AOV classes. The British Belgian Bantam Club did not have enough funds, or wealthy members, to guarantee show organizers against losses from the generous prize money offered in those days. Even if there were classes, they were often poorly assessed by unsympathetic judges who seemed to positively refuse to learn about any breed of which they did not approve. Fortunately, now almost all UK shows have several classes of Barbu d'Anvers, which are properly judged. The British Belgian Bantam Club, along with some other True Bantam breed clubs, holds its main annual show in conjunction with the Reading Bantam Club Show, now held at Newbury.

They have been known in the USA since the 1920s, but have not been as popular there as in Belgium, Germany, the Netherlands or (eventually) the UK. Several names for them seem to be used in the USA: Belgian d'Anver, Belgian Bearded d'Anver or Antwerp Belgian. The highest show entry in the USA found by the author was at the 1998 Ohio National Show where 221 were entered by twenty-five exhibitors. Fewer colour varieties are bred in the USA than elsewhere, as seen in this breakdown of the Ohio total: 183 Quail, 20 Self Blue [Lavender?], 11 Black, 5 Blue-Quail, 1 White and 1 Blue.

BARBU D'ANVERS, TYPE DESCRIPTION

This is a small breed. Exact weights differ in standards books around the world, the clearest weight requirements appearing in Dutch standards: 500g (17oz) pullet, 600g (21oz) hen and cockerel, 700g (25oz) cock. They should be compact and cobby, appearing to have almost no back at all as the profuse neck feathering reaches halfway along the back, and the plumage of the lower back rises to the tail at the same point. The tail is long and held high. On males, the sickle feathers should be fairly straight: more like a sabre than a sickle. Wings are carried pointing down to the ground.

Head characteristics are very important on Barbu d'Anvers, starting with the compact rose comb with a leader (rear spike) following the skull, pointing down the neck. Ideally, wattles should be completely absent as they detract from one of their main features, the well developed beard. This should be in a tri-lobed formation. Neck hackle feathers should be very profuse, with the breed's characteristic 'boule', some of the feathers on the side of the neck pointing to the rear.

Eye, beak, shank and feet colours vary according to plumage colour variety, all being almost black on Blacks. Many other varieties have red eyes and slate-blue beak, shanks and feet. Cuckoos and Whites have white shanks and feet.

BARBU D'ANVERS PLUMAGE COLOURS

This breed is best known for the Quail pattern, which exists in five colour versions, detailed below. Millefleur and Porcelaine, colour varieties usually associated with Barbu d'Uccles, are also recognized in Barbu d'Anvers, but are comparatively rare. Other, more conventional, colour varieties of Barbu d'Anvers are Black, Black-Mottle, Blue, Blue-Mottle, Cuckoo, Ermine (as Columbian in other breeds), Fawn-Ermine (as Buff Columbian in other breeds) and Lavender. Self Buff, Black-Red/Partridge and Silver Duckwing (Silver Partridge) are listed as recognized varieties, but rarely seen.

The general colour scheme of Normal Quails consists of light ochre beard, breast and legs contrasting with dark brown ('umber') neck, back and tail plumage with bright ochre or golden feather shafts and lacing. Tail feathers on males are glossy greenish-black, again with light shafts and edging. Consult a standards book for full details. Neck, back, wing and tail plumage is not as dark as it should be on many birds. This is because correct, dark 'top colour' often brings faulty dark markings on the breast. Breeders, understandably, wish to avoid double mating, but may not achieve the best compromise colours with single mating.

Quail Barbu d'Anvers in Germany and the Netherlands have darker beard, breast and legs than Normal Quails in Belgium and the UK. The shade is a rich buff. These have appeared in the UK, where they are called Red Quail.

Blue Quail have the same pattern as Normal Quail but with all umber brown and black

Black Barbu d'Anvers, male. Photo: John Tarren

Lavender Quail Barbu d'Anvers, female. Photo: John Tarren

parts replaced by blue, in parts with a brownish tinge.

Lavender Quail Barbu d'Anvers are the same pattern with the ochre underparts changed to creamy shades and the dark upper parts changed to lavender-blue with cream shafts, and so on.

Silver Quail are the same pattern, crisply defined in black and white.

It is normal practice to cross Normal Quail with Blue, Lavender or Silver Quails, but these three should not be mated together. If Lavender Quails are mated together for several generations they can become very faded, so it is important to breed them together with a related group of Normal Quails which are carrying the recessive Lavender gene. At time of writing (2007) most Silver Quails were too large, so some really good quality Normal Quails, small and with neat, low combs, will help to improve your Silvers.

Returning to the conventional colour varieties, Black Barbu d'Anvers are usually much better in size, shape, comb, beard and so on, than Cuckoos and Blues, so similar crossing is useful. Again, do not mate Blues with Cuckoos. In the case of Cuckoos, from a Cuckoo male × Black female mating, the resulting pullets should be excellent Cuckoos, but the cockerels will be poorly marked, very dark Cuckoos. They may be useful for mating with rather light Cuckoo females. Whites are sometimes mated with Cuckoos as the barring (Cuckoo) gene helps to minimize brassiness or odd-coloured feathers in Whites.

Enthusiasts should resist the temptation to keep too many varieties. Although they are small birds, there are limits to the number of colours a hobbyist can breed successfully. They sometimes start feather pecking, especially at beards, when moulting, so may need to be kept individually for a month or so at this time.

CHAPTER 6

Barbu d'Uccles/Ukkelse Baardkriel/Belgian d'Uccle

This Belgian True Bantam is essentially an offshoot from the much more ancient Booted/Federfüßige Zwerg/Sabelpoot Bantam, which was covered by the author in *Rare Poultry Breeds*. Some Booteds were bearded, and some had spangled plumage patterns, especially in the Netherlands, both to become features of Barbu d'Uccles when they were established as a separate breed. Their French name, in bilingual Belgium, is used internationally, rather than Ukkelse Baardkriel, their Flemish/Dutch name.

The main creator of Barbu d'Uccles as a distinct breed (rather than just being a strain of Booted) was Michel van Gelder of Brussels. Robert Pauwels (who also lived near Brussels) and L. Vander Snickt joined his project: Uccle/Ukkel is a suburb on the southern edge of Brussels. The breeding programme started by crossing Booted Bantams with the then very new Barbu d'Anvers breed in about 1895–99. They started showing their new breed in 1905 and 1906, producing four colour varieties in the first couple of years: Millefleur, Black, Cuckoo and White. Their aim was to make a breed with the single comb and heavily feathered legs and feet of Booteds with the beard, smaller size and compact form of Barbu d'Anvers. As this breed was still in its infancy, and not yet very uniform, some chicks had single combs. It was one of these which was used, which would have been culled from Barbu d'Anvers breeding anyway.

Word of their existence was first spread outside Belgium by C.S.Th. Van Gink, when he saw them at the 1909 Brussels Show. Van Gink lived in the Netherlands, but contributed to poultry magazines all over the world. Barbu d'Uccles was among the breeds taken to Crystal Palace Shows in London, 1911 to 1913. The British Belgian Bantam Club was formed in 1915. There had never been a Booted Club in the UK, so almost all Booted breeders here joined the new club and started crossing their Booteds with Barbu d'Uccles. The leading exhibitor of Booteds in England in 1915 was Mr Kenneth Ward from Yorkshire, but even he had entirely switched to Barbu d'Uccles by 1930, when a flock in Ipswich were the last known Booteds in the UK.

Possibly partly as a lasting legacy from this early crossing with Booteds, Barbu d'Uccles do not seem to have ever been as small and compact as Barbu d'Anvers. Enough winning show birds were photographed from 1915 onwards, the photos appearing in books and magazines, to reveal that they never, in the UK at least, had the desired ultra-short back, which we know from the Barbu d'Anvers chapter was partly due to their general small size, and partly a visual effect caused by their profuse neck feathering reaching to their back plumage rising to the tail. The American Standard of Perfection classes both breeds together as non-bearded and bearded Booteds, despite there being a 'Belgian d'Uccle and

Millefleur Barbu d'Uccles and Black Barbu du Grubbe (rumpless Barbu d'Anvers), some of the first Belgian Bantams, sketched at the 1911 Crystal Palace Show. Artist: unknown

Booted Bantam Club'. White Booteds were in the first, 1879, edition of American Standards, with Millefleurs (with or without beards) being added in 1914. A very detailed article by Bob Jarvis in the November 1988 issue of *Poultry Press* magazine clearly shows that at least some enthusiasts in America clearly understand the history of the two breeds, and the differences there should be between them. Sadly, one sees references to 'Millefleur Bantams' (as if it was the breed's name, rather than its colour) in the UK and USA, so clearly many bantam keepers need more breed education.

The names of this and other spotted-plumage colour varieties which are so characteristic of Barbu d'Uccles and Booteds differ between countries, with English speakers at least partly using French variety names. English/French 'Millefleurs' are the same as Dutch 'Porselein' and German 'Porzellanfarbig'. However English/French 'Porcelaines' are the same as Dutch 'Blauwporselein' and German 'Blauporzellanfarbig'. To add to the confusion,

this diluted version of the Millefleur pattern is caused by the Lavender gene, not the Blue gene. There is a new version of this pattern, which really is diluted by the Blue gene. On these the ground colour is a slightly lighter version of the orange-red of normal Millefleurs, not the creamy shade of (UK) 'Porcelaines'. When this blue gene version is standardized in the UK it will probably be called 'Blue-Millefleur'. What will they call them in Germany or the Netherlands?

Barbu d'Uccles have been bred in greater numbers, and more colour varieties, since the 1960s than at any time before then. They are widely distributed around the UK, with at least one class for them at almost every local show. However, the quality and presentation of many of the birds shown is often quite poor. Their leg and foot feathering is brittle, so easily broken, and they need to kept inside very clean houses to keep them in show condition. Even if only intended to be garden pets, they should never be allowed outside in muddy conditions.

Barbu d'Uccles, Blue female and Millefleur male. Artist: René Delin, an early breeder

BARBU D'UCCLE
TYPE DESCRIPTION

Belgian and Dutch standards require weights of 550g (20oz) pullet, 650g (23oz) hen, 700g (25oz) cockerel, 800g (28oz) cock. Probably as a result of the Booted crosses, British standards allowed higher weights: 700g (25oz), 800g (28oz), 800g and 900g (31oz). Most British fanciers would like smaller Barbu d'Uccles, if they had good leg and foot feathering, beard, colour and markings, and so on.

They have a smaller than average sized, straight, single comb. Wattles should be as small as possible, so as not to detract from the well developed, tri-lobed beard. The beard covers the small ear lobes, which are red. Eye, beak, shank and feet colour vary with plumage colour variety as for Barbu d'Anvers: very dark, nearly black for Blacks, brown or red eyes for the other colours. Beak, shanks and feet are slate-blue on most other varieties, white on Cuckoos and Whites.

As with Barbu d'Anvers, neck feathering is thick, profuse and partly swept back. The body is compact and cobby and the wings point to the ground. Legs need to be long enough for the 'vulture hocks' (cluster of stiff feathers pointing down and back from the hock joint), shank and foot feathering to be well displayed. Some seem too tall when young, but look fine when adult.

BARBU D'UCCLE
PLUMAGE COLOURS

The most popular varieties are several colour versions of the Millefleur pattern, which are described in more detail below. Continuing the spotted theme, there are also Black-Mottles, Blue-Mottles, Buff-Mottles (buff with white spangles) and Lavender-Mottles. Other varieties are Black, Blue, Cuckoo, Ermine (Columbian or Light in other breeds), Lavender and White.

Black-Mottled Barbu d'Uccle, male. Photo: John Tarren

Most feathers on both sexes of Millefleurs are orange-red (various shades, especially on specific parts of males), with a large round black spangle, and a small V-shaped tip at the end. The black spangle should not be so large that it makes the birds look almost black. Black markings in the lower, orange-red, part of the feathers constitute a serious fault. The white tips are small on young birds (often absent on many feathers), and get progressively larger and more numerous with each annual moult. As this is a breed which improves with age in terms of cobby type and wealth of plumage in all parts, birds which are underspotted when initially reaching maturity (at about 6–8 months of age) may have to stay at home their first winter, but should go on to have a long and successful show career. Eventually most Millefleurs have to be retired from showing because their white spots become far too big and the main wing and tail feathers are white for over half their length.

The main tail feathers of both sexes on Millefleurs are mainly glossy black with a small white tip and dark golden edging. Their beards are black. Main wing feathers are golden-brown on the outer web (the part showing when the wing is folded), a mix of golden-brown and black on the inner web (details not important), and a neat white tip.

Porcelaine (in the English sense) Barbu d'Uccles, especially males, often have poor feather quality. It is believed that lavender plumage affects riboflavin metabolism, or requires more riboflavin than normal. Tail feathers in particular are frequently short, stringy and fretted. The short feathers on the upper part of the wings often do not grow properly, remaining as stubs. If Porcelaines are bred together for many generations the colour eventually fades to an indistinct creamy shade, combined with a loss of distinct spangling. Most fanciers also keep Millefleurs,

and routinely cross the two colour varieties, which also helps improve feather quality. The Lavender gene is recessive, but there has been so much crossing over the years that many, possibly most, Millefleurs carry the Lavender gene. A few Porcelaines may appear with a rich (too rich) apricot ground colour. Although too dark for showing, they are useful for breeding with birds that are too light, perhaps an even better mating than Millefleur × Porcelaine.

There are several more colour versions of this pattern: Citron (Lemon) Millefleurs and Silver Millefleurs, but these are more often seen on Booted/Sabelpoot Bantams than Barbu d'Uccles.

Porcelaine Barbu d'Uccle, female. Photo: John Tarren

CHAPTER 7

Barbu de Watermael/ Watermaalse Baardkriel

This tiny bantam breed was created by Antoine Dresse and his son Oscar on their farm, Les Fougères at Watermael-Boltsfort/ Watermaal-Bosvoorde, a borough on the south-eastern edge of Brussels, Belgium. They never divulged any details of the breed-ing programme, started about 1900, to make their new breed; but the then very new Barbu d'Anvers and bearded varieties of Poland Bantams would have been two of the breeds used. Antoine Dresse might have used some crossbred bantams of unknown parentage as well. Progress was halted by the disruption of the 1914–18 war, so he was unable to exhibit his new creation until the 1922 Brussels Show. It has not been possible to discover details of what other fanciers in Belgium thought of Barbu de Watermael then, but the breed seems to have only been bred in the Brussels area until well after 1945. A few Dutch and German fanciers started to keep them in the 1950s, but they were not brought to the UK until about 1978. The British Belgian Bantam Club produced an English version of the original French/ Flemish standard, which was accepted by the PCGB Council in 1987. At time of writing (2007) Barbu de Watermael could not yet be honestly described as a popular breed, but a few could be seen, even at small local shows, in many parts of the UK. They will probably go on to become more popular in the future than at any time in the previous century.

Normal Quail Barbu de Watermael, male. Photo: John Tarren

Normal Quail Barbu de Watermael, female. Photo: John Tarren

BARBU DE WATERMAEL DESCRIPTION

This is a small breed, with standard weights of 450g (16oz) pullet, 550g (19oz) hen, 600g (21oz) cockerel, 700g (25oz) cock. General body shape and proud carriage is similar to Barbu d'Anvers, although Watermaels show more length of back and have slightly lower tail carriage. Watermaels also have a well developed tri-lobed beard, but differ from other Belgian Bantam breeds by having a bushy head crest and a unique comb formation. The crest is on both sides and to the rear of the comb and appears swept back. It is smaller than crests on Polands and must not interfere with their sight. They have a small rose comb, the unique part being the three small leaders (spikes) at the rear. All colour varieties of Barbu d'Anvers and Barbu d'Uccles are also allowed on Barbu de Watermael although not all of them may have been made yet. They are suitable for novices, as long as they do not keep them with larger breeds who will bully these midgets.

'Amerikaansche Nuthoenders'. A picture of the actual birds (prototype Gold Laced Wyandottes) imported in 1898 by B.H. Bertels to make Barnevelders.

CHAPTER 8

Barnevelder

Barneveld, a town east of Utrecht in the middle of the Netherlands, is the traditional centre of the Dutch poultry industry. A wholesale egg market was established there in the late nineteenth century, its annual throughput rising to 30–40 million eggs during the 1930s. Barneveld also has an agricultural college which concentrates on poultry, and now there is also a poultry museum providing a permanent record of this aspect of local, agricultural and social history.

The Barnevelder breed is one of many made in Europe and America in the late nineteenth and early twentieth centuries by crossing imported heavy Asiatic fowls with previously existing local chickens. Dutch poultry farmers had no doubt tried crossing their local breeds with Shanghais since the 1850s (Bredas are believed to have been significantly modified by such crosses) but more significant for Barnevelders was the arrival of dark brown-egg laying Langshans in the 1870s. Major Croad in Sussex, England, was the main importer of Langshans from China, but there were others. It is not known whether the Langshans used in the Barneveld area came via Sussex or other sources. During the period 1870–1900, egg production was beginning to be transformed in the Netherlands from being a very minor part of general farming into an industry in its own right. Wholesale dealers, later to include organized producer co-operatives, were changing the Netherlands from being a net importer of eggs to a major net exporter. Sea freight costs were relatively

modest at the time, and the docks and huge population of London made it a major market for the Dutch egg traders. English consumers would pay extra for large brown-shelled eggs, so producers in the Barneveld area made sure they had birds to produce them.

The first step towards establishing the eventual main Double Laced plumage pattern of the Barnevelder breed was done by B.H. Bertels when, in 1898, he imported some prototype Gold Laced Wyandottes from America (this breed was not fully established then) to his estate near Barneveld to add to the mix. Other significant breeders who helped to refine the breed between between 1900 and 1910 were Jan Berkhof, J.H. Sandbergen, Frans van Deelen, W. Schimmel and J. van Droffelaar. Their new breed was first exhibited in 1911 at an agricultural show at Den Haag (The Hague). They continued to improve the colour and pattern of Barnevelders at shows until 1915, after which further progress had to wait until the First World War ended in 1918. By this time the general colours of glossy green-black and rich red-brown were established, but their markings were still variable, including single lacing, double lacing, peppering and partridge patterned. Markings on hens were more variable than markings on cocks.

Luckily for the Barnevelder breeders, the first World Poultry Congress was held at Den Haag, 5–9 September 1921. All the world's poultry experts gathered for the event, including Edward Brown and William Powell-Owen from England. Both regular contributors in

Barnevelders. Originally a free gift with Feathered World *magazine, 22 October 1926. At this time it can be seen that British breeders had not yet adopted laced breasted males. Artist: A.J. Simpson*

British poultry magazines, they praised the Barnevelders (and their dark brown eggs) they saw at the WPC when they returned home. Another visitor to the Congress was Mrs J.M. Walker of Chatteris, Cambridge (she later moved to Newdigate, Surrey). Shortly after the event she arranged for a shipment of day-old Barnevelder chicks to be delivered by plane, believed to be the first such international consignment in the world. She easily sold as many of the birds reared as could be spared from her breeding plans. The British Barnevelder Club was formed in 1922.

The Club's first job was to examine the still variable plumage patterns. A breed standard for the shows could not be published until these matters were settled. It should be remembered that plumage patterns were not yet fully settled in the Netherlands, so the British Barnevelder Club could not simply translate the standard of the breed in its homeland, the present general policy with imported breeds. The British Club committee asked leading members here and in the Netherlands to send in sample feathers for examination. This process resulted in the first Barnevelder standard, passed by the PCGB Council in 1923. At this stage there was one standard male plumage pattern, with a solid black breast, legs and tail; the neck, back and wing plumage being mainly deep glossy red-brown with black markings. Confusingly to many, two alternative female patterns were

Double Laced Barnevelder, large male. British Standard with single laced breast plumage. Dutch Standard Barnevelder males have solid black breast plumage, and it is impossible to breed males with double laced breast markings. Photo: John Tarren

Double Laced Barnevelder, large female. Photo: John Tarren

allowed to go with these males, Double Laced and Partridge. The first of these, which has gone on to become the main variety of the breed, was very similar to the already familiar pattern of Dark Indian Game (= USA Cornish). Partridge hens had single outer lacing with random black peppering in the feather centres on all parts except for predominantly black neck feathers required on both female patterns.

This standard created several problems. Many breeders already regarded the Double Laced as the main variety, regarding Partridge hens as no better than rejects as far as showing was concerned. The solid black-breasted males were not ideal for breeding Double Laced hens. Some breeders resorted to crossing with Indian Game to improve the pattern, and almost ruined the Barnevelder's reputation as good layers of dark brown eggs by doing so.

The British Barnevelder Club revised its standard at its 1931 Annual General Meeting at the London Dairy Show. The new Double Laced males had single laced breast and wing bar feathers. Partridge males kept to the original standard, with a solid black breast and wing bar. Club members would probably have liked double laced breast feathers on males, but only single lacing was achievable. Partridge Barnevelders are still standardized, but are extinct.

In the Netherlands, they have only standardized Double Laced Barnevelders, the males of which should ideally have solid black breast plumage, although in reality many feathers have brown centres. Partridge females have never been recognized there.

BLACK BARNEVELDER

Double Laced and (when they existed) Partridge Barnevelders have always had a tendency to be too dark, some appearing almost completely black at first glance. There were divided opinions among Barnevelder breeders about what to do about them. Some, including W. Powell-Owen in the UK, thought it would be a good idea to selectively breed from these dark birds to create Black Barnevelders as a new variety. Others regarded them as rejects, thinking all efforts should be concentrated on perfecting the Double Laced pattern.

Because of these divided opinions a separate Black Barnevelder Club was formed in the UK in 1925. They published a standard for their new variety which was accepted by the PCGB in 1928. As can be imagined, almost all Black Barnevelders still had some brown plumage. The obvious way to obtain completely black birds was to cross with established breeds of similar body size and shape, black plumage and yellow shanks and feet, Black Plymouth Rocks and Black Wyandottes being prime candidates. The rose combs of Wyandottes would not have been a problem as there would have been several years of selective breeding ahead, with plenty of opportunties to establish single combs again. However Barnevelders, including Black Barnevelders, must lay dark brown eggs if they are to be proper representatives of the breed, and Plymouth Rocks and Wyandottes both lay tinted or, at best, light brown eggs. Once lost by crossing, dark brown eggs are very difficult to restore.

Such crossing was regarded as a major threat to the new variety, so new members to the Black Barnevelder Club were required to sign a pledge saying they would not resort to such malpractices. They had to sign the pledge again every time they won a club cup to affirm that the winning bird was a pure bred Barnevelder, with nothing added.

In another policy designed to concentrate efforts on ensuring Black Barnevelders remained primarily good layers of dark brown eggs, the standard was designed to avoid the need for double mating to produce show-winning black-plumaged, yellow-legged birds of both sexes. Therefore, white underfluff was allowed on males, which made them the equivalent of pullet-breeder males in Black Plymouth Rocks and Black Wyandottes.

The two clubs eventually settled their differences, and in 1937 the Black Barnevelder Club merged with the main British Barnevelder Club. Black Barnevelders are also standardized in the Netherlands, as were Whites. A separate breed club, the Nederlandse Zwarte en Witte Barnevelder Vereniging, had 28 Blacks and 7 Whites at their 1930 show at Utrecht.

OTHER COLOURS

White Barnevelders have been bred for a long time in the Netherlands, but no records have been found of them in the UK. Silver Barnevelders, with the Double Laced pattern in black over a white ground colour, were standardized in the UK in 1938. A few have been seen from time to time at British shows, but they remain rare, probably because faulty markings are glaringly obvious on Silvers, whereas similarly poorly marked normal Double Laced do not look nearly as bad unless closely examined. Silvers have never been recognized in the Netherlands. A blue version of the Double Laced pattern, with blue lacing over a red-brown ground colour, is a very attractive new colour variety developed by Dutch and German fanciers which will probably become very popular in the future.

BARNEVELDERS AS LAYERS

Mrs Walker entered a pen of Barnevelder pullets in a laying trial organized by *Feathered World* magazine towards the end of 1922. They won a silver medal, laying an average of 200 grade 1 eggs each. Over the next few years their performance at other laying trials gradually improved to 240 eggs, not as many as laid by Rhode Island Reds, the main commercial laying breed at the time, but as Barnevelder

Double Laced Barnevelders, bantam pair. Photo: John Tarren

eggs were dark brown, they were good enough for producers who supplied customers prepared to pay extra for a quality product. There were not many such consumers during the Great Depression. A few hens were recorded which laid up to 287 eggs in 52 weeks in one case, but this was exceptional, and everyone knew it to be so. They certainly never lived up to the claim made by some Dutchmen, that a Barnevelder hen would lay exactly 313 eggs in 52 weeks, an egg a day Monday to Saturday with every Sunday as a day of rest. Dutch people were very religious then, but still had a sense of humour.

BARNEVELDER BANTAM

Several strains were made, the first record of them being exhibited being at Utrecht Show in 1921, where Mr Van Dyk won the class. Dietrich Giesenof Mülheim-Ruhr, Germany started to make his strain in 1922 by crossing undersized large Barnevelders with several bantam breeds: Rhode Island Reds, Indian Game, Red German Langshans and Gold Laced Wyandottes. He exhibited them at Berlin, Dresden, Essen and Hannover Shows, 1927–30. Few pre-war Barnevelder Bantams laid dark brown eggs, but they died out during the war anyway.

After the war another German fancier, Hans Altheinz of Kirkhain made Black and White Barnevelder Bantams by crossing the Double Laced variety with Black and White Wyandotte Bantams, *circa* 1954–60.

Barnevelder Bantams were first made in England during the 1920s by Mrs Mainwaring and her poultry manager, Mr William Foote. Another leading breeder then was Lady Bromley-Wilson, who won first prizes (presumably in AOV Bantam classes) at Great Yorkshire, Harrogate, Hornsey, Otley and Penistone shows with her Barnevelder Bantams in 1928.

Light Brahmas. Originally a free gift with Poultry *magazine, circa 1912. Artist: J.W. Ludlow*

Dark Brahmas in 1873. Note less foot-feathering then. Artists: C.E. Brittan (female) and Harrison Weir (male)

CHAPTER 9

Brahma

The origin of this breed was once a great cause of controversy among poultry experts, a series of arguments which gave rise to many column inches in magazines, chapters in the major poultry books and even a few smaller books which are more or less devoted to the subject. The row lasted some forty years, from about 1850 to 1890. It consisted of one group who thought Brahmas came from India and another which thought Brahmas were selected forms of Shanghais, closely related to Cochins and Langshans. Generally, the latter theory is now thought to be correct, although some stock bred in India were used to refine Dark Brahmas. Light Brahmas could be regarded as an American breed as their standard plumage pattern, pea comb, and so on, were all fixed by American breeders. Similarly, the intricate plumage markings and heavily feathered feet were perfected by British fanciers.

'Shanghaes' had only been coming into Boston, New York and other east coast ports for a few years when the birds destined to become Light Brahmas arrived in 1847. The ship they were on was said to have come from 'Luckipoor', believed to be somewhere in the Ganges delta in present day Bangladesh. The Brahmaputra River merges with the Ganges a relatively short distance inland and, going upstream, goes through Assam (north-east India) and into Tibet. The ship may have started from Shanghai and stopped off in the Ganges area *en route*.

It is well known (*see* Chapter 10: Cochin) that very large feathery chickens with feathered feet were unknown to Europeans (in Europe or America) before China was forced to open up for international trade following the Opium Wars in 1840. Shanghai became an international port in 1842. These chickens, initially called 'Shanghaes', caused a sensation throughout the whole of society. In those days almost everyone kept a few hens, and knew about poultry breeds.

The British had been in the Ganges delta area of India (Bangladesh became a separate country in 1971) since the seventeenth century. The British East India Company effectively ruled the region from 1757 until 1858, after which the British government took over until 1947. Further up the Brahmaputra River is Assam, and the British were there from about 1825. Although Tibet has never been ruled by Britain, several explorers must have visited. In all this time no large feathery chickens were reported; the local poultry consisted of either smallish chickens (like farmyard flocks everywhere) or Asil type fighting cocks. If any Shanghai type chickens were in India, some British person would have spotted and reported them.

Mr Nelson H. Chamberlain was the buyer of the birds (mentioned above) from the ship in New York in 1847 (some accounts say 1846), which he took to his farm in Connecticut. It is not clear if he thought of the name Brahma-Pootras, it could have been another dockside poultry buyer, Dr Kerr of Philadelphia, or even Dr John C. Bennett of Plymouth City, Massachusetts. One story says that 'Brahma-

Pootra' was decided by sticking pins into a map of Asia until an exotic name was found. Perhaps the name was too exotic: a lot of people seem to have got confused. Buram-Pootras, Burram-Putras, Brama-Poutras, Burma-Porters, Bahama-Paduas and Bohemia-Prudas all appeared in print. It was eventually shortened to Brahma.

George P. Burnham of Roxbury, Massachusetts got involved in 1849, as a result of being interested and amused by the enthusiasm of Dr Kerr. They formed the first poultry club in America, The New England Society for the Improvement of Domestic Poultry. Its name was not Burnham's idea; he later sarcastically remarked, 'Now, the only objection I ever raised to this title was that it was not sufficiently lengthy'. In November 1849 the new society organized the first poultry show in America, in marquees erected in Boston's main public park. This event started 'the hen fever', a period when exotic chickens became very fashionable and changed hands for extraordinary prices – $50 a pair or more – a fortune in those days. Burnham could see a lot of money could be made from the fancy hen trade, so he bought stock from Dr Kerr and regularly visited the docks in Boston and New York to select the best arriving from Asia. He started by buying all colours, including Buffs which later became Cochins. Chamberlain, Kerr and others were promoting Brahma-Pootra/Grey Chittagongs above other colours, so Burnham followed their lead. He had first pick of over a hundred Shanghaes on a ship in New York in 1851, and found enough good 'Greys' to be able to specialize in these only from then on, and sold off all other colours.

Burnham was well ahead of his time when it came to realizing the value of publicity, and knew that despite America having been at war with Britain twice (War of Independence and War of 1812), Americans were still fascinated by the British royal family (as they are today). He sent nine (two cockerels, seven pullets) of his best birds in a 'black-walnut-framed cage' to Queen Victoria in December 1852, which arrived in London on 22 January 1853,

initially to London Zoo, to be sent on to 'The Royal Poultry House' at Windsor. Burnham naturally made sure the newspapers on both sides of the Atlantic were kept fully informed. He enjoyed a few profitable years selling Grey Shanghaes, until 1854, when another American dealer flooded the market by sending too many to London in one consignment.

The Queen's Grey Shanghaes were drawn by Harrison Weir, the picture appearing in the *Illustrated London News*. They had single combs (although others had the pea comb which became the only recognized type by about 1860) and were tall birds with lightly feathered legs and feet, roughly similar to Langshans today. At this stage there was one main plumage colour variety, roughly halfway between the eventual Darks and Lights. Cocks were more like Lights, but had some black or grey markings on their legs and belly. Hens had black-and-white striped neck feathers, a white breast and belly (as Lights) and grey pencilling on their back and wings (as Darks). Many British poultry experts, including Rev. W.W. Wingfield, George Johnson, W.B. Tegetmeier and Harrison Weir tended to agree with Burnham, that Brahmas were essentially a strain of Shanghaes, perhaps with some Malay crosses. Lewis Wright sided with Chamberlain, with the Assam and Bengal (Bangladesh) origin theory.

Brahmas developed in different ways in the USA and UK during the 1860s and 1870s, in response to different circumstances in each country. American breeders concentrated on Light Brahmas, which they kept as a practical breed, retaining the modest leg/foot feathering and rather tighter body plumage (more Langshan than Cochin). They were still being used as table chickens, in contrast to the UK, where Brahmas were already just used as they are now, for showing and as ornamental garden pets.

Dark and Light Brahmas were established as two distinct varieties during the 1860s, but by the early 1870s British exhibition breeders had realized that it was not possible to breed perfectly marked Darks, according to the new,

Light Brahmas. Originally a free gift in Geflügel-Börse, *August 1941 (during the war). Artist: W. Jennrich*

stricter breed standards of both sexes from one strain.

Double mating (separate 'cock-breeder' and 'pullet-breeder' strains) would be essential. They were already familiar with the general principle from Hamburgh breeders. Dark males were required to have a solid black breast, legs and tail, to contrast with the pure white back and shoulders, and white with black stripes neck and saddle hackles. Dark females were to have fine concentric pencilling over all parts except for the striped neck. They discovered that good males could only be bred from very dark grey females, with hardly any pencilling; and good females could only be bred from males with a lot of white markings on breast and thighs. At their peak as a popular show breed there were 268 Dark and 237 Light Brahmas at the 1875 Crystal Palace Show. The Brahma Club may have been formed by then, but the author was not able to find definite evidence of it before 1900. Some cock-breeder

strains of Darks may have been developed by British fanciers living in India, who could get feather-legged stock from China, and useful pea-combed, silver-hackled, black-breasted, Asil type cocks locally.

American breeders concentrated on Lights, with the American Light Brahma Club being formed in 1902 (it had 200 members by 1912), and a separate New England Light Brahma Club which also existed in 1912 (no details have been found about when it started or finished). There was no club for Darks in the USA at this stage. All of the (few) Dark Brahmas in America had come from England, where they had been bred on exhibition lines, partly from crosses with Partridge Cochins, intended to improve plumage pattern and increase foot feathering. This type did not suit American Brahma breeders who were trying to keep them a reasonably practical breed.

This level of popularity could not last, partly because the period from 1870 to 1900 saw the creation of several other large breeds in many attractive colours and patterns which did not have feathered feet, which were, and still are, difficult to keep clean and unbroken. These new breeds included Orpingtons, Plymouth Rocks, Wyandottes and eventually (1904–5) Rhode Island Reds. The decline was quite gradual until the First World War, as can be seen by the numbers entered at the Crystal Palace Show, London: 1901, 180; 1909, 91; 1910, 96; 1911, 102; 1912, 101; 1918, 89.

After the war the club struggled for a couple of years, then recovered quite well considering this was the era of the Great Depression and Wall Street Crash. However, show prize money was still generous, and Brahma strains were uniform by then, so only twenty youngsters had to be bred annually for a team of birds capable of winning AOV classes at local shows all year.

Brahma Club Show entries between the wars (those known) are: 1919 Birmingham 27; 1920 Birmingham 50; 1921 Crystal Palace 51; 1925 Olympia 80; 1928 Crystal Palace 84; 1929 Crystal Palace 69; 1931 Crystal Palace 69.

The last Brahma Club Show would have been in 1938 or 1939; it was not revived after 1945. Brahmas may even have died out in the UK by 1945. They started to be seen at shows here again in the 1960s, most stock coming from Germany and the Netherlands, where fanciers managed to preserve breeding stock through the destruction of war. The 1964 Hannover Show had 82 large Brahmas on display. In the UK, Brahmas came into the Rare Poultry Society when it was formed in 1969, until a new Brahma Club started in 1973.

Additional colour varieties of Brahmas have all been relatively recent creations. Buff Columbian Brahmas, the same pattern as Lights, but on a buff ground colour, seem to have first been bred in significant numbers in Germany from 1958 onwards, although a trio bred in the USA was exhibited at the World Poultry Congress in London in 1930. It is not clear whether a new strain was made in Germany, or imported from America.

White Brahmas were included in *British Poultry Standards* in the 1950s, but very few were actually seen. Friedheim Weitkamp of Epe, Germany was a leading breeder of Buff Columbians, and he went on to create the Gold Partridge (1970) and Blue-Gold Partridge (1976) varieties. Danish and Dutch fanciers have made blue-marked versions of Lights, Buff Colombians and Darks since then. Barred, Birchen, Black, Blue and Exchequer Brahmas have all been made, but have attraced very little interest.

BRAHMA BANTAM

William Flamank Entwisle of Calder Grove House, near Wakefield, Yorkshire started to make the first Brahma Bantams in the 1880s, with a German fancier, Louis Neubert, of Niederbritzsch in Saxony following closely behind with a second strain. Entwisle and his son and daughter made several more miniature breeds, including Indian Game, Malays, Partridge Pekins and Poland Bantams. Dark and Light Brahma Bantams started (by Entwisle) from a small Grey Asil cock running with a mixed pen of Black, Buff, Partridge and White Pekin and White Booted hens. This pen of oddments was only put together to breed some crossbred broody hens, the idea of them being the foundation of Brahma Bantams only occuring to him when he saw the potential as the crossbreds grew. The crosses with the Black and Partridge Pekins seemed to do the trick, after a few more years of selective breeding, for making Dark Brahma Bantams, the Lights being refined by a further mating with an undersized large Light Brahma cock, although this obviously required further selection to reduce size. A cross with a Black-Tailed White Japanese cock was also tried, but abandoned as the resulting birds had poor combs and very long tails. Brahma Bantams became quite popular during the 1890s.

Louis Neubert made his strain from undersized large Brahmas, Silkies and Booted Bantams. He first exhibited his strain at Dresden in 1889, then at Leipzig in 1891.

Buff Columbian Brahma, large female. Photo: John Tarren

The Brahma Club only covered large fowl, so a separate Brahma Bantam Club was formed some time between 1902 and 1909, the secretary being T.H. Bowen, of The Park, Woburn, Bedfordshire. He was succeeded by J. Greaves from Ben Rhydding until the Brahma Bantam Club folded in 1928. Brahma Clubs in all countries today cover large fowl and bantams.

The Brahma Bantam Club was very successful before the First World War, but rapidly declined in the 1920s, possibly because of fanciers switching to Pekins and the then very new Wyandotte Bantams. Annual Club Show entries were: 1909, 92; 1910, 96; 1911, 63; 1912, 70; 1913, 79 (all at Crystal Palace); 1915 Manchester, 45; 1919 Kendal, 46; 1920 Bradford, 30; 1921 Crystal Palace, 52; 1923, 37; 1924, 34; 1925, 25 (these three at Olympia, an exhibition hall in London). There was no club show in 1926, the last one being back at Crystal Palace in 1927, where 27 were entered.

As with large Brahmas, some Brahma Bantams were kept going by Dutch and German fanciers during the war. A strain of Dark Brahma Bantams owned by East Anglian fancier J. Hepburn also survived. They were advertised in *Poultry World* magazine after his death, by his son in the spring of 1984, and bought and revived by Swindon-based fancier P.R. ('Dick') Ricketts, one of the founder members of the Rare Poultry Society. These were a cock-breeder strain, comprising males with beautiful solid greenish-black breast plumage and rather dark and mossy females. Mr Hepburn senior had bred them for about forty years; and it is believed he got his first birds from W.F. Entwisle's son.

The other colours of Brahma Bantams were made in Germany (Buff Columbians in 1950, Gold Partridge in 1980, Blue-Gold Partridge 1988), and the Netherlands (Blue-Gold Columbian and Blue-White Columbian, both in 1991).

Gold Partridge Brahma, large female. Photo: John Tarren

BRAHMA DESCRIPTION

Full details are given in all the world's poultry standards books. American standards continue to require less heavily feathered birds than elsewhere. In all countries large Brahmas should be as big and as heavy (that is, not just a giant heap of feathers with not much chicken inside) as possible. Aim for 3.5kg (7½lb) pullets and up to 5.5kg (12lb) adult cocks. Bantam males are 1000g (36oz), females 900g (31oz). Some Dark Brahma Bantams are too small, thus losing the breed's substantial style. By contrast some Light Brahma Bantams are not greatly overweight, but appear too big because their legs, neck and tail are all too long. At time of writing, in the UK at least, Buff Columbian Brahma Bantams are usually best for representing true large Brahma type in miniature.

Brahmas should have a neat pea comb, over-large and irregularly shaped combs being a common fault. Walnut-combed chicks, which should be culled, usually occur in large Golds. They are a legacy from the Partridge Wyandottes used to make some strains (pea comb × rose comb gives walnut comb). The beak is yellow, eyes are orange-red and lobes are red.

Large Brahmas are very big birds, so in reality they have a long back; but it looks very short because the thick plumage on the back rises towards the high-carried tail from a point very near where the flowing neck feathers touch the back. Brahmas are tall birds, not much different in height from many Malays, although the profuse plumage of Brahmas means they do seem as tall at first glance. Breast, thigh, shank and foot feathering are all very profuse, but not quite as profuse as on Cochin. Vulture hocks are permitted in the UK but not in the USA. The tail should be no more than medium in length, carried high and fanned. When viewed from above, the tail is almost as broad across as the body.

Plumage colour varieties, including the newer ones which have not yet been standardized in all countries, have been mentioned in the text above. Darks, Gold Partridge and Blue

Dark Brahma, bantam male.
Photo: John Tarren

versions of the same pattern should be double mated for reliable breeding of correctly marked specimens. Lights, Buff Columbians, and their Blue versions do not need to be double mated, but undercolour needs to be mentioned. Birds with clear white or buff body feathering down to the skin look better than those with slate undercolour, which often shows at the surface; but if only birds with white or buff under-colour are used for breeding there will be a loss of neck striping, wing markings and black (or blue) tail colour. Therefore birds with slate undercolour are often mated with birds that have white or buff undercolour. Slate under-coloured birds can be successfully exhibited if the dark shading does not show at the surface too much. Judges may in any case place more emphasis on size and presentation, especially clean, unbroken foot feathering. The white parts of the plumage on Darks, Lights and their Blue variants must be pure white, not brassy. Shaded runs are preferred when they are allowed outside.

SPECIAL MANAGEMENT REQUIREMENTS

As a breed with heavily feathered feet, Brahmas are often kept inside houses with the floors covered with clean wood shavings. They will certainly be happier and healthier if they are let out on your lawn, but only in good weather. Brahma, should never be allowed anywhere near mud. The controlled housing needs of Brahmas are much easier to provide for bantams than large fowl. Do not provide perches for large Brahmas, they usually sleep on the floor, another reason why they need very regular cleaning out and generous provi-sion of wood shavings.

Large Brahmas, being very large indeed, need unlimited access to as much chicken food as they will eat. They will eat a lot, plus they need generous housing. As they are expensive to keep, fanciers will have to be well organized and willing to cull all sub-standard birds. Do not try to keep too many colour varieties.

Buff Cochins. Originally a free gift with Poultry *magazine, circa 1912. Artist: J.W. Ludlow*

White Cochin hen and Buff Cochin cock in 1873. Note less foot-feathering then. Artists: unknown (cock) and C.E. Brittan (hen)

CHAPTER 10

Cochin

Some large chickens called Cochin-Chinas were brought to Britain from the Far East in 1843, but these were not the ancestors of present-day Cochins, although they did leave a legacy to today's birds – their name. They caused a sensation when they arrived because of their great size. A drawing of them appeared in the 23 December issue of the *Illustrated London News*. The artist, Samuel Read, normally did architectural drawings, but enquiries by famous poultry expert Harrison Weir at Windsor (the birds had been presented to Queen Victoria) confirmed the drawing was accurate. The birds, two cockerels and five pullets, were very tall, did not have feathered feet, had single combs, and plumage was orange-red with black tails. Cochin-China was a French colony in what is now the southern region of Vietnam.

The first big, fluffy, feather-legged chickens from the Far East were brought to the UK in 1847 from Shanghai, a long way north of Vietnam. Poultry experts naturally called them 'Shanghaes', but ordinary poultry keepers were used to the names 'Cochins' or 'Cochin-Chinas' for any big chickens from Asia, so the old name stuck on the new chickens.

It was a very long trip from Shanghai to London, even for 'tea clippers', the fastest sailing ships of the period. It was also long before the invention of refrigeration equipment, so merchant ships bought an assortment of livestock to provide fresh eggs and meat for the crew *en route* at the beginning of each outward and return journey.

Alfred Sturgeon became an early leading breeder of Shanghaes/Cochins because he supplied these ships. He had a business by the Thames at Grays, Essex and a farm at nearby South Ockenden (near where the M25 Thames tunnel and bridge is now). Mr Sturgeon's clerk was instructed to buy anything interesting from the ships' crews, including antiques, porcelain and unusual livestock. His first Shanghaes came in on *The Fiery Cross*, a tea clipper, in 1849. After his first trio, Sturgeon told his clerk to buy any more which came in. On one occasion Mr Sturgeon went out in a rowing boat to meet an incoming ship before rival fanciers could get to it as he was determined to buy the best birds. He succeeded, despite having to be rescued when swept out by strong winds and tides.

At this time Shanghaes were broadly similar to today's Cochins, but had less foot feathering, and the plumage colours were not genetically fixed, with a mixture of youngsters being hatched even from uniformly-coloured breeding groups. Most of them had a basic ground colour of various shades – from yellow to orange-red, with variable amounts of black markings. Some had a black tail, others were marked as Buff Columbian Brahmas (*see* Chapter 9), and many had variable amounts of partridge, pencilled and peppered markings.

Mr Sturgeon preferred the lighter-coloured birds, so started the long process of selective breeding, which eventually led to Buff Cochins as they are today. Charles Punchard, of Blunts Hill, Haverhill, Suffolk, had been a friend of

Mr Sturgeon's for many years (Punchard had been an executor of Sturgeon's father's will), and admired the new birds when he visited the South Ockendon farm in the autumn of 1850. Sturgeon gave Punchard some of his darker patterned birds, which started Mr Punchard on the development of Partridge Cochins.

It took a long time to establish Buff and Partridge Cochins as we know them today, probably well into the 1880s. From 1850 until about 1875, most breeders and judges were still trying to make sense (for the purposes of show judging) of the mixed range of colours that were still coming in from China. The 1874 *Standard of Excellence in Exhibition Poultry*, which was used in both the UK and USA, described the following colour varieties of 'Cochins' (indicating that the experts had given up on persuading the public to call them Shanghaes): Buff, Demon, Silver Buff, Silver Cinnamon, Cinnamon, Grouse, Partridge, White and Black. The first three were eventually merged into Buffs as they are now. Cinnamons and Silver Cinnamons died out. When Partridge Cochins became a competitive exhibition variety they had to be double mated to produce perfectly marked males and females. Grouse Cochins became cock-breeder Partridge Cochins, and early Partridge Cochins became just pullet-breeders.

White Cochins were quite rare in the 1850s, two of the early breeders being Mr Bowman, of Penzance, Cornwall and the Dean of Worcester. This was the beginning of the Industrial Revolution, and white chickens did not stay white if you lived in a town or near a railway line. Rural fanciers soon discovered that White Cochins needed shaded runs, as sunlight made them brassy, an unattractive yellowish shade. They also needed a lot of show preparation. However, clear Whites were easier to breed than uniformly coloured Buffs or well marked Partridges. This is still true today. A large, clean White Cochin will impress most judges, and if you can provide appropriate housing and care, a full trophy cabinet is assured.

Black Cochins were also rare for many years; in fact there have probably been more good ones bred and shown since 1970 than there were from 1850 to 1960. For a long time almost all Black males had more or less red and gold edged neck and saddle hackles. Some were solid black as cockerels (so could be shown for one season) but the red came when they moulted in their second year. It was a lot easier to breed solid Black females, but most of the best coloured hens had solid black shanks and feet which should have been yellow. After about 1900 dusky yellow or 'lizard' shanks and feet were accepted, but still not solid black. Black Cochins can win well at the shows, but are less saleable than the brighter colours.

Cuckoo Cochins have appeared in small numbers since the 1850s, but the markings have never been clear and sharp enough to attract many breeders. Most competitive, perfectionist poultry fanciers who like large birds with this pattern have preferred Barred Plymouth Rocks.

Silkie Cochins or 'Emu Fowl' were mentioned in all the major Victorian poultry books, most of the few ever seen being coloured, like most of the early Shanghaes, somewhere between Buff and Partridge. Similar birds may still exist in China, but they are extinct as far as hobbyists in Europe and America are concerned.

Blue Cochins are a relatively new creation, made by Mr Herbert Whitley and his poultry manager, Mr Billy Wilkinson, of Primley Hill, Paignton, Devon. They started about 1930, and produced two hens good enough to enter in the AOV class at the 1932 Birmingham Show. Mr Whitley was already keeping Black Cochins, Blue Orpingtons and Blue Wyandottes, so we can guess how Blue Cochins were made. They went on to breed a beautiful trio which won the breeding pen class at the 1934 London Dairy Show. The other members of the Cochin Club saw the potential of Blues, and accepted them as a new variety at their AGM a few weeks later at the Birmingham Show. Curiously, the PCGB Council did not recognize Blues until 1948.

The Cochin Club had been formed at the 1902 London Dairy Show. This is a surprisingly late date when you consider that

Shanghaes/Cochins had been a popular exhibition breed since 1850. Even if you allow for the great changes made to the breed in shape and colour, both issues had been more or less stabilized since 1880, and several other breed clubs started about then. Mention should be made of Sidney J. Ballard, from Chelmsford, Essex, the Cochin Club's second secretary, serving a marathon thirty-eight years, from 1908 to 1946. The club was virtually dormant from 1954 until 1972, when a new generation of enthusiasts started to join up. By 1976 the numbers of Cochins at major shows was back up to levels last seen in the 1930s. Here are some Cochin Club Annual Show entry figures, which illustrate the changing fortunes of the breed in the UK.

Most club shows from 1902 to 1938 were held as part of the Birmingham Show. When the club was revived in the 1970s, the first few successful shows were part of Malpas Poultry Club's annual Easter Monday Shows held at Whitchurch, Shropshire.

1902, 147; 1903, 174; 1904, 179; 1909, 179; 1910, 144; 1911, 135; 1912, 131; 1913, 133; 1920, 55; 1921, 105; 1924, 63; 1925, 72; 1931, 69; 1934, 94

Very few records have been found of Cochin entries at major UK shows from 1935 to 1975, but it was generally very few. There were 88 Cochins at Malpas in 1976, the first display to confirm that a major revival was happening. Entries have fluctuated, usually between 50 and 100, since then.

COCHIN BANTAM

As this book is being written in the UK it naturally has a British perspective. After a lot of heated debate over several decades it

White Cochin cockerel and Buff Cochin pullet, 1910. Artist: A.F. Lydon

Partridge Cochin, large male. Photo: John Tarren

was decided that the approximate bantam version, which had initially been looted from the Emperor's Palace in Beijing (Peking) was different enough to be classed as a separate breed; therefore *see* Chapter 25: Pekin,

Bantam section. The 'Cochin Bantams' shown in almost every other country are not very different from UK Pekins, rather too low and rounded to be accurate miniature versions of large Cochins.

COCHIN DESCRIPTION

Full descriptions are given in American, British, Dutch, German and other standards books, so only key features are emphasized here. They must fill a standard show cage, the size coming from a combination of masses of feather covering a substantial chicken. Standard weights vary from country to country, ranging from 3.5kg (7¾lb) pullets up to 6kg (13lb) adult cocks.

Carriage is sedate, so Cochins do not look quite as tall as Brahmas when seen in show pens. Their very profuse body plumage on breast, belly and thighs, to which is added the thick thigh, shank and foot feathering, makes them appear to be a solid mass of feathers down to the floor. The plumage on the back forms a thick 'cushion', which starts rising just behind where the neck hackles reach the back, and rises gently to the short tail. Tail carriage

Partridge Cochin, large female. Photo: John Tarren

Cuckoo Cochin, large female.
Photo: John Tarren

is lower than that of Brahmas, and its tip just projects a little out from the rounded mass of tail coverts. Wings are short, the tips neatly tucked in between the tail coverts and thigh fluff.

Combs are single, fairly small, and straight. The whole head seems quite small in relation to the very large size of the birds as a whole. Ear lobes are red on all colour varieties. Eyes are dark on Blacks and Blues, red on other varieties. The beak, shanks and feet are yellow on the lighter varieties, again with darker shades allowed on Blacks and Blues.

The colour of Blacks, Blues, Buffs and Whites should be as even as possible. Blues naturally have a darker neck and (on males) saddle hackles. Remaining plumage should have as little dark lacing as possible. Buff males still sometimes have dark tails, a fault which has remained for 160 years because clear buff tails usually bring another fault, white in wing feathers. Cuckoo Cochins are seldom very clearly marked, so this variety is unlikely to win 'Best Cochin' awards, but they can be useful for crossing with Whites. The barring gene helps to reduce traces of colour and the tendency to go brassy in sunlight when carried by Whites of all breeds. Few, if any, Partridge Cochin breeders today have separate cock- and pullet-breeder strains, most of those seen tending towards pullet-breeders. There is probably scope for a keen fancier somewhere to develop a really good cock-breeder strain.

SPECIAL MANAGEMENT REQUIREMENTS

These are generally the same as given for Brahmas. White Cochins should not be allowed to eat much, if any, grass or maize when moulting. The pigments in these foods give a creamy tinge to the growing feathers. Once the moult is complete they can be allowed grass and maize again, which helps to keep the beak, shanks and feet a nice bright yellow.

'Mr Arthur C. Major's Silver Grey Dorking Hen'. Originally a free gift with Feathers *magazine, 25 August 1899. Artist: F.J.S. Chatterton*

CHAPTER 11

Dorking

Fine table fowls with distinctive extra hind toes were mentioned 2000 years ago by Columella when the Romans ruled England; perhaps not identical to Dorkings today, they were similar enough for Dorkings to be regarded as a very ancient breed. They were mentioned occasionally over the intervening centuries, at Dorking market in 1683 and 1824, for example.

The extra hind toes were well known in Kent, Surrey and Sussex as the key characteristic of the true old local breed. Before 1845 some plumage colours were more common than others, although there was no reason to stick to precise patterns. Some farmers chose to breed a distinctive colour, different from other flocks in the locality to deter chicken thieves. White and Cuckoo Dorkings may have been established for this reason. 'Old Red and Tawnies' were common varieties, eventually stabilized as Red Dorkings. Reds have remained most like ancient Dorkings, slightly smaller, tighter feathered and more active than the other varieties. Wingfield and Johnson's *Poultry Book* (1853) lists several more colours bred before 1845 which, because they were not recognized for showing, were already beginning to die out. 'Japans' were mostly black, with silver or gold neck hackles. 'Greys' were very variable, eventually becoming two varieties, Darks (or 'Coloured') and Silver Greys. 'Goldens' were a light version of Reds. 'Red Speckles' were either marked as Spangled OEG or as Speckled Sussex.

Lewis Wright mentioned that before 1850 the breast feathering of Dorking cocks of all colours except Cuckoos and Whites often had white speckles. He quoted from a Mr Meall who recalled that from 1854 onwards most had solid black breasts, larger combs than previously and partly white ear lobes (previously red). Some prominent breeders in Sussex and Surrey (particularly around Wokingham) had crossed Dorkings with Spanish (popular layers then). Partly white lobes remained a common fault long after show standards required red.

Wright also quoted from Mr John Douglas, a prominent breeder in the process of converting variable old flocks into standard-coloured exhibition strains. This was written about 1872, and covered Mr Douglas's recollections over the preceeding fifteen years. He started by confirming that their plumage colours were very variable before 1857, and that they were smaller than Dorkings in 1872. In 1857, 9½lb (4.3kg) cocks and 7½lb (3.4kg) hens were considered 'good'. In 1857 Mr Douglas obtained 'a dark grey cock, which had come from India, weighing thirteen pounds [5.8kg]. This bird was a model single-combed Dorking in all but the fifth toe, which was absent.' We can only guess what it was. He crossed this huge Indian cock with seven Dorking hens. Luckily for him, most of the birds he bred from this pen inherited their father's size and their mothers' extra hind toes. His new birds were more uniform in colour than his old stock, becoming a champion strain of Dark Dorkings. Until the 1860s, poultry shows mainly consisted of classes of pens of a cock and three hens. Mr Douglas recalled, '...before this time [1857] almost every

Dorkings. Originally a free gift with Feathered World *magazine 1903. Artist: A.F. Lydon*

hen was different in colour, so much so that out of a hundred hens in a yard it was a difficult matter to get three out of the lot to match'.

Silver Grey Dorkings were established with their present pattern and colours, particularly the salmon breast on hens, by crosses with Silver Duckwing OEG. Lord Hill's strain of Game were mentioned as being used by some Dorking men, including Mr Oswald E. Cresswell JP, of Morney Cross, Hereford (out of the main Dorking area), who tried this cross about 1868.

Dorkings can have single or rose combs, but specific rules were established about this time regarding which colour could have which comb. Then, and now, Cuckoos and Whites could only have rose combs, Reds and Silver Greys only single combs, Darks could have either, but most have had single combs since then. It was suggested that Cuckoo Dorkings were bred from crosses between White and rose-combed Dark Dorkings.

For the rest of the nineteenth century Dorkings were still used for commercial table chicken production and were an established exhibition breed. They were popular enough for separate breed clubs to be formed for the main colour varieties. The White Dorking Club was formed in 1884, the Silver Grey Dorking Club in 1888, and the Dark Dorking Club a little later, exact date unknown, possibly early in 1891. These latter two amalgamated to form the Dorking Club some years later, perhaps around 1900. The White Dorking Club became dormant during the 1890s, but was briefly reactivated from 1910 to 1915. There was also a short-lived (1910–13) Red Dorking Club and a Scottish Dorking Club (1919–39). It is believed that neither the Scottish nor main Dorking Clubs were revived after the Second World War. Arthur C. Major, followed by his son A. John Major, from Langley, Buckinghamshire were leading Dorking breeders from the 1880s through to

Silver Grey Dorkings. Originally a free gift with Poultry *magazine circa 1912. Artist: J.W. Ludlow*

1970, when a new Dorking Club was formed. Dorkings owe their continued existence from 1939 to 1970 to the dedication of A.J. Major and Mr S. Oatey from Cornwall.

Dorkings were a popular exhibition and table breed up to the beginning of the First World War in 1914, but rapidly declined from then, down to near extinction by 1945. As they became more uniform show birds they deteriorated as table birds. From 1920 to 1940, general farmers reared the cockerels from the popular R.I.R. × Light Sussex sex-linked cross, with specialist table chicken producers using Indian Game × Light Sussex crosses. Dorkings suffered at the shows during the same period (1920–40) from having classes at major shows cancelled because there were not enough entries to cover prize money. The

Dorking Club did not guarantee prize money (promising to make up deficits to show organizers) until after the 1932 AGM when, after a lot of 'plain speaking' a new secretary, W.O. Aitkenhead, of Cranbrook, Kent took over from A.J. Major. It was a good move, but too late to stop the rot. Here are some Club Show entry numbers to illustrate the rise and fall of Dorkings (most shows at Crystal Palace):

1909: 12 classes, 145 birds
1910: 12 classes, 108 birds
1911: 12 classes, 123 birds
1912: 13 classes, 170 birds
1913: 14 classes, 150 birds
1920: 10 classes, 75 birds
1921: 8 classes, 84 birds
1923: 4 classes, 29 birds

Red Dorkings. Originally a free gift with Poultry World *magazine, 21 February 1913. Artist: Ernest Wippell*

1929: 13 classes, 98 birds
1954: 2 classes, 20 birds (no active club).

Entries at Dorking Club Shows 1970–2006 have been about forty large and fifteen bantams in the better years. This is quite low considering how many members there are in the Dorking Club now. It is hoped that more members realize the importance of showing in breed conservation.

DORKING BANTAM

W.F. Entwisle said (*Bantams*, 1894) 'We have also heard of Silver-grey Dorkings and White Creve-Coeur Bantams, but as neither of these kinds has been exhibited recently, we fear they have died out through lack of appreciation'. Mr R. Scott-Miller of Uddington, near

Glasgow made a strain of Silver Grey Dorking Bantams several years later, about 1910–12, which he kept going until the 1950s, although not many, if any, other fanciers helped him with the project. Dorking Bantams are still not kept by many people today, although since 2003 some fanciers have been making some of the other colour varieties, primarily Reds.

DORKING DESCRIPTION

Standard weights of large Dorkings vary greatly in different countries. British weights are highest, and can best be described as 'aspirational': 3.6kg (8lb) pullets up to 6.3kg (14lb) adult cocks. They may have been this big in their heyday (1890–1914), but several decades of inbreeding (1940–70), when they were kept going by Mr Major and Mr Oatey,

Red Dorking, large male. Photo: John Tarren

Red Dorking, large female. Photo: John Tarren

have reduced them to a shadow of their former selves. German standards only require them to be from 2.5kg to 4.5kg (5½–10lb). Progress is being made at restoring their size, but there is a lot more work to do.

Dorkings generally appear rather long and low. They have fairly short legs which seem even shorter on all except Reds because of their profuse and somewhat 'loose' plumage. Reds are still tighter feathered, slightly smaller and more active than the other colours, so can claim to be nearer the pre-1850 type. All Dorkings have a long back, horizontal when they are standing normally, and a long tail which is carried 'well out' (that is, not very high).

Single combs on Dorkings are quite large, upright on males, partially falling to one side on females. Rose combs are quite large too, and some are of 'unconventional' shapes, which does not help their chances at shows. All facial skin, including lobes, are red, as is the eye colour. The beak is white or horn, darker on Darks. Shanks and feet are white, and the extra hind toe is an essential breed feature.

The ideal colours of Cuckoos and Whites are obvious, but (because both varieties remain rare) are seldom achieved, especially not on males. Cuckoo males are often too light, sometimes with partly white tail and wing feathers. White males are often brassy. We hope that an expert in the arts of showing white chickens

adds White Dorkings to his/her flock to 'raise the game' in the Dorking classes.

Silver Greys are similar to Silver Duckwing Game in colour; Silver Grey Dorking hens differ by the back and wing colour being a softer, lighter shade than that of most Game hens.

Darks are a darker version of Silver Greys, with heavy black striping in the male neck and saddle hackles, sometimes with yellowish rather than white edging. The back and wing colour of Dark females has cream-white shafts, black lacing and the remainder of the feather centres are peppered with dark grey, sometimes with a brownish tinge. Breast feathers on females are salmon-red with grey or black spangles.

Reds are a dark version of the normal Black-Red/Partridge pattern, with black spangles (as Darks) on the breast of Red females if possible. Not all have spangling at present.

SPECIAL MANAGEMENT REQUIREMENTS

Both sizes of Dorkings are on the road to recovery, and need dedicated specialist hobbyists who are prepared to breed large numbers annually and select the best for future breeding and showing. Continue to breed and feed for increased size of large fowl, and solid, substantial looking, but on a small scale, bantams.

'Hollandsche Partrijs-Kriel' (Partridge Dutch Bantams). Originally a free gift with Aviculture *magazine, 17 October 1913. Artist: C.S.Th. van Gink, who also bred them*

Silver-Wheaten and Salmon Dutch. Artist: C.S.Th. van Gink

CHAPTER 12

Dutch Bantam/Hollandse Kriel

Single-combed Black-Red/Partridge Bantams have been bred all over Europe since bantams in general were first brought here from southeast Asia in the sixteenth century. Modern and Old English Game Bantams in the UK, Belgische Kriel in Belgium, Deutsches Zwerghuhn in Germany, Pictaves in France and Swedish Bantams were all made from the same ancestors as Dutch Bantams when standardized breeds and shows were established in the nineteenth century. Fanciers in the Netherlands are believed to have started to view 'Hollandse Kriel' as a specific breed about 1886. A few were entered in AOV classes at Utrecht in 1895 and 1896, but they had to wait until 1906, when they were standardized, for a class of their own, when at least two males were entered. Only the Gold Partridge variety was standardized at first, with Black, White and Silver Partridge (then called Silver Duckwing, as in the UK) varieties added in 1911. English Game and Yokohama/Phönix Bantams were imported to help reduce size and refine plumage colours around this time. The 1913 Utrecht Show had eleven Gold Partridge and two Whites entered. Interest was boosted by an article and colour plate by C.S.Th. Van Gink in the 17 October 1913 issue of *Avicultura*, followed in 1919 by prints of Gold Duckwings, Piles and Millefleurs. It is not known if all these varieties existed then, or were still 'work in progress'.

Poultry World magazine in the UK reported Dutch Bantams in the Netherlands several times, but without tempting any British fanciers to keep them until the 1970s. The 30 December 1921 issue reported on the recent Utrecht Show, 'The Partridge, Duckwing and White Holland Bantams were very fine, especially the Partridge.' At this stage though, the reporter only perceived them as a means to a different end, as he continued 'English fanciers anxious to improve their Brown Leghorn Bantams should secure some of these.'

The 27 January 1922 issue included a report on a show at Den Haag (The Hague), which included: 'The Dutch S.C. Bantams, Partridge, Duckwing, White, Black, Laced and Cuckoo, are very pretty and quite different to anything we have in England.'

Photos of male and female Whites followed in the 17 March issue, and revealed that they were a long way from finished (more like White Plymouth Rock Bantams), but a photo of a Partridge male owned by Mr Ostermann, one of the leading breeders then, in *Poultry World* 12 May 1922, was essentially as they are now, but probably larger. Laced Dutch (possibly from Sebrights) died out.

It is not known when Blue Dutch were made, but a photo of a Blue hen appeared in *Avicultura* in 1942 (exact date unknown), which had been bred by F. van der Mark, of Leiden.

Their breed club, Hollandse Krielenfokkers Club, was not formed until 1 December 1946. It is not known why there was no club back in the 1920s or 1930s.

The first Club Show was held in early 1948 at the 'Avicultura Show' at Den Haag (The Hague), where there were 150 single birds and seven trios entered in these colours: Partridge, Silver Duckwing, Gold Duckwing, Black, Blue, Pile, Black-Mottle and Cuckoo. Salmon Dutch (Wheaten-bred Gold Duckwing) and Silver-Salmon (Wheaten-bred Silver Duckwing) also existed in the late 1940s; the former was the same colour as French Standard Salmon Faverolles.

A.L.A. van der Sande started to make Crele/Cuckoo-Partridge Dutch in 1970 by mating a Partridge cock with a Cuckoo hen. Two of the cockerels from this mating, gold-hackled Cuckoos, were mated with Partridge hens in 1971. The flock was increased from there.

F.M. van Oers started to make Normal Quail and Blue Quail Dutch Bantams in 1977, by crossing Partridge and Blue Partridge Dutch with Quail and Blue Quail Barbu d'Anvers. All first crosses were rose-combed, but F2 generations included a percentage of single-combed chicks. In 1980 an F3 generation Normal Quail cockerel was mated with a Silver Duckwing/Silver Partridge hen to begin making Silver Quail Dutch Bantams. Normal Quail were good enough to be accepted by the breed club and Nederlandse Standard Commission in 1985, with Silver Quail being accepted in 1988.

P. Schendstock made Buff Columbians and Blue-Buff Columbians, J. Voets made Lavenders, and E. Korte made Yellow Partridge, a variety which has caused much confusion. There are two genetically different, but visually similar, colour variations of the Black-Red/Partridge pattern: Yellow Partridge (a diluted Gold) and Gold Duckwing (genetically Silver with autosomal Mahogany).

From the statistics available, the first time a Hollandse Krielenfokkers Club Annual Show had over 200 entries was in 2003 at the Noord show, where there were 204 single bird entries and seven trios. The record high entry (statistics only available up to 1989) was at the 1989 special show to commemorate the fortieth anniversary of the club held at a restaurant's hall at Grave-Velp. There were 405 single bird entries and five trios, comprising 167 Gold Partridge, 36 Silver Partridge, 11 Blue-Gold Partridge, 1 Blue-Silver Partridge, 17 Yellow Partridge, 3 Red-Shouldered Silver Partridge, 10 Pile, 15 Cuckoo Partridge (Crele), 23 Cuckoo, 54 Black, 10 Blue, 16 White, 14 Lavender, 2 Black-Mottle, 12 Salmon, 1 Blue-Salmon, 3 Quail, 1 Blue-Quail, 5 Buff-Columbian, 3 White-marked Buff-Columbian, 1 Lavender-marked Buff-Columbian.

DUTCH BANTAMS IN OTHER COUNTRIES

Dutch Bantams in all colours started to be bred in other countries, Germany, Switzerland, the UK and USA, in significant numbers in the 1970s. Breed clubs were formed in the UK and Switzerland in 1982 and in the USA in 1986. American Dutch Bantam Society members have had less direct contacts with experts in the Netherlands because of the distance than English, German and Swiss fanciers who regularly visit Dutch fanciers and shows. One Hollandse Krielenfokkers Club Show Champion was exhibited by (UK) Dutch Bantam Club secretary Mike Banks. Dutch Bantams are now (2008) more popular in the UK, both as show birds and pets, than many other breeds which have been bred here for a century or more.

The first mention found of Dutch at a major show in the UK were G. Roper's (Blaby, Leicester) male and two females in the AO Rare Bantam class at the 1978 National Show. At the 1981 Stafford Show, Dutch's last major event within the Rare Poultry Society before the Dutch Club was formed here, had twenty-three Golds and seven Silvers from twelve exhibitors. The first of the new club's annual shows, Stafford 1982, also had twenty-three Golds, plus thirteen Silvers and three AOC. Among the other colours, there was some confusion, and still is to an extent, between the Gold Duckwing (genetically Silver, plus autosomal Red or Mahogany genes) and Yellow Partridge (genetically Silver, diluted by another gene, possibly recessive White). Apart from these, by 1990

Silver Partridge Dutch, female.
Photo: John Tarren

British fanciers also had Blue-Reds, Blacks, Blues, Whites, Cuckoos and Creles. Ten years later, there were also Blue-Silver-Partridge, Pile, Salmon, Lavender and Silver Quail varieties in the UK. Stafford Show in 2000 had the highest entry of Dutch seen in the UK so far: 213 single birds and nine entries in the Pair of Pullets class.

A Dutch Bantam Club was also started in Switzerland in 1982, Dutch having been first brought to Switzerland in 1968 by Edi Landolt; they were recognized by Switzerland's National Poultry Club in 1970. The Swiss Dutch Club had about fifty members in 2008.

Dutch Bantams were first taken to the USA about 1945–47, appeared at a few shows in

Blue-Gold Partridge Dutch, male. This colour variety is called Blue-Red in other breeds in the UK. Our Dutch Bantam Club prefers to use direct translations of variety names used in the Netherlands.
Photo: John Tarren

the eastern states until about 1955, then died out. American fanciers took a greater interest when further importations were made to Wisconsin (*circa* 1970) and Tennessee (*circa* 1980), resulting in the American Dutch Bantam Society being formed in August 1986. The Society now (2008) has about eighty members.

DUTCH BANTAM DESCRIPTION

Standard weights range from 400g (14oz) pullets up to 550g (20oz) adult cocks. They must be very close to this weight range to be considered acceptable. General type, style and shape is elegant, but conventional. Dutch do not have a single main feature for non-specialist judges to latch on, who have all too often demonstrated they do not understand them. Type, carriage, colour markings, head (comb,

lobe, eye, and so on), legs/feet and condition all need to be considered.

Dutch have fairly small, straight and upright single combs. The comb should ideally have five serrations. Double pointed or 'fish-tail' serrations are considered serious defects in the UK and the Netherlands, especially on males. Ear lobes are small, oval and white. Eyes range from orange-red to brownish-red, depending on plumage colour. Most varieties have horn or bluish beaks and slate-blue shanks/feet, except for Cuckoos and Cuckoo-Partridges (Creles), where these parts are much lighter, almost white.

Dutch really need to be double mated for plumage quantity and style to produce ideal show birds. Exhibition males have luxuriant, plentiful neck and saddle hackles, and a large fanned tail with well developed sickles and side hangers. Exhibition females also

White Dutch, male. Photo: John Tarren

Silver Partridge Dutch, male. Photo: John Tarren

have a large and well spread tail, accentuated by quite tight feathering on their back and (body) sides. The hens needed to breed exhibition males have rather looser, fluffier back and body plumage – the genetic female equivalent of the desired luxuriant male saddle and side hangers. Cocks used to breed exhibition females have relatively scanty neck, saddle and tail plumage. 'Cock-breeder' and 'pullet-breeder' strains may also differ on plumage patterns which are double mated.

COLOUR VARIETIES

The British Dutch Bantam Club has adopted direct English translations of Dutch terminology, which has one advantage: Dutch terminology is arguably more logical, and therefore more understandable to novices. Traditional English terms follow in parentheses, many of which were coined centuries ago by the cock-fighting fraternity.

Gold Partridge (Black-Red)
Silver Partridge (Silver Duckwing)
Yellow Partridge (Golden Duckwing). This is debatable, as two visually very similar, but genetically different varieties have been seen on Dutch, causing much confusion. One type is genetically 'Gold', but with an autosomal diluting gene, the other is genetically 'Silver', but with autosomal Mahogany gene.
Blue Gold Partridge (Blue-Red)
Blue Silver Partridge (Blue Silver Duckwing)
Blue Yellow Partridge (more debatable!)
Red Shouldered White (Pile)
Cuckoo Partridge (Crele)
Cuckoo
Self colours: Black, Blue, Lavender, White
Salmon and Blue-Salmon (as Faverolles)
Columbian and Blue-marked Columbian
Buff-Columbian, Blue-marked Buff-Columbian, White-marked Buff-Columbian, Normal Quail and other Quail variants (as Barbu d'Anvers)

Salmon Faverolles. Originally a free gift with Feathered World *magazine, 16 July 1909 Artist: J.W. Ludlow*

'Lachsfarbige Lachshuhner' (Salmon Faverolles). Originally a free gift with Geflügel-Börse *January 1941.
Artist: W. Jennrich*

seen at shows since then, but never by enough enthusaistic fanciers to revive their quality or numbers securely.

Ermine Faverolles Bantams were made by William Croft in the UK *circa* 1945–50. Additional strains were made by other fanciers in the 1960s and 1970s. John Kraft has been the leading breeder and exhibitor here since then, at the head of a small group of Faverolles Society members with this colour variety.

As with birds of this pattern in other breeds, there has been a consistent problem of trying to achieve good black neck hackle striping without getting a lot of black showing in what should be the white parts.

WHITE

As can be seen from the Faverolles Club Show entry figures earlier in this chapter, large White Faverolles were very popular in the years shortly before the First World War. It is believed that they were kept by many table chicken producers as well as show exhibitors. Although Whites are easier to breed than most patterned varieties, they need shaded runs, careful feeding and extra show preparation if perfectly snow-white specimens are to be presented before a judge. Many White Faverolles males have been rather brassy over the past century, but this did not matter to table bird producers – brassy cockerels are white enough to look 'clean' when plucked. Whites virtually died out during the war, with the Whites seen at shows in the 1920s being accused of being 'half-bred Cochine'. Dr T.W.E. Roydon, Faverolles Club President from Fleggburgh, Norfolk, was the leading exhibitor of Whites during the 1930s. John Milner, his daughter Janet, and William Croft were the main (possibly the only) breeders here during the 1950s and 1960s. There have been few in the UK since then, but there are some in Germany and the Netherlands.

Although a strain of White Faverolles Bantams briefly existed *circa* 1910–14, they were not really established until a strain was made by Clifford Lowe in the 1960s. He

Cuckoo Faverolles, bantam female. Photo: John Tarren

obtained some very light-coloured, nearly white, birds which had hatched from a friend's flock of Salmon Faverolles Bantams. He selected from these and bought a White Sussex Bantam cockerel to cross with them to obtain pure white plumage. A few other Faverolles enthusiasts joined this project, notably John F. Morris.

FAVEROLLES DESCRIPTION

Because of the differences between countries, which are sometimes more imagined than real, interested readers should study the standards of several of the relevant countries and live birds at shows. The basic features (great size, 'cloddy' build, beard, extra hind toes) are the same everywhere, but details of back line and tail carriage, the colour of Salmons, and other points vary. Faverolles Bantams are one of the biggest miniatures, which has sometimes caused differences between Faverolles specialists and general judges. Bantam hens can look 'cloddy' and still look acceptable in a bantam show cage for most general judges, but some bantam cocks hardly fit in these cages and are probably way over their official (British) weight of 1360g (3lb). Large cocks can weigh a very impressive 5kg (11lb), and everyone agrees – the bigger the better.

Hamburghs. Originally a free gift with Feathered World *magazine, 13 May 1910. Artist: J.W. Ludlow*

Gold Spangled Hamburghs. Originally a free gift with Poultry *magazine, circa 1912. Artist: J.W. Ludlow*

CHAPTER 14

Hamburgh (UK)/Hamburg (USA)/ Hollandse Hoen (Netherlands)

Hamburghs are the most popular of a large group of European light breeds, the remainder of which were described by the author in *Rare Poultry Breeds*. The 'Turkish Rooster and Two Turkish Hens' in Ulisse Alrovandi's book on poultry in 1600 were similar to Silver Pencilled Hamburghs, apart from one hen being single-combed and tasselled.

Competitions among cottagers for specific local breeds (hens only) were held in northern pubs, mostly Lancashire and Yorkshire, long before the first general poultry show at

Silver Spangled Hamburghs. Originally a free gift with Poultry *magazine, circa 1912. Artist: J.W. Ludlow*

London Zoo in 1845. Few details of the small, relatively informal gatherings have survived, but they may have been held as far back as 1700. Black Pheasant Fowl, later to become Black Hamburghs, were concentrated in Lancashire and around Keighley in west Yorkshire. They were described by Thomas Sutlief in 1702 in his book *A Trip to the North of England*. Lancashire Moony Fowls eventually became the basis of 'pullet-breeder' strains and Yorkshire Pheasant Fowls 'cock-breeders'. Gold Pencilled and Silver Pencilled Hamburghs are mainly of Dutch origin (related to Assendelftse Hoenders), but were also represented in Lancashire as 'Bolton Bays' and 'Bolton Greys'. One of the later local clubs, not formed until 1842, was the 'Society of Fanciers at Hollins' (near Oldham) which had standards for hen 'Red Mooned Pheasant' (Gold Spangled), 'Silver Pheasant' (Silver Spangled), 'Black Pheasant' and 'Creel Poult' (possibly Silver Pencilled).

Local standards and strains were not viable once general poultry shows were established. Derbyshire's version was almost extinct by 1870, but was revived as a separate breed, the Redcap, just in time. The name 'Hamburgh', with the extra 'h' at the end, was adopted, after meetings at Birmingham Shows, 1848–50, of experts led by Rev. E.S. Dixon. They would have known about the identical 'Hamburgers' in Germany and Dutch 'Hollandse Hoenders', and their long history in northern England, so it is not known why he chose the German name over the alternatives. Many British breeders objected, including Mr B.P. Grant (letter in *The Cottage Gardener and Poultry Chronicle*, 15 April 1856), who thought the older names, Bolton Greys, Bolton Bays, and so on, were more accurate, citing references to 'Hamburghs' (E. Albin, *Natural History of Birds*, 1736; J.M. Bechstein, *Natural History of Germany*, 1793), which described spangled, bearded and crested birds like Brabanters.

Once the new name and standard had been imposed, fanciers started to modify their old strains to suit. It was soon discovered that separate strains would still be needed to breed

perfectly-marked males and females in all five (Black, Gold and Silver Pencilled, Gold and Silver Spangled) of the now 'official' varieties. In Spangleds, Yorkshire Pheasant Fowls became the basis of the new 'cock-breeders' and Lancashire Moonys the basis of 'pullet-breeders'. Both still needed some modification, so (as with Derbyshire Redcaps) the old strains almost died out. This process of refinement was blamed by some for a loss in size, vigour and productivity. A group of breeders who held this view found surviving old-type Yorkshire birds *circa* 1919–14 and relaunched them as 'Old English Pheasant Fowl'. Yorkshire Pheasant Fowls were smaller than Lancashire Moonys, had smaller spangles, had good white ear lobes and the males had (on Silvers at least) full cock-feathered tails, clear white with neat black spangles at the end.

Lancashire Moonys were bigger, had bigger round spangles, partly or completely red lobes, and many males were hen-feathered. Pullet-breeder Pencilled males were, and still are, hen-feathered; so there were at least two groups who promoted the acceptance of hen-feathered males for showing. After much more argument it was eventually decided that only cock-feathered males would be exhibited except at Hamburgh Club shows where there were special classes for 'pullet-breeder males' and 'cock-breeder females'. There were originally two colour versions of 'Golden Moony', a lighter bright gold and a darker golden-red type, the latter becoming the standard form. It would probably have been possible to produce the lighter version with clear tail feathers and black spangles, but it proved virtually impossible to have other than solid black tails on the darker form with its desired rich ground colour. Some old strains of the dark type had males with a solid black breast and red lobes, like Redcaps.

Many of the original Yorkshire Pheasant males had clear (gold or silver) neck and saddle plumage, but the new standard required centre stripes and tips on these feathers: hence some Lancashire Moony crosses, followed by back-crossing to Yorkshire Pheasants and further selection. These crosses also led to larger, rounder spangles, resulting in exhibition males and their mates, 'cock-breeder' females.

Although represented by Bolton Bays (bay = brown, as in bay horses, from Latin *badius*, 'chestnut-coloured') and Bolton Greys in England, Pencilled Hamburghs are essentially a Dutch breed. There would be good historical justification for adopting their name Hollandse Hoen internationally for the increasing range of colour combinations of the Pencilled pattern, and then limiting the name 'Hamburgh' for the Spangleds, Blacks and newer self colours. There are other breeds in the Netherlands with this or very similar patterns: Assendelftse Hoenders, Friesians and Groninger Meeuwen. All these breeds are fairly small breeds, Friesians being very small; Pencilled Hamburghs have always been smaller than Blacks and Spangleds. Their small size and rather small, although

plentiful, eggs, meant they were never used by large scale producers. For a thousand years, probably much longer, the ancestors of these birds were rather small for a very good reason: their owners could not afford to give them much of their valuable grain. The birds had to find almost all or their own food by foraging around the countryside, so needed to be active and with a small appetite. Their owners provided a safe and warm perching place in the days when people and livestock shared a single 'longhouse'.

Black Hamburghs were originally much the same size as Spangles, that is, slightly larger than the Pencilleds. In the nineteenth century many were crossed with Spanish and Minorcan, resulting in Black Hamburghs being larger in general, and with much larger white ear lobes, than other varities. Photographs of prize-winning Blacks in the 1920s and 1930s show birds almost identical to rose-combed

Buff/White Pencilled Hamburghs. Artist: C.S.Th. van Gink

Minorcas. Blacks were rare in the 1850s, with usually only one or two in the AOV classes at shows with huge entries of the four patterned varieties. But by 1930 there were full classes of Blacks, with all the others together in AOC Hamburgh. Minorca-type Black Hamburghs are extinct, present-day birds being elegant birds of correct size and shape.

Blue, Buff and White Hamburghs have all been bred and exhibited from time to time in several countries over the past 150 years. Lewis Wright mentioned strains of Buffs and Whites in the 1880s and 1870s (the Whites were in Lancashire). They soon died out in England, but some had been exported to America, where they fared better. It is believed these strains were made from very lightly marked cock-breeder Gold and Silver Pencilled Hamburghs, some of which were crossed with Buff or White Leghorns. Some of the resulting birds had white shanks and feet, instead of the slate-blue required on all other varieties of Hamburgh. This caused several years of argument among the American fanciers who had taken up Whites in the period 1870–1905. Two leading figures were Lewis F. Allen, who preferred white shanks, and Rev. C.W. Bolton, who thought slate-blue correct for all Hamburghs. John H. Robinson said in his book, *Popular Breeds of Domestic Poultry* (1924), 'that it had been all but impossible to find good models to photograph for illustrations.' He succeeded, though; the two Whites illustrated are excellent. Charles Holt was trying (in the UK) to make Buffs and remake Whites in 1913, but he died in 1915. There were later attempts, but none survived for long.

Another colour version of the Pencilled pattern, 'Geelwitpel' (as Gold Pencilled, but with white replacing black markings), were first exhibited in the new varieties class of the 1899 Utrecht Show. They continued to be bred in small numbers in the Netherlands (14 in 1921, 3 in 1984 at Utrecht). Two were shown in the 1901 Crystal Palace Show, but were not seen in the UK again until the 1990s.

The British Hamburgh Club was certainly well established by 1891, but it is not known when it was formed or whether any of the previous local clubs had amalgamated to start the process. There was also a Scottish Hamburgh Club, a Northern Hamburgh Club, a Southern Hamburgh Club, possibly also a Welsh Hamburgh Club. At least around the turn of the century, they seem to have operated as a federation. Following some complaints about which shows should have prize money guaranteed, the British Hamburgh Club's AGM at Liverpool on 22 January 1901 agreed that each of the four regional groups could keep a third of the subscription money in their area to support whichever shows they considered suitable. There was also a Hamburgh Bantam Club, formed about 1905 or 1906 which amalgamated with the main club in 1960. The Northern Club had 27 members when it held its AGM at the Red Lion Hotel, Silsden on 9 February 1901, but no later mentions of it have been found. The Southern Club folded during the First World War, with the Scottish Club lasting until some time during the 1930s. The latter probably lasted longer than the others because its annual show was often held on New Year's Day, after a good party in a local hotel the previous night.

In the first decade or so of general poultry shows Hamburghs were one of the leading breeds, their breeders having the advantage of previous showing expertise over supporters of most other varieties. Mainstream shows (unlike previous Hamburgh competitions) were primarily for pens (trios or quartets). The Birmingham Show of December 1854 had over 220 pens (1m: 3ft) of Hamburghs, followed by about 215 similar pens in 1855.

There were 216 large Hamburghs entered at the 1868 Birmingham Show, an impressive figure which suggests the British Hamburgh Club may have already been formed by this time. This level of popularity did not last, but most of the main shows (Alexandra Palace, Crystal Palace, London Dairy, Olympia and Birmingham) could still muster between 100 and 150 from 1880 until 1914. The Scottish Club Shows were almost as good, with about 80 to 100 birds.

Some British Hamburgh Club Show entry numbers indicate their popularity:

- January 1901 Liverpool, 29 Black, 11 Gold Spangled, 11 Silver Spangled, 17 Gold Pencilled, 4 Silver Pencilled, 22 Novice, 21 Selling
- December 1901, Alexandra Palace London, 47 Black, 17 Gold Spangled, 25 Silver Spangled, 36 Gold Pencilled, 19 Silver Pencilled
- 1912 Leeds, 18 classes/120 birds: 25 Black, 8 Gold Spangled, 11 Silver Spangled, 10 Gold Pencilled, 11 Silver Pencilled, 3 pullet-breeder male, 4 cock-breeder female + (?selling; ?novice)
- 1913 York, 18 classes/145 birds: 28 Black, 9 Gold Spangled, 30 Silver Spangled, Gold Pencilled cancelled, 14 Silver Pencilled, 10 pullet-breeder male, 8 cock-breeder female.

Hamburghs declined sharply during the First World War and the Great Depression which followed, and have never recovered in the UK. Wartime shortages and economic hardships were one obvious cause, but more significant was the death of several of the leading exhibitors between 1914 and 1924. There were few new fanciers to replace them, partly because of the general difficulties from 1914 to 1945, and partly because old Hamburgh fanciers had a bad reputation for being secretive and unhelpful, some even resorting to faking to create winners. The most infamous type of faking was transplanting well marked tail feathers of males, fixed into the hollow lower shaft of the original feathers. Ideally spangled or edged (Pencilled males) sickles didn't appear very often, and then not necessarily on cockerels which excelled in comb, lobe or body markings; and 'experts' didn't want to waste these good feathers, did they?

Some Hamburgh stalwarts had seen this decline coming before the war, as described

Black Hamburgh, large female. Photo: John Tarren

by Charles Holt in the 1912 *Feathered World Yearbook*. After reporting the ousting of the previous club secretary, he said, 'To outsiders, like me, all the newly-organized club appears to have done is to appoint eighteen club judges. I don't know whether all the paid-up members of the club have been appointed judges. If not, then they have a grievance, for that is all they can expect in exchange for their subscriptions. Just fancy, "eighteen Hamburgh judges". What an absurdity! It puts Gilbert and Sullivan in the shade. I wonder what they expect to judge. Very few shows give classes for Hamburghs, and when they do very few Hamburgh fanciers support them. What the Hamburgh Club ought to do is to appoint exhibitors, not judges.'

His words proved to be true. In 1926 only Bingley, Harrogate, Hebden Bridge, Keighley, Utley, Royal Lancashire, Silsden, Skipton, York and the London 'International' Show offered classes for Hamburghs, a situation which was not going to encourage anyone living outside Lancashire or Yorkshire to start with Hamburghs. Even this limited number of shows was sending the Club into financial ruin as they could only persuade the show organizers to keep putting on Hamburgh classes if they 'guaranteed' to finance the prize money if there were few entries. The Club President privately paid the prize money at some shows

Silver Spangled Hamburgh, large male. Photo: John Tarren

until 1930. The British Hamburgh Club Shows in 1920 at York had 80 entries, followed by 90 birds in 1921 at Bradford, both of which were reasonable, but there was no show at all in 1923, 1925 or 1927, and entries (not found) were generally described as poor from then until 1939.

Large Hamburghs have only survived in the UK because of the efforts of a few enthusiasts, most club members keeping the bantam version. At the 1954 National Poultry Show, Olympia, London, there were only two large Blacks in the AOV classes, improving in 1962 (same venue but this time incorporating the Hamburgh Club Show) to fifteen Silver Spangleds and six others. During the 1970s the Hamburgh Club Show was part of the Birmingham Show. Two entry figures were found by the author: 1971 (7 Silver Spangled, 6 AOC), 1978 (9 Silver Spangled, 4 AOC). Interest gradually increased during the 1980s, the highest entry found being at 1988 Stafford Show: 21 Silver Spangleds, 16 Blacks and 11 AOC. Since then Gold and Silver Pencilleds have become more numerous and Chamois Pencilleds and others have been imported.

A similar situation occurred in America and Canada: a steady decline in the early twentieth century after a popular spell in the late nineteenth century. From about 1890 onwards Hamburgs (USA spelling) were concentrated in Ontario, Canada and the north-eastern states, especially Massachusetts and New York. There were two breed clubs, the Hamburg Fanciers' Club (founded 1903), which was mainly based around the Chestnut Hill suburb of Boston; and the New York Silver Spangled Hamburg Club, which had 32 members in 1913. Hamburgs have revived recently, and are once again regularly seen at poultry shows all over America.

Hamburghs, or 'Hollandse Hoenders' as they are named there, had a slightly smoother history in the Netherlands. Entries of the large fowl at Utrecht ranged from 102 to 191 between 1899 and 1921 (of those known). Obviously they were affected by two world wars, but since 1950, they have been bred in limited numbers, but more than in the UK.

HAMBURGH BANTAM

Many miniature versions of large breeds were first made by W.F. Entwisle of Wakefield, Yorkshire; but although he had a go at making Hamburgh Bantams (possibly in the 1880s), he gave up on them to devote his time and housing to other projects. Another British breeder, John William Farnsworth (died 1915) saw the project through from beginning to end, *circa* 1880–90. The initial matings he used to make his strain of Silver Spangled Hamburgh Bantams are recorded in Pringle Proud's book *Bantams as a Hobby*, where a letter by Mr Farnsworth is quoted. 'A really good but undersized silver spangled Hamburgh cockerel of notable descent, having been mated to a couple of rather large silver Sebright hens, resulted in my being, the following year, in possession of a fairly good Moony cross cockerel, which was mated to a somewhat large blue-legged white rose-comb hen, a black rose-comb hen, and his sister, a Moony cross pullet. Another similar pullet was bred to a pure White Rosecomb cock. The remaining Mooney cross pullet, the smallest of the three, was put back to her sire, the

Hamburgh cock, the services of the Sebright hens being at once and for ever dispensed with.' Mr Farnsworth, who lived at Frampton Place, Boston, Lincolnshire, continued his breeding programme with selected birds from these matings, more Black and White Rosecombs, and another undersized (3½lb) large Silver Spangled Hamburgh cock.

A Hamburgh Bantam Club was formed in 1905 or 1906. Silver Spangleds remained the most popular variety, but other fanciers tried to make Gold Spangleds and Gold and Silver Pencilleds. Large Pencilled Hamburghs had always been the smallest variety, so the smallest of these were selected to further reduce their size. There was not much difference in size between many so-called 'large' and 'bantam' Pencilled Hamburghs, which is often still the case today, a century later. Gold Spangled Bantams were probably made by crossing Silver Spangled Bantams with Gold Sebrights. The way things were headed was made obvious in 1925 when the British Hamburgh (for large fowl) Club did not have a show because of lack of money (to guarantee prize money), but the Hamburgh Bantam Club had an excellent show at Birmingham with 32 Silver Spangleds, 14 Gold Spangleds and 12 Gold Pencilleds. This was one of their best shows before the war, exceeded only by a display of 65 birds at Mansfield in 1923, but a total entry of about 35 was usual.

The Hamburgh Bantam Club suspended all activities during the Second World War, re-activated in 1945 by its new secretary Harry Snowden of Cononley, near Keighley, Yorkshire. It had 26 members by May 1947. The British Hamburgh Club and Hamburgh Bantam Club combined to form a single Hamburgh Club about 1960.

Hamburgh Bantams remained rather too big in the UK, although Jim Owen and others imported some of the much smaller birds from Germany and the Netherlands in the 1990s, as well as some much needed large Hamburghs.

Gold Spangled Hamburgh, bantam female. Photo: John Tarren

Silver Spangled Hamburgh, bantam female. Photo: John Tarren

Many stalwart British fanciers stuck to their larger bantams, claiming that the markings on their old strains were superior to the European strains. Black Hamburgh Bantams are to be included in the 2008 edition of *British Poultry Standards* for the first time, earlier generations of fanciers thinking they would be too similar to Black Rosecomb Bantams. It is now considered that there is enough difference in shape between the two breeds for this not to be a problem.

Silver Pencilled Hamburgh, bantam exhibition male. Photo: John Tarren

Silver Pencilled Hamburgh, bantam pullet-breeder male. Photo: John Tarren

Hamburgh Bantams gradually increased in popularity from 1950 onwards, and at least a few have been entered at most shows since then, but few specimens are good enough to win 'Best in Show', which has limited their appeal to regular exhibitors. Bantam entries at Hamburgh Club Shows (usually at Stafford) have fluctuated, some of the best appearing below (pbm = pullet-breeder Pencilled male, nov. = novice exhibitors, ns = non-standard colours):

- 1981: 116 (58 Silver Spangled, 6 Gold Spangled, 36 Gold Pencilled, 6 Silver Pencilled, 5 pbm, 3 nov., 2 trios)
- 1984: 133 (75 Silver Spangled, 10 Gold Spangled, 21 Gold Pencilled, 13 Silver Pencilled, 9 pbm, 5 nov.)
- 1985: 144 (80 Silver Spangled, 7 Gold Spangled, 27 Gold Pencilled, 10 Silver Pencilled, 10 pbm, 10 nov.)
- 1995: 119 (65 Silver Spangled, 12 Gold Spangled, 25 Gold Pencilled, 8 Silver Pencilled, 7 pbm, 22 nov.)
- 1999: 117 (57 Silver Spangled, 19 Gold Spangled, 18 Gold Pencilled, 9 Silver Pencilled, 4 pbm, 3 nov., 7 ns).

None of the club shows since 2000 have had over 100 bantams entered.

HAMBURGH DESCRIPTION

Close study of American, British, Dutch and German poultry standards and photos of winners (or live birds for globe-trotting enthusiasts) will show considerable differences in size, shape (especially tail carriage), headpoints (especially male combs), and markings from country to country. Some British Hamburgh fanciers have used Dutch and German Bantams to reduce size and produce tidier combs on our frequently oversized version, while retaining UK standard markings and colours. Spangles on British birds have consistently been larger and more round than on Spangleds elsewhere. The ground colour on Gold Spangleds is darker in the UK than elsewhere. Gold Spangleds have had solid black tails for most of their history, instead of the spangled tail feathers on Silvers. It was argued that this concession was necessary for Golds as early attempts at producing spangled tails also brought light feather shafts on body plumage. Some attractive Gold Spangled Bantams have been

Silver Pencilled Hamburgh, bantam exhibition female. Cock-breeder females have clear white upper back and breast plumage, with tail markings which run along the feathers, not across them. Photo: John Tarren

Gold Pencilled Hamburgh, bantam exhibition female. Cock-breeder females are marked as described for cock-breeder Silver Pencilleds, but with gold ground colour. Photo: John Tarren

exhibited since 2000, and it is not yet clear whether they will be accepted as an alternative or as the new preferred pattern.

Double mating is essential for the Pencilled varieties and preferable, but not essential, on Blacks and Spangleds. In these varieties it obviously depends on how competitive classes are. In the case of Blacks the problem is related to obtaining maximum sized white lobes without white extending into the face, and maximum green sheen on plumage without getting yellow hackle feathers in males. As males are the problem, partly white-faced, yellow-hackled males have been used for breeding exhibition females. To avoid these problems when trying to breed exhibition males, small lobed, matt black plumaged females have been used as cock-breeders.

Hen-feathered Spangled males have been used as pullet-breeders, but otherwise differences between cock-breeders and pullet-breeders are complex. Consult an expert for details.

Hen-feathered males are certainly essential for breeding exhibition Pencilled females, which most fanciers concentrate on anyway,

so are readily available. Exhibition Pencilled males are hardly pencilled at all, having clear (gold or silver) body plumage, with the tail feathers being the main point of interest. They should be black with white edging on Silver Pencilleds, black with gold edging on Gold Pencilleds and white with orange-buff edging on Chamois Pencilled (Dutch Geetwitpel). Cock-breeder females have clear head, neck and upper body plumage, with indistinct markings on lower body and tail more like that of Pencilled Wyandottes (going around each feather in concentric rings) than that of exhibition Pencilled Hamburghs (bars across feathers).

Hamburghs are active birds, so must have large, grassed outside runs. To avoid their long tail feathers getting broken, give them large houses with perches well away from house walls. Chicks will need to be petted as much as possible, followed by periods in show training cages, to get them reasonably tame for showing. Hamburgh males are noisy and frequent crowers, so this is not one of the best breeds for suburban poultry keepers.

'Dr. J. K. Goodall's Indian Game Cock'. Originally a free gift with Feathers *magazine, 8 December 1899. Artist: F.J.S. Chatterton*

Jubilee Indian Game female. Originally a free gift with Profitable Farm & Garden *magazine, 16 April 1904. Artist: unsigned, but probably F.J.S. Chatterton*

CHAPTER 15

Indian Game (UK)/Cornish (USA)

The different names for this breed represent its history: made in Cornwall, England from birds imported from India. Early 'Cornish Indian Game' were used for cockfighting, but since about 1880 they have been bred for exhibition or for breeding table birds. Specialist breeders sold surplus cockerels for crossing with Dorking (UK), Plymouth Rock (USA) or other hens. Most of today's broiler hybrids are a sophisticated version of White Cornish × White Rock crosses.

ANCIENT HISTORY – THE PHOENICIANS

The Phoenicians, an ancient Mediterranean civilization, have frequently been mentioned as the people responsible for bringing the first Asiatic fighting cocks to Britain, and therefore the beginning of the Indian Game breed. When the Romans invaded Britain in 55BC they noted that the British primarily kept chickens for cockfighting, with table birds and eggs being secondary considerations. Many centuries had already passed between Phoenician visits and Roman times, and almost 2000 years before 'Indian Game' as known today were made. The author does not know if any ancient chicken bones found by archaeologists in Cornwall are big enough to be clearly Oriental Game rather than normal European light breed type chickens.

Ancient Phoenicians certainly did visit Cornwall. Theirs was an empire built on trade, and they came to Cornwall for tin. They were based in the area which is now Lebanon and the coastal part of Syria, plus major Phoenician settlements in southern Spain, Sardinia, Sicily and the north African coast from (present-day) Rabat, Morocco to Tripoli, Libya; they were at their peak about 850 to 750BC, 700 years before the arrival of the Romans in Britain.

THE EIGHTEENTH CENTURY

Large scale British trading links with India and other parts of southern Asia started in the seventeenth century, but British East India Company ships did not regularly call in at Falmouth and other south-west harbours until well into the eighteenth century. Returning ships, fully laden with Indian goods, called in to receive instructions from messengers who rode down from the ship owners in London, perhaps with revised delivery instructions. These ships started their voyage with crates of live chickens on board, to provide the crew with fresh eggs and meat for the trip, and the occasional cockfight to relieve boredom. Any birds still alive by this time were sold to local farmers and cockfighting enthusiasts while the ship was waiting.

A new breed was gradually formed in Cornwall, called 'Indian Game' (informally 'Injees'). Some poultry books have given detailed family trees of crosses between Asils, Malays and English Pit Game used to make them, but these should be regarded as a very general outline of what happened. A great many ships brought exotic chickens to Devon and Cornwall between 1750 and 1850, possibly a few as early as 1550. Who knows what matings happened then?

Harrison Weir said that a few 'Indian Game' (*circa* 1858) had short, thick legs and wide bodies like we see today, but the majority were fairly tall; perhaps not as tall as the best Malays or Shamo of today, but of similar general appearance. The plumage colour and pattern of Indian Game was (roughly) already established by this time, not surprising as similar markings have been known on some Asil, Shamo and Malays for many centuries. The pattern, particularly on hens, was called 'Pheasant' on these three breeds. Cockfighting was banned in England in 1849, although the new law was not vigorously enforced in rural areas. However, demand for table chickens was increasing, a result of a growing population and the new railways for rapid transit of produce into towns, so their value as table bird breeders was becoming more important.

Indian Game did not become a fully recognized breed until 1886, so their development in the period 1846–86 is not well known. Harrison Weir said the Cornish 'Indian Game' were first exhibited in the 1858–59 show season at Crystal Palace and some west country shows, with Lewis Wright adding that he saw 'a fine display' of them at the 1870 Plymouth Show. All the Victorian poultry experts agreed they were virtually unknown outside Devon and Cornwall. However, in the course of researching for this chapter, the author found two earlier exhibitors of 'Indian Game' (in AGV classes): Messrs Jessup Brothers, of The Aviaries, Cheltenham, at Gloucester Show, November 1854, and Rev. John Meredith, Donnington, Shropshire, at Birmingham Show, December 1854.

THE INDIAN GAME CLUB

The club was formed at a meeting which started at 2.30pm, on Thursday 15 April 1886 at The Royal Hotel, Plymouth. John Frayn was elected President, Julius J. Mosenthal became Secretary, John Pomroy the treasurer, and others present were James Frayn, John's brother (James later changed his surname to Frayne, after a family argument), William Brent, and Messrs Crockford, Henwood and Site. They decided to produce a provisional breed standard, which was agreed at another meeting on 1 December 1886. There was a major argument at some stage (possibly the cause of the Frayn family fall-out), which caused the club to be suspended for a while (details not found), until it was reactivated at a meeting at Bridgwater in 1891. The breed standard was finally published in 1896, the wording of which has not changed much since, although the birds have changed beyond recognition. Back then some hatches included a mixture of pea- and walnut-combed chicks, which were successfully exhibited as Indians (pea comb) and Malays (walnut comb), under general judges at least, despite being siblings. Since 1946 Indian Game have been very broad bodied and short legged. The changes were gradual until 1920, followed by rapid change up to 1940.

'Indians' are often criticized for being 'horrible, deformed looking things', and even enthusiasts freely admit there are chronic fertility and hatchability problems. People were making similar comments back in the 1920s, quite early in their transformation. They were countered by Indian Game Club secretary A.H. Brownson in the 1928 *Feathered World Yearbook*, who said that in the course of trying to breed the oft-criticized short-backed, short-legged show birds, a lot of longer-backed, longer-legged (and more fertile) cockerels were also bred, which were ideal for table bird crossing. This is still true today, and some free-range/organic producers still use them, and even exhibition breeders use slightly longer legged males for breeding.

JUBILEE INDIAN GAME

This variety is the same pattern as original (now usually called 'Dark') Indians, but with all black parts of the plumage changed

Jubilee Indian Game, large male. Photo: John Tarren

Jubilee Indian Game, large female. Photo: John Tarren

probably correctly, that 'Indian Game' would deter people who would think they were still a fighting breed. This could have happened in two ways: by practical poultry breeders who worried about batches of cockerels killing and injuring each other just before they were ready to be sold; second, any connection to cockfighting would not go down well with the general public, especially in the north-eastern states where the infant USA broiler industry was beginning to develop.

White Cornish were added to American Standards in 1898. They were a completely American production, with no connection to British strains, instead being a mixture of White Asil, White Malay, White Wyandotte and White Georgia Game (a strain of Pit Game). White Cornish were more feathery than Darks, a legacy from the Wyandottes.

Jubilee Indian Game, bantam male. Photo: John Tarren

They were ideal for broiler chicken breeding, but mere mongrels to British Indian Game enthusiasts, hence their hostility to Henry

Double Laced Blue Indian Game, bantam male.
Photo: John Tarren

Double Laced Blue Indian Game, bantam female.
Photo: John Tarren

Hunt's Jubilees, which they suspected had been made by similar means.

A few years later some American breeders tried to import Jubilees from Mr Hunt, but he did not have any to spare. He had already reduced his flock following their hostile reception, and some of these were killed by a neighbour's dog. Mr W.H. Card, of Bristol, Connecticut decided to make something similar from scratch, but ended up by making White Laced Red Cornish, a similar pattern to Buff Laced Wyandottes. White Laced Red Cornish and Jubilee Indian hens do not look very different, from a distance anyway, but the males are completely different. He used some roughly Buff Laced crossbreds (believed to be Dark Cornish × Light Brahma), White Cornish, White Wyandottes and, possibly, Shamo.

Indian Game Bantams were first shown in America at the 1904 St Louis Show, where two exhibitors, Dr Phelps and Roberts & Co., entered fifteen birds. Interest was limited to a handful of fanciers until about 1930, when a lot more people started to keep them. In addition to stock imported from the UK, additional strains were made by American fanciers, in one case using Chibi-Shamo from Japan. The long

delay before many American fanciers took an interest explains why they were not standardized there, as 'Cornish Bantams', until 1933. American Cornish Bantams are rather smaller (with a sloping back and tail) than British Indian Game Bantams, possibly a legacy from those Chibis. Many British Indian Game Bantams are rather too big, however, although a few excellent specimens have been exhibited in the UK, Germany and the Netherlands, which are the perfect balance of size and type.

Buff Cornish were standardized in 1938, having been developed since 1925. APA Standards require even Buff plumage, but they were more like Wheaten Piles when first made, with white neck, wing and tail feathers, and have been called 'Palomino', rather than 'Buff'.

White and White Laced Red Cornish Bantams were added to American Standards in 1942, by crossing Dark Cornish Bantams with White Chibis and Buff Laced Wyandotte Bantams. Blue Laced Cornish were added in 1965, also using Wyandottes. British Standard Jubilees are also bred in the USA, but are rare. American Standards also list Blacks, Blues, Columbians, Spangles and Black-Mottles.

INDIAN GAME/CORNISH DESCRIPTION

For full details, read *British Poultry Standards*, or its equivalent for overseas readers. In the case of British Standards, most of the wording is the same as the 1896 Standard. Words such as 'medium' or 'short' can be made to mean anything you want them to mean. Extremely short and broad birds usually win, but have been criticized for associated infertility problems.

There has never been any argument over required head characteristics: a strong head and beak with a compact pea comb and small wattles. Eyes are usually yellow or light orange. The beak is yellow, with some horn coloured striping on Darks.

Plumage should be tight and close to emphasize their muscularity. Wing and tail feathers are usually rather brittle and easily broken, so exhibitors need a 'reserve show team'.

As all three British varieties are simply different colour versions of the same pattern, it is usual, indeed advisable, to cross Darks with Blues or Darks with Jubilees, but not Blues with Jubilees. Jubilees soon become too light, the females losing most of their lacing if repeatedly bred pure. This is why Jubilee males are 'dirty white'; it is necessary to breed well marked hens. The lacing of Blue females deteriorates unless regularly crossed back to Darks.

SPECIAL MANAGEMENT REQUIREMENTS

Indians need exercise and grass to keep fit and fertile, plus the grass to keep those shanks and feet a really rich orange-yellow. Nutrition needs special attention: a good start to get initial development of muscle and bone, followed by slightly restricted feeding to avoid them building internal body fat, which reduces their fertility and egg production further. Taller, less extreme, cockerels are often mated with winning short-legged, wide-bodied hens for best results.

Black-Mottled Cornish, bantam pair in US. Photo: John Tarren

Japanese Bantams. Originally a free gift with Feathered World *magazine, circa 1905. Artist: A.F. Lydon*

Japanese Bantams. Originally a free gift with Poultry *magazine, circa 1912. Artist: J.W. Ludlow*

CHAPTER 16

Japanese/Chabo Bantams

These very distinctive bantams, with very short legs and a long tail, held vertically, are called Japanese in English speaking countries, but their name in Japan and other countries, Chabo, is more correct. The name Chabo is derived from the old Japanese name for southeast Asia, present day Vietnam, Thailand and Malaysia. Chabos were depicted on Japanese paintings from 1603, so it must be assumed they were first imported to Japan about then.

European explorers and traders started to travel to the Far East in significant numbers from the late sixteenth century onwards. The rulers of Japan feared these new outside influences would disrupt their structured society, especially Christian missionaries. In 1636 Japan was closed off to the outside world, and any Japanese people who managed to leave their homeland were not allowed back; any that did return were executed. This policy continued until the mid-nineteenth century, when some 'gunboat diplomacy', initially by the American Navy in 1853, forcing Japan to fully reconnect to the rest of the world by 1867.

Throughout these two centuries or so of seclusion virtually the only contact between Japan and the outside world was a small Dutch trading post on the tiny island of Decima, just off the coast of Nagasaki. A handful of Dutch seamen and traders were allowed to live there, no missionaries allowed! Dutch artist Jan Steen included a Black-Tailed Buff Chabo cock in his painting *The Poultry Yard* (circa 1660), presumably taken to the Netherlands from Decima.

Apart from the bird in this painting, nothing seems to have been recorded of Chabo Bantams in Europe or America until about 1860 (possibly 1855), which suggests that they had died out in their original homelands. There were plenty of European traders in these countries though, indeed (present-day) southern Vietnam became the French colony of Cochin-China, Malaysia became a British colony and Indonesia a Dutch colony. If any Chabo Bantams had existed in any of those countries they would surely have been taken back to Europe during the eighteenth century. It is not known how long they had existed in Indonesia or Malaysia before 1600.

Among the earliest European importers, *circa* 1855–60, were Herr von Albrecht (Dresden), Bailey & Sons (London), Mrs A. Woodcock (Leicester), H. Marten (?) and Berlin Zoo. The first recorded importers in America were Mr J.D. Nevius (Philadelphia), J.H. Fry (Staten Island) and E.G. Stadley (Claverack, NY), all importing during the 1860s. The tail carriage of Chabos was a controversial point in Europe and America from the beginning, and continued to be so ever since this period. There were no comparable breeds, and 'squirrel tail' (tail held forward of vertical, that is, pointing towards the head) was considered a serious fault on all breeds. An exactly vertical tail was taken as the ideal in most of Europe and elsewhere, despite evidence that in Japan (it was their breed, after all) forward tails were considered correct.

Lady Brassey, in her *Voyage of the Sunbeam*, writing from Kobe in Japan in 1877, described some she saw: 'They seem generally very small, and one I saw today had its head far behind its tail, which divided in the middle outwards, and fell forward on either side of its neck, in a most extraordinary manner.'

Debate about tail carriage was set off again many years later (1913, 1926, 1937) when Chabos which were known prize-winners in Japan (clubs and shows as we know them had been established in Japan from 1889) were sent to England and Germany, and all of them had forward-pointing tails. The two main importers during this period were Major G.T. Williams and J. Graf von Welczek.

Godfrey Trevelyan Williams first became interested in poultry in 1890 through a tutor for an army exam. His childhood was spent at Burton Joyce, Nottinghamshire, but he moved to Perranwell, Cornwall as a young man. His full-time career in the army (14th Hussars) limited his opportunites for poultry keeping, including periods in India, (probably) South Africa (the 14th Hussars served in the Boer War) and the First World War. He was able to keep a few bantams though, and his first Chabo Bantams were obtained by two men from his regiment in 1901 who went on a trip round the world. After 1918 he retired to his estate in Perranwell, where he kept a wide range of breeds, and was secretary of the Variety Bantam Club, Japanese Bantam Club, Frizzle Club and a local poultry club. Around 1945 he was promoted to Colonel, although he was quite elderly by then, and it is known he was at home most of the war. He may have been on 'secret duties' (see next paragraph). He died in the early 1960s.

Johannes Graf von Welczek had an estate at Labland in eastern Germany (pre-1945 borders). He was the German Ambassador in Paris from 1936 until 1939 (or 1940?), so would not have had much contact with Major Williams until 1945. He was replaced as ambassador by Foreign Minister Ribbentrop, so may not have been a loyal Nazi. He died in 1972. No details of his bantam keeping in later life were found by the author.

The first international poultry breed club was the International Chabo Bantam Club formed in 1937. Its secretary was Dr Renhold in (neutral) Switzerland. We can only imagine whether these three gentlemen met to discuss matters other than bantam breeding.

CHABO VARIETIES IN JAPAN

Early paintings, both in Japan and Jan Steen's in the Netherlands, indicate that the first Chabos were Black-Tailed Buffs. A wide range of additional colour varieties were developed over the following centuries, for many years the main ones being Black-Tailed Whites, Whites, Blacks, Birchens and Brown-Reds. At some time there must have been some crossing with Silkies, which resulted in a Black-Skinned Black ('Shinkuro') variety in addition to normal (red facial skin, yellow skin elsewhere) Black

Black-Tailed White Japanese/Chabo, female. Photo: John Tarren

Chabos, and Silkie-feathered Chabos (with normal red facial skin and yellow skin elsewhere). There were also bearded Chabos, frizzle-feathered Chabos, hen-feathered Chabos (on Millefleur, Red-Mottle, Black-Mottle) and 'Daruma' Chabos. These had, and still have, an exceptionally large comb and wattles, combined with a shorter tail than those of normal Chabos. Ideally the tail of a Daruma Chabo should reach to the same height as the bird's head and be well fanned, giving the whole bird an almost circular profile, apart from the very large comb on top. Large single combs can suffer from frostbite in cold weather, which is no doubt why Daruma Chabos originated on Kyushu, the southernmost of the major islands of Japan. There is also a rumpless bantam breed in Japan, the Uzaro, which has quite short legs and a similar body shape to Chabos, but it is debatable whether they could be classed as a variety of Chabo. Normal Chabos in Japan are not required to have a very large comb. Large combs on Chabos in Europe may have been included in breed standards because fanciers here did not then realize Daruma Chabos were a separate sub-variety.

CHABO HISTORY IN THE UK

From the first imports in the 1860s until 1914, Chabos were most popular in the south-western counties of England, although some of the leading breeders lived elsewhere. Taking show entries in 1901 as an example, the three best displays of them were at Birmingham (19), the 'International Show' at Alexandra Palace, London (20) and Taunton, Somerset (17). Their popularity surged just before the First World War, with show entries between 63 and 103 at the Crystal Palace (London) and Variety Bantam Club's Annual Shows (Sheffield or York) from 1911 to 1913. The Japanese Bantam Club was formed at the Crystal Palace Show on 12 November 1912, initially with Mr Darty

Birchen-Grey Japanese/Chabo, male. Photo: John Tarren

as secretary. Club activities were suspended during the war, being re-activated in 1919, with Major Williams taking over as secretary until 1939. The breed was gradually revived, with the Japanese Bantam Club Annual Show having entries of 55 (1920), 60 (1921), 46 (1922), 70 (1924), 71 (1925), 69 (1926), and 'over 80' in 1928 and 1929.

The club's activities were suspended again 1939–45, and a meeting was held in 1946, chaired by (now) Colonel Williams. Here it was decided to form a joint Japanese and Frizzle Club, but this only lasted a few years (probably until 1954). The present Japanese Bantam Club was formed in 1961. Its Annual Show is held at Reading Bantam Club's show (actually at Newbury), and has had about 200 entries since 2000, more than ever before.

JAPANESE/CHABO DESCRIPTION

Full descriptions are given in *British Poultry Standards* and its equivalent in other countries. The comb should be single, large and straight.

White Japanese/Chabo, female. Photo: John Tarren

legged' (by Chabo standards – they still have much shorter legs than other breeds) males with very short-legged females. This mating will give 25 per cent short-legged males (the best kept for showing), 25 per cent long-legged males (the best can be used for breeding), 25 per cent short-legged females (keep the best for showing and breeding) and 25 per cent long-legged females (sell as pets). Long-legged males kept for breeding are selected for quality of comb, plumage colour pattern, and so on. Their shanks and feet should be bright yellow, with black shading on Birchens, Blacks (red-faced) and Brown-Reds. There is also a rare Black-Skinned Black which obviously have completely black shanks and feet.

The body should be compact, quite broad and chunky within their small overall size. The breast should be full and rounded. As the ends of their wings drag along the ground their flight feathers are often damaged. Judges are aware of this inevitable problem, and will make allowances for it when judging, although they might be reluctant to make the 'Best of Breed' up to overall Show Champion if there are many other 'Best of Breeds' which are almost perfect in every feather.

The tail should be very large, long (with the sickles on males 'sabre' shaped) and upright. Novice breeders should consult experienced breeders regarding how far forward of vertical is currently, and in your country, considered correct. Remaining tail feathers should be well spread, not closely 'whipped'. Classic Chabo shape is obviously much less evident on the Frizzle and Silkie feathered sub-varieties, this being another aspect which should be discussed with the specialists to ascertain how good they need to be.

COLOUR VARIETIES

British Poultry Standards only gives 10 points out of 100 for colour, emphasizing that their unique shape is more important. As a consequence, many prize-winning Chabos of the patterned varieties are some way short of the idealized birds depicted by specialist poultry

There has been less emphasis on large combs on 'normal' Chabos since the 1980s, when more breeders and judges became fully aware that the very large-combed Daruma Chabos are classed as a separate sub-variety in Japan. The comb is allowed to tilt over somewhat on hens, but a perfectly straight, perfectly upright comb, with (ideally) five even serrations is essential on a winning male. Wattles should be fairly large (the comment regarding Daruma Chabos also applies to their wattles) and nicely shaped, with no creases. Ear lobes should be medium sized and red, although some birds have lightish lobes from being housed inside to be kept clean.

Their legs should be as short as possible, most Chabos appearing to be sitting down even when they are standing up. Extremely short legs are caused by the incompletely dominant, lethal 'Creeper' gene. Embryos with Creeper genes from both parents all die during incubation. Very short-legged males also have trouble mating, so most Chabo fanciers solve both problems by breeding 'long-

Birchen-Grey Japanese/Chabo, Silkie feathered male. Photo: John Tarren

artists. Closely examine show winners to see how good plumage colour really needs to be.

Black, Blue, Cuckoo and White Chabos are as other breeds with these colour varieties, and the same considerations apply in keeping them, such as the genetic instability of Blues and the need for extra care to keep Whites really white.

Black-Tailed Buff and Black-Tailed White are the two main traditional colour varieties of Chabos. Some of their main tail feathers are required to have a buff or white edging, which in the real world is hardly ever as perfect as in the paintings. They also have some black markings in their flight feathers, hardly visible when their wings are folded normally. Birds with a little black in body or neck feathers (which should be buff or white) are useful for breeding as naturally clear-coloured birds, if bred from for several generations, can have reduced black in the tail. If there are only a few black neck and body feathers, they can be removed for showing.

British Poultry Standards allows three variations of 'Grey' in addition to the main exhibition 'Birchen Grey', the only version allowed in some other countries. Brown-Red is the gold version of the Birchen-Grey pattern, with a similar latitude allowed in the UK.

Millefleur, Black-Mottled, Blue-Mottled, Red-Mottled and Buff-Mottled are all spotted patterns which should be as even as possible, but are never as neat as Ancona spotting. These varieties were traditionally hen-feathered in Japan, but henny Chabo males are seldom seen in Europe. Black-Red, Blue-Red, Silver Duckwing and Gold Duckwing are all allowed, and can all be either 'Partridge-bred' or 'Wheaten-bred'.

SPECIAL CARE AND HOUSING

Chabos are for specialists, not suitable for farmyard conditions. Housing must be designed with their limited mobility in mind, and must be kept very clean. Their needs would take up too much space to describe in this book, so everyone keeping, or even thinking of keeping Chabos should buy and study one of the specialist books such as *Japanese Bantams* by A.C. Banning Vogelpoel or *Understanding Japanese Bantams* by John K. Palin.

Brown Leghorns. Originally a free gift with Poultry *magazine, 11 October 1912. Artist: J.W. Ludlow*

Pile Leghorns. Originally a free gift with Poultry *magazine, circa 1912. Artist: J.W. Ludlow*

CHAPTER 17

Leghorn/Italiener

Early editions of Lewis Wright's *Book of Poultry* describe Leghorns in the American breeds chapter, not in a Mediterranean or Italian breeds chapter as might be expected. He knew that although their ancestors came from Italy, they were refined into a stable breed in America. No details have been found of their earlier history in Italy. Similar birds were bred all over Italy, and were exported overland to northern Europe, hence their German name, Italiener. All of the early exports to America were shipped from the port city of Livorno, 'Leghorn' being the Anglicized version of the city's name, hence their name in English speaking countries. They eventually became the most important commercial egg production breed in the world, and a popular exhibition breed. They have been developed along different lines in various countries, resulting in commercial versions and distinct American, English and Dutch/German show types.

It is believed the first Leghorns arrived in America in 1828 or 1829, but details were recorded many years later by men who by then were elderly, and who might not have remembered every detail correctly. These first Leghorns were probably in a mixture of colour varieties. Mr N.P. Ward of New York City was recorded as the first importer of (specifically) Brown Leghorns in 1834. He bred a few, and sold some to friends, including Mr J.C.C. Thompson of Staten Island, quite a rural place in the 1830s. Mr Thompson was so impressed with them he arranged another importation; however, this stock had disappeared long

before the next significant importations of Brown Leghorns by Captain Gates, of Mystic River, Connecticut in 1852 and 1853. Mr F.J. Kinney of Worcester, Massachusetts bought a trio from a ship in Boston harbour in June 1853, the foundation of a strain he refined over the next twenty years. They varied greatly in plumage patterns at first, and many had red ear lobes. Early White Leghorns were also a long way short of pure snow-white, most being 'brassy' and with odd-coloured feathers. A Mr Simpson of New York obtained some in 1853, followed by 'the Lord importation' in 1858 and 'the Stetson importation' in 1863. For the next decade or so American breeders of Brown and White Leghorns began to select for uniform appearance, presumably after agreeing on white ear lobes and the plumage pattern of Browns. At this stage Leghorns had rather large combs and upright, well fanned tails: broadly similar to future 'utility type Leghorns'.

Reed Watson of Connecticut imported the first recorded Black Leghorns from Genoa in 1872, but the offspring bred from them came out in all colours. Mr Watson sold this lot off in disgust, but decided to try again. His next shipment, two cocks and three hens, arrived in New York on the barque (a type of sailing ship) *Ironsides* in July 1876. Black Leghorns were standardized by the American Poultry Association in 1875, so there must have been more importations.

There was a real financial incentive for breeders to improve the appearance of early

Leghorns. As layers, Leghorn pullets were worth about $5 then, not enough to be really profitable. By introducing show standards requiring white lobes, pure white Whites, pure black Blacks and a specified pattern for Browns, they intentionally created breeding difficulties, and so a market for $25, or even $50 show birds, and could still sell their less perfect birds for $5.

LEGHORNS IN THE UK

The first recorded importation of Leghorns to the UK came to William Bernhard Tegetmeier, a Victorian poultry author who also assisted Charles Darwin. These were a trio of Whites, which arrived in 1869 having won first prize at a show in New York in 1868. They were probably sent by C.H. Wyckoff of Aurora, NY. Tegetmeier sold all his White Leghorns after just one year of breeding them. Lewis Wright, also a major poultry book author, received Whites in 1870 or 1871, and Browns on 17 June 1872 from A.M. Halsted of New York City (publisher of first *American Standards Book* in 1867). Wright hatched a brood of Brown chicks on 1 August, and after rearing them to maturity to see how uniformly they bred (he suspected they might be crossbred White Leghorn × Black-Red Game), he sold the lot to R.J. Walker of Edgwarth, Bolton, in 1873. Wright was impressed by the hardiness and egg production of Brown Leghorns, but not (like several other poultry judges at the time) by the appearance of the first imports. The next known White Leghorn importer was A. Kitchen (then an undergraduate at Oxford, later Rev A. Kitchen). He also received Browns in 1872 or 1873, bred from them, and unlike Tegetmeier and Wright, persevered with them. In 1875 Mr Kitchen (still a student) became secretary of the 'Leghorn Fanciers Club', remaining so until 1896, when William Clarke took over in 1896, until the club fizzled out about 1926, to be replaced by other Leghorn Clubs.

Another club was formed at the 1876 Crystal Palace Show, and rather curiously catered for three apparently unrelated breeds, being 'The Leghorn, Plymouth Rock and Andalusian Club'. This club was very successful for over forty years, with 568 birds in 47 classes at the 1913 Crystal Palace Show. This club collapsed around 1926, by which time there were several other Leghorn Clubs, Plymouth Rock Clubs and an Andalusian Club. Black Leghorns were probably brought to the UK during the 1870s. They were much more popular in the UK than the USA. Buff Leghorns, although not very good ones, were first exhibited in 1885 at Copenhagen. They were probably made by crossing Chamois Polish with various brown or red Leghorn type birds. J. Pedersen-Bjirgaard entered some in the 1888 Crystal Palace Show, which were bought by L.C. Verrey. More British fanciers bred them, improving colour by Buff Rock crosses, followed by selective breeding to restore Leghorn type and white lobes. They were very popular until about 1900, with entries of forty Buffs at some shows. Cuckoo Leghorns were also established here by L.C. Verrey, probably from stock imported directly from Italy in 1883. 'Blue Leghorne' (Lavenders really) were probably first made by British fanciers about 1900, details unknown.

Captain George Payne, of Woking, Surrey, made Pile, Gold Duckwing and Silver Duckwing Leghorns; Mr R. Terrot of Maidenhead also made Duckwings, independently (Mr Terrot also promoted Coucou Malines in England). Captain Payne started in 1881 with a White Leghorn cock × Brown Leghorn hen mating. After five years of selective breeding he exhibited some pullets in 1886. Some fanciers who bought birds from Capt. Payne tried crossing them with Pile Game to improve colour and markings, obviously causing setbacks in Leghorn type. He made Duckwings from birds from his Pile programme, plus a Duckwing Yokohama cock he bought at Antwerp Show in 1889. Mr Terrot's strain was a combination of Brown Leghorns, Duckwing Game and Silver Grey Dorkings. Duckwing Leghorns were also first exhibited in 1886, but for several years some had short legs and fluffy plumage, a legacy of Mr Terrot's use of Dorkings.

were sent from Mr and Mrs Lister-Kay, of East Close, Christchurch, Hampshire to Mr August D. Arnold of Dillsburg, Pennsylvania between 1890 and 1893. Ezra Cornell of New York and George & Barnes, of Battle Creek, Michigan also took up Buffs, the latter becoming secretary of the American Buff Leghorn Club formed in 1891. Buffs became, for a while at least, very popular, the club having 480 members by 1912.

In addition to the Buff Club, there were, as in Britain, several single-variety clubs for the breed, although this included one which tried to cover all colours. These included:

American Leghorn Club, formed 1895; 50 members *circa* 1909, up to 500 members 1912/13.

American Single Comb Brown Leghorn Club, formed 1900; approx. 300 members 1912/13.

American Rose Comb Brown Leghorn Club, formed 1899; approx. 160 members 1912/3.

Rose Comb Buff Leghorn Club of America, formed 1910; 60 members 1912/13.

National Single Comb White Leghorn Club, formed 1903; 425 members 1912/13.

National Rose Comb White Leghorn Club, formed 1902; 55 members 1912/13.

American Black Leghorn Club, formed 1891; collapsed before 1900.

American breeders gradually changed and refined Leghorns, but in the opposite direction to British exhibitors. Whereas the 'Brits' went for bigger birds, with bigger combs and lobes, and closely whipped tails (from Minorca and Malay crosses), American breeders went for smaller birds, with rather small combs and lobes, and extravagant, widely fanned tails.

One source of the new American-type Leghorn may have been W.W. Babcock of New York who in 1865 started to make rose-combed White Leghorns by crossing single-combed White Leghorns (possibly some of the earliest imports) with White Hamburghs. The Hamburgh ancestry could have brought in the smaller combs and larger tails of American Leghorns and kept size down to USA standard weights of the 1920s between 5½lb (2.5kg) cocks to 3½lb (1.6kg) pullets. The extreme differences between American and British exhibition Leghorns were fully apparent after 1919, as there was little transatlantic poultry contact during wartime. At the annual meeting of the American Poultry Association at Chicago in August 1919, one of the most significant differences between the USA and UK was formalized: the division of Brown Leghorns into Dark Brown (ex-cock-breeders) and Light Brown (ex-pullet-breeders). There were few, if any, more transatlantic shipments of standard-bred Leghorns either way after the First World War as each type was of no use in the other country.

Charles H. Wyckoff, of Aurora, New York, coined the phrase 'America's business hen' for White Leghorns, and was responsible for selling the variety on the path to becoming the basis of layer hybrids. He established a very large (for the time) egg production farm in 1881 to supply New York City. He never entered shows, did not worry about poor shaped combs or a few coloured feathers when selecting breeding stock, and was criticized for this attitude at the time by others who associated breed characteristics with general quality. He realized, as did the hybrid companies much later, that genetic progress can only be made by concentrating on a few factors at a time, and he concentrated on egg numbers, egg size and low food consumption.

Douglas Tancred, of Kent, Washington, was a pioneer of testing egg laying performance by using trapnests (nest boxes which shut a hen in when it lays, so its leg ring or wing tag number can be recorded by attendants before it is released) from 1904 until his death in 1923. L.C. Beall of Vashon, also in Washington State, continued with Tancred's system until about 1950. John E. Kimber started breeding Leghorns at Fremont, California in 1925, and introduced strain crossing: Leghorn based hybrid layers. In 1943 Kimber Farms became the first commercial poultry breeding company

UK type White Leghorn, bantam male. Photo: John Tarren

to employ a fully qualified (PhD) geneticist. Several other breeding companies started during the 1940s, which grew to become the international hybrid corporations Babcock, DeKalb, Hy-Line and Shaver. Their stories are outside the scope of this book, but are mentioned to mark the final parting of the ways between traditional breeds and commercial egg production.

LEGHORNS IN THE NETHERLANDS AND ITALIENERS IN GERMANY

Despite the different breed names used, both Dutch and German exhibition breeders kept to a breed type very similar to the original birds as bred in Italy, and as 'utility type' in the UK. They did refine exhibition aspects such as ear lobes and plumage colours/patterns, of course, but restrained themselves from creating extreme body shapes like the very tall, large-combed British birds or the American

and Canadian show Leghorns with tails to rival a Yokohama.

They began in the 1870s and 1880s with stock imported from the UK, USA and directly from Italy, including Buffs from Mr and Mrs Lister-Kay, and Duckwings and Piles from George Payne. Some colour varieties were first made in Germany:

Blues and Blue-Reds by E. Schneider, Niederoderwitz, *circa* 1878–80
Millefleurs by Gebruder Rentsch, Werther, first exhibited at Bielefelder Show in 1880
Columbians by O. Goldmann, Pölitz/ Pommern, *circa* 1922.

Leghorns/Italieners became a popular exhibition breed in both countries, as indicated by these entry figures for the main Dutch show at Utrecht:

1896: 142 (out of a total of 546 large fowl of all breeds)
1899: 231 (total 1,185); 1902: 222 (1,426); 1907: 139 (1,076); 1910: 129 (1,173).

UK type Black Leghorn, bantam female. Photo: John Tarren

LEGHORN BANTAMS IN THE UK

W.F. Entwisle mentioned (*Bantams* 1894) that some breeders (not named) had attempted to make Brown, White, Duckwing and Pile Leghorn Bantams by crossing the relevant colours of Game Bantams with undersized large Leghorns. He was not impressed, so didn't keep them. This continued to be the situation until the 1930s, Leghorn Bantams remaining as rarities at shows in the UK, with very few strains taken up by anyone other than their originators. Those mentioned in *Feathered World Yearbooks* being:

1916: Blues, shown by Mr Collier at Penistone

1924: Crystal Palace Show, British Black Leghorn Club had a class for bantams, 7 entered

1925 and 1926: Whites, shown by Mr Shackleton of Silsden

1927: Blacks and Whites (as above) still seen at shows, plus an Exchequer at Richmond

1928–30: as above, plus Browns (Mr W. Potts) and Duckwings (Miss Budd)

1932–35: W.H. Baker (secretary of Red Leghorn Club) making Red Bantams

1935: Herbert Whitley had Blue Leghorn Bantams, part of his 'Blue Collection'.

Leghorn Bantams were quite big in comparison to their large fowl equivalent, which probably accounts for their limited credibility as a show breed before the Second World War, and their little publicized, but very real, boom during the war. They were ideal back garden birds, good layers of fair sized eggs and low in food consumption.

The Leghorn Bantam Club was formed in 1947, which amalgamated with the main Leghorn Club in 1975. The situation was somewhat confusing during this period as the Black Leghorn Club and Brown Leghorn Club both covered bantams (in their respective colours) before they merged in 1950. Black, Brown and White Leghorn Bantams became very popular show breeds during the 1950s and 1960s, plus good overall entries in 'AOC Leghorn Bantam' classes, but no one colour attracting sustained or significant support. White Leghorn Bantams have been the most popular variety among really competitive exhibitors, although since 2000 a few have given them up, and have not been replaced by new hobbyists. They are a very demanding variety, each bird having a short show career

US type Light Brown Leghorn, bantam female.
Photo: John Tarren

(so more have to be bred constantly), and they need expert show preparation. Most fanciers concentrate on showing pullets, cockerels only being good for a few shows before white spreads from lobes to face and the comb flops over.

LEGHORN BANTAMS IN THE USA

A few White Leghorn Bantams were shown about 1904–6 (no details of their owners found); but they died out. Arthur O. Schilling (1882–1958, also a leading poultry artist and photographer) made a new strain in 1927, which he started to show in 1934. He used undersized large Leghorns, White Rosecombs, White Japanese/Chabos (long-legged specimens), a smooth feathered bird from a flock of White Frizzle Bantams, White German Bantams (Deutsches Zwerg), and a White Leghorn (large) × Modern Game (bantam) crossbred. J.A. DeBee made Buff Leghorn Bantams. Other colours were made, but details were not found by the author.

LEGHORN DESCRIPTION

As this breed is so complex, interested readers should read and compare American, British, Dutch, German and other standards books. The photographs and old pictures in this chapter will give the general idea. Unfortunately the two extreme versions, British and American show types, are seldom to be seen in the same country, never mind the same show hall (except, just possibly, at some of the largest Dutch and German shows), so it is difficult to appreciate how different they are from each other. About the only thing they have in common is their name! (The same comment applies to UK/USA Old English Game Bantams – *see* Chapter 23.)

SPECIAL MANAGEMENT REQUIREMENTS – DOUBLE MATING

The large single combs on Leghorns, especially in the UK, should be upright on males and flop over on females. Most strains are effectively pullet-breeders. Cockerels are good for one or two shows just as they reach maturity, with their combs 'going over' after a month or so. The best of them are then just kept at home for breeding. Should anyone wish to develop a proper cock-breeder strain, select for slightly smaller-combed males and females with upright combs.

Genes for large comb size have affected the few rose-combed strains of Leghorn still existing, with the combs of males becoming rather misshapen, even 'gross', as they get older. There are probably neater rose-combed birds in Germany and the Netherlands.

British-type Leghorns were also double mated for tail formation, although there may not be many fanciers who continue to do so. Exhibition females are required (UK standards only) to have a closely folded or 'whipped' tail, so similarly tailed 'pullet-breeder cocks' are used to produce them. Exhibition males

Wheaten Malay, large female. Photo: John Tarren

Cinnamon Malay, bantam female. Photo: John Tarren

The females to go with Black-Red males have a range of colours, from light to dark, appropriate to their mates; 'Cinnamon' is the name given to the darker females, the colour of this spice with black markings in neck, wings and tail. Malay hens can be any shade from this to light, creamy wheaten. This lighter shade is preferred in Germany. Partridge hens are rare, but sometimes appear. General colour and markings are indistinct, and somewhere between Wyandottes and Modern Game. They usually have a lightly marked breast, not salmon (as in Moderns). Although the standards describe females similar to Pile Moderns, they are really a pinkish-wheaten colour with white markings in neck, wings and tail.

Spangled Malays can also come in a range of colours and markings, but the traditional ideal is for dark Black-Red males with white spots and light Millefleur females.

Other colours sometimes seen include:

Blue-Reds, with blue-tailed wheaten females

Duckwings, with silver-wheaten females

Cuckoos and Crow-winged Creles, with Cuckoo females, perhaps with gold in head and neck

Creles, with wheaten females showing 'ghost' barring on neck, wing and tail.

SPECIAL MANAGEMENT REQUIREMENTS

Malays need lots of food and lots of space if they are to reach their potential size. Some fanciers use turkey crumbs to get chicks off to a good start, but only for the first month. Once off heat, they need space for exercise to build muscles on those long legs. They can be bullies, so need to be kept in small groups. No more than four hens should be mated with each cock. Some Malays are monogamous.

Coucou de Fiandre, one of the breeds used to make Marans. Artist: Rene Delin

CHAPTER 19

Marans

Because of their dark brown eggs, Marans are one of the most popular breeds with hobbyist poultry keepers. The birds seldom win major awards at the shows, but plates of their eggs regularly win 'Best Egg Exhibit'.

Marans in Britain and France are effectively two separate breeds, which shows how little real communication there was between these neighbouring countries until very recently – the two versions of the breed were established in the 1920s and 1930s.

Marans is a small town (population approx. 5,000 *circa* 1930) north-north-east of the coastal city of La Rochelle. The importation of Langshans, and therefore dark brown eggs, about 1876 is the real starting point of the Marans breed, although the Marans Club de France also points out that poultry in this area had been modified by English Pit Game since the twelfth century. King Henry II of England was also Duke of Anjou, and his wife was Eleanor of Aquitaine, links which obviously meant that a lot of English ships were going in and out of La Rochelle harbour.

There were three main importers and breeders of Langshans from 1876 onwards in the area, Mr Geoffrey Saint Hilaire, Mr Foucault, and Mr Louis Rouille, the latter from Fouras, about 30km south of La Rochelle. He had a large flock of Langshans by standards of the time but, as his interest was focused on dark brown eggs, did not worry about keeping to all-black plumage. He sold birds to his neighbours, many of which no doubt crossed them with their existing flocks. Thus, Copper-Black

French type Marans were born, but at this stage alongside brown egg layers of other colours as well. Some were exhibited as 'country hens' at a show at La Rochelle in 1914.

Madame Rousseau of L'lle d'Elle, a few kilometres north-east of Marans, took an interest in 1921, and started a programme of selective breeding to improve and make more uniform the colour and size of both the birds and their eggs. In 1928 she exhibited a uniform pen of Cuckoo Marans at La Rochelle. Paul Waroquiez, editor of *Aviculteur Francais* magazine, was at the show, and wrote about this new 'Marandaise' breed several times, the main article being in the 1 July 1929 issue. This publicity generated enough interest for the Marans Club Francais to be formed at a hotel at Charente, north of La Rochelle, on 12 September 1929. A little later Lord Greenway saw Marandais fowls in several colour varieties at the 1929 Paris Show, and took some fertile eggs back home to begin the English thread of the Marans story.

The new breed club established a standards committee, comprising Prof. Sebileau, Paul Waroquiez, Mr Mace and Mr Sangali, who visited about a hundred farms during 1930. They held two committee meetings (the second on 2 April 1931) at the Manor of l'Aulnaie to collate their findings and write a provisional breed standard. It was published in French poultry magazines so all breeders had a chance to study it in time for the general club meeting on 22 November 1931. This standard was adopted, although there continued to be some arguments about clean legs as opposed to feathered legs. The standard was deliberately a bit vague, as Marans were always going to be a utility breed, even though they could be shown as well. The club had 53 paid-up members by the end of 1931, but the Marans breed was already declining by the beginning of the war. The club was reformed in 1946, but few pure-bred Marans had survived the war. They initially concentrated on reviving the Silver-Cuckoo, Golden-Cuckoo, White and Copper-Black varieties, adding self Blacks in 1949, but interest was still limited. There were still only thirteen club members in 1963, the worldwide low point for all pure breeds, when farmers switched to hybrids and few hobbyists yet realized or cared that traditional breeds were rapidly dying out. New signs were erected at all the roads into the town, '*Marans, capitale de la poule aux oeufs extra roux*' in 1965, but it was a long time before many people did much to help them survive. The club's 1966 AGM was its last until it was revived at a meeting on 19 January 1991. Progress has been steady since then, the number of members being: 140 in 1992, 190 in 1994, 250 in 1996, and up to over 540 in 2005. The club leg ring scheme, established in 1997, issued over 12,000 rings in 1999. The club's 2000 annual show had over 400 birds entered.

BRITISH TYPE MARANS

Marans were introduced to the UK by Lord Greenway and his poultry manager, J.S. Parkin. Lord Greenway was an interesting person, worth describing in more detail. He was the second Baron Greenway of Stanbridge Earls, his father (Charles Greenway, 1857–1934) having been first knighted (1919), then raised to the peerage (1927) for services to industry – he was one of the founders of the Anglo-Persian Oil Company, which later became British Petroleum (BP). The first baron bought the Stanbridge Earls Manor estate in 1917, and the family also had a racehorse stud at Kemsing in Kent. The second baron, Charles Kelvynge Greenway (1888–1963) is

believed to have kept his Marans and other poultry at both sites. Poultry was very much a hobby for Lord Greenway, as he eventually became Chairman of the oil company, and used his Middle East contacts to help the government. Most of the Middle East was part of the Turkish Ottoman Empire, until it was broken up after the First World War (the empire sided with Germany and the Austro-Hungarians). The British had a League of Nations (forerunner of United Nations) mandate to make new independent countries in the region, and Lord Greenway is believed to have played a 'behind the scenes' role in the establishment of the present state of Iraq.

Moving on to his involvement with Marans chickens, there is an equally 'behind the scenes' story to tell, this time – allegedly – involving his poultry manager, J.S. Parkin. Mr Parkin gave the 'official' story in the 1935 *Feathered World Yearbook*. 'Lord Greenway's attention was drawn to its [the Marans breed] merits by specimens exhibited at the 1929 Paris Exhibition and decided to import them to this country'.

> There are White, Buff, Black, Cuckoo and Ermine colours of the breed, and he imported the most popular of these colours, *viz.*, Cuckoo, White, Black and Ermine. He gave each of these varieties a thorough trial the first year and found – just as the French claim – that the cuckoo-coloured ones were the best all-round birds, being much quicker growers and superior as a table bird. They were also the best layers of good, large brown eggs. Finally he discarded all the other colours for the cuckoo-coloured variety.

A photo of a Cuckoo Marans cockerel, without feathered legs, appears with this article, one of the first Lord Greenway exhibited in the 'New Breed Class' at the 1934 Crystal Palace Show.

That was the official version, but people (who would rather not be named) who knew Lord Greenway and J.S. Parkin have said the truth was rather different. First, it must be remembered that there was only a

Dark Cuckoo Marans, large male. Photo: John Tarren

provisional standard in France, and that was not published until April 1931. Furthermore, Greenway and Parkin knew French breeders were still arguing about the clean leg versus feather leg issue when the article mentioned above was written in 1934.

Lord Greenway certainly imported more than one batch of fertile Marans eggs which Mr Parkin incubated as instructed. However, the 'unofficial story' is that Parkin, a man with strong views of his own about poultry breeds, thought the chicks hatched were such a mongrelly looking lot, he killed them all. He was already working on another project for Lord Greenway, a strain of clean-legged, cuckoo-coloured table birds, which also laid nice brown eggs. They are believed to have been mainly a mixture of Noord Hollandse, Coucou de Rennes

Dark Cuckoo Marans, large female. Photo: John Tarren

Dark Cuckoo Marans, bantam trio. Photo: John Tarren

and similar Belgian, Dutch and French breeds (see the companion volume *Rare Poultry Breeds*). If this version is true, and it came from 'reliable sources', then British type Marans have never really been Marans at all! Lord Greenway, and others who knew this version of events, no doubt justified their actions by the 'provisional' state of French Marans then, and that both types were only intended to be practical chickens, not show birds.

Lord Greenway's birds were still variable, so when they were standardized by the PCGB in 1935, three colour varieties were described: Dark Cuckoo, Silver Cuckoo and Golden Cuckoo. The British Marans Club was not formed until after the Second World War, at a meeting at the Grosvenor Hotel, on 18 February 1950. A self Black variety was added to British Standards in 1952, but has not survived, and Whites were fairly popular for a while.

Marans have become one of the most popular hobbyists' breeds because of their egg colour, but they do not lay well enough to be used commercially, although they have all been used to make the 'Speckledy' hybrid. Although a few Marans can be seen at almost every show in the UK, their fuzzy cuckoo barring has not

attracted competitive exhibitors. The highest entry of large Marans found at National and Stafford Shows from 1954 to 2007 was back in 1962, when J.S. Parkin was judging at Olympia, and had 61 Dark Cuckoos and 22 AOC (probably most or all Whites) to sort out. Since 1980 the biggest entries have been 48 Dark Cuckoos at Stafford in 1981 and 7 AOCs at Stafford in 1988. French type Marans are now bred here as well, and 20 were entered at Stafford in 2003.

The British Marans Club has applied to the PCGB to pass a standard for the French type, but they had not been accepted by the PCGB Council at time of writing in 2008. The Marans Club de France is, apparently, quite hostile to the British type. As both types have been standardized breeds since the 1930s, it is time relevent bodies in all countries recognized them.

MARANS BANTAM

British type Marans Bantams have existed far longer than French type Marans Bantams. The British type were first exhibited at the 1953 National Show, Olympia, presumably in a

New Breeds class, with a class being added for the 1954 event, which incorporated the Marans Club Annual Show. Fourteen were entered, including six from one of their creators, Mr J.H. Fines, of Crown Farm, Wingland, Sutton Bridge, and two from the other, Ken Bosley, of Wantage, Oxfordshire. They, and the other four exhibitors, realized that Marans Bantams would only be viable if they also laid dark brown eggs, so it is believed they bred down from undersized large Marans. They were no doubt aware that early Barnevelder and Welsummer Bantams were crosses that looked correct, but laid tinted eggs, and deservedly flopped. Some other breeders were not so scrupulous, however, making strains by crossing. They gave Marans Bantams a bad name for some years.

There have been very few Marans Bantams in other colours over the years, with the highest entry of Dark Cuckoos found being 48 at Stafford in 2002. At local shows up and down the UK, there are usually a few Marans Bantams, seldom more than a dozen.

French Marans Bantams are quite new, probably made about 1990, but no details about who made them and how they did it have been found.

MARANS DESCRIPTION

British and French Marans are similar to each other in general body shape, allowing for natural variation from one bird to another. The French birds have lightly feathered shanks and feet, whereas the British type is clean-legged; there are the different plumage colours. Large fowl weights are also similar, with French standards allowing a broader range. British standards range from 2.7kg (6lb) pullets up to 3.6kg (8lb) adult cocks. French standards have a minimum pullet weight of 2.2kg (5lb) and a maximum cock weight of 4kg (9lb). French bantam standards have 1.1kg (39oz) males and 0.9kg (31oz) females. British standards give lower weights, but are a fiction, so take the French bantam weights as good for both.

Marans are broad bodied, with a prominent breast, yet active and with tight plumage. The

Golden Cuckoo Marans, bantam female. Photo: John Tarren

tail is not particularly long, carried between 45 and 60 degrees above horizontal. They have a single comb, normal wattles, red lobes, red or orange eyes and white skin.

Dark Cuckoo females are darker than males, although very light coloured males are far from ideal.

Silver Cuckoo are allowed to have areas of clear white, mainly the head, neck and upper body.

Golden Cuckoo are similar to Silver Cuckoos but (obviously) golden coloured on the head, neck and breast.

Copper-Blacks and Silvered-Blacks are similar to some Brown-Red and Grey Pit Game, but without breast lacing. The copper should be just that, neither lemon nor deep red.

Whites, Blacks and Ermines (Columbians) are as these varieties on other breeds.

Wheatens consist of orangey-shaded Black-Reds; males have minimal hackle striping, and females are a darkish type of wheaten.

Black-tailed-Buffs can have a range of ground colours, and are allowed black tips on their neck hackle feathers.

'The MacNab', Lord Dewar's famous champion. Originally a free gift with Feathered World *magazine, 13 February 1925. Photo: Arthur Rice*

CHAPTER 20

Minorca

Some of the ancestors of Minorcas came from the island of Menorca, others were from other parts of Spain, possibly some from Portugal, but the standard breed was made in England. Original imports were smaller, and with much smaller ear lobes, than Minorcas as bred and exhibited now. The Castilian breed was standardized in Germany in 1957 to represent the common ancestor of Andalusian, Minorca and White-faced Spanish.

Black Minorcas. Originally a free gift with Poultry *magazine, 1 March 1912. Artist: J.W. Ludlow*

Detailed and reliable information about their history is only available from the memories of those living when W.B. Tegetmeier, Harrison Weir and Lewis Wright were researching for their books from 1850 onwards. John Harwood, of Tiverton, Devon (secretary of the first Minorca Club) provided the earliest reference to 'Minorcas', saying that around 1780 they were kept in his locality by French and Spanish prisoners of war (colonial wars with UK) who decided to settle here rather than go home when released. Before then they were regarded as a sub-variety of Spanish. Mr Harwood also mentioned a picture of a trio of Minorcas painted in 1810 which was shown to him by an old breeder in 1876. Many more similar chickens, and a lot more French prisoners of war, were brought to Cornwall, Devon and Somerset during the Peninsular War waged by Wellington and Napoleon, *circa* 1807–12.

Mr Leworthy (Barnstaple, Devon), Rev. Thomas Cox (Castle Cary, Somerset) and Sir Thomas Acland (Holnicote, Somerset) bred them during the 1830s, the latter having imported some in 1834 or 1835 directly from Menorca. Although called 'Minorcas' in the West Country, most poultry books, if they described them at all, called them 'Red faced Spanish' in a footnote at the end of the Spanish chapter, until the 1870s. The 1853 Bristol Agricultural Show is believed to be the first to give separate classes for Spanish and Minorcas; however, Minorcas remained virtually unknown north of Gloucestershire or east of Wiltshire until some breeders started to promote them in *Live Stock Journal* in 1875–76.

Minorcas rapidly progressed around the rest of the country after two classes were provided at the 1883 Crystal Palace (London) Show, in which a total of thirty-two birds were entered by south-western breeders. This was followed by 2 classes/69 birds in 1884 and 4 classes/98 birds in 1885. The Minorca Club was formed in 1888, and its first show was part of the Crystal Palace Show of that year, with 6 classes/140 birds, all large, single-combed Blacks.

As Minorcas were spread around the country, fanciers in other areas decided they could improve on the breed which, in the West Country, had remained much the same as they had been since 1830. Northern fanciers were, and still are, a competitive lot, and they had realized that 'size matters' in poultry showing. The colder climate of the north of England gave them both advantages and problems. The problem was that of frostbite in Minorcas' large combs, but this could be solved by heated winter houses for selected show birds. Their advantage was that spring hatched birds were slower to sexually mature in the autumn, so grew larger than birds in the south which often started laying (and stopped growing) in early autumn. The major shows were in November and December, so ideally pullets would have started laying, and cockerels would have properly developed comb, lobes, and adult tail feathers, shortly before show day. To further increase size, northerners crossed Minorcas with Langshans or Orpingtons. After each cross, fanciers then had to do several years of selective breeding to restore Minorca features. One permanent change was from silvery-black to greenish-black plumage.

Meanwhile, back in Bristol, fanciers with a heritage of increasing the size of white faces on Spanish, increased the size (but different structure) of Minorca lobes. There must have been some swapping between the two groups, as large-lobed, large-sized, Minorcas were being exhibited in both southern and northern counties after a few years. Smaller-sized, smaller-lobed Minorcas survived in Cornwall and Devon, later revived as 'utility type Minorcas'.

Minorcas rapidly became a popular exhibition breed, and several regional clubs were formed in addition to the main breed club. Bristol Minorca Club, probably formed about 1890, seems to have been the first. Its last secretary, 1909–16, was D.G. Porter, of 5 Avonside Cottages, Feeder Road, near Bristol's historic Temple Meads station. In 1923 it was replaced by the Western Counties Minorca Club, which covered a wider area; its first

CHAPTER 21

Modern Game

Cockfighting was banned in the UK in 1849; so Game Fowl breeders naturally turned to the arena of poultry competition showing. For a few years they were judged reasonably well because many of the breeders and judges were former 'cockers'; some probably still were in secret. Even judges who had never been cock-fight enthusiasts had seen plenty of Game Fowl around, probably at least one fight as well. By 1870 there was a new generation of judges and exhibitors who had never seen a cockfight. We must give them the benefit of the doubt as far as motives are concerned, but Game Fowl began to change. They thought tall cocks would have an advantage in a fight, and were told that tight, 'hard' feathering was an essential characteristic of Game Fowl, so they gave top prizes to the tightest, hardest-

The Development of Exhibition Game, with John Douglas's 1870 champion illustrating the intermediate stage. Artist: J.W. Ludlow

feathered birds. Some exhibitors tried crossing with Malays to get taller, tighter-feathered birds, although they emphatically deny doing so. As early as 1860 some judges were giving top awards to taller, tighter-feathered birds, this style achieved then by 'hackle drawing', removing some neck, saddle and tail side hanger feathers for showing.

Eventually this fashion for taller, tighter-feathered Game Fowl became a new breed, 'Modern Game'. J.W. Ludlow drew a set of three pictures to demonstrate the process, a full feathered Pit Game from 1850, a really tall Modern Game from 1900, and the intermediate type from 1870, sometimes called 'Exhibition Game'. This drawing was based on a bird which won at Crystal Palace in 1870 for John Douglas. Poultry books and magazines from 1870 to 1871 almost all criticize these changes; although the exhibitors and judges concerned presumably thought their winning birds were wonderful. It will no doubt surprise readers today, but most poultry experts, certainly those who wrote books and magazine articles, were pro-cockfighting. The following passage is the only evidence found supporting 'Exhibition Game'.

John Douglas, who had been an active 'cocker' before 1849, later a successful exhibitor, was one of the few who put pen to paper (quoted in Lewis Wright's *Poultry Book*) in support of Exhibition Game as they were in the 1870s, saying they had 'perfection in beauty, symmetry, purity of feather, more muscle, less but stronger bone, and more hardness of flesh' than the cocks of thirty years previously.

The name 'Old English Game' was not used until 1883, when classes were provided for them at some shows in the north of England by breeders who decided to go their own way, giving up on ever persuading the judges who were favouring the tall birds. OEG rapidly became very popular exhibition birds in their own right, but not without further arguments and divisions, which are covered in Chapter 23: Old English Game.

There were still some people who clung to the fiction that their taller birds were still

Golden Duckwing Modern Game, large male. Photo: John Tarren

the same as historic fighting cocks, and they stuck to the name 'Exhibition Game' for a very long time. The reality that there were now two breeds was certainly established by 1910, and the new name 'Modern Game' was widely adopted by then, but the author did not have much source material *circa* 1903 to 1908 to accurately date universal acceptance of the name change.

Similar changes happened with Game Bantams, which are covered in more detail later in this chapter and in Chapter 23, but were a few years behind. There was a key difference: Old English Game Bantams did not exist as a recognized, regularly exhibited breed before the 1890s, although thousands of (possibly delinquent) schoolboys had fought bantams which could have been given the name at least as far back as the eighteenth century.

Large Exhibition/Modern Game were a very popular breed for about thirty years, say 1884 to 1914, with some winning birds changing hands for very high prices. Samuel Matthews had one of his winning Black-Reds 'claimed' at the catalogue price of £100 at the 1884 Crystal Palace Show. All birds had to be offered for sale at shows in those days, so exhibitors who did not want to sell their birds gave a prohibitive price (£100 in 1884 would be equivalent to several thousand pounds today) in the hope that either none of his main competitors would buy the bird or there would be, as in this case, someone with more money than sense!

Game Fowl were, of course, exhibited in large numbers from 1849 to 1884, but this chapter does not concentrate on them since they were established as a separate breed from Old English Game.

Example Show Entries of large Modern Game:

1892 Crystal Palace, 299
1901 Birmingham, 325 (137 Black-Red, 60 Pile, 55 Duckwing, 48 Brown-Red, 13 Black or White, 12 AOC, which included Birchen, Blue and Mottled)
1904 Birmingham, approx. 270? (107 Black-Red, 50 Pile, 54 Duckwing, 40 Brown-Red, unknown number of other colours)
1909 Birmingham, 133+? (54 Black-Red, 8 Pile, 44 Duckwing, 27 Brown-Red, ±? AOC). It is clear that large Moderns had considerably declined by 1909, compared to the display of them in 1901, which may have been the largest number ever entered in one show. Then there were four classes (cock, hen, cockerel, pullet) for each of the main colour varieties, but show organizers gradually reduced the number of classes as entries declined.
1912 Birmingham, 111 (54 Black-Red, 31 Duckwing, 10 Brown-Red, 20 AOC, including Piles)
1913 Birmingham, 111 (61 Black-Red, 25 Duckwing, 8 Brown-Red, 17 AOC, including Piles).

Large Moderns were not seen in such numbers again after the First World War, despite the

support of the Modern Game Club, which had been formed some time between 1902 and 1909 (exact date not found). There was also a United Game Club, a Welsh United Game Club and a Scottish Game Club, but it is not known if these were just for Moderns, or covered OEG as well. There were also several specialist clubs for single colour varieties, but these seem to have only covered Modern Bantams, so are mentioned again later in this chapter.

There were three main reasons for the decline in the popularity of large Modern Game, the first being a lot of breeders switching to OEG. Secondly, food shortages during the war, rapidly followed by the Great Depression meant

Partridge Modern Game, large female. Photo: John Tarren

141

that few people could afford to keep purely exhibition breeds of large fowl. There was another, self-inflicted reason for the decline of large Moderns: most of the leading exhibitors had a 'dog in the manger' attitude, insisting on very high prices for birds and refusing to sell hatching eggs at any price. Apparently there were several young fanciers in the 1920s and 1930s who wanted to try them because of their unusual appearance and reputation as one of the 'classic' exhibition breeds, but were unable to buy decent stock.

As numbers declined, so did the quality of the remaining flocks of large Moderns, even those kept by the 'old hands'. In their efforts to obtain maximum overall height, breeders neglected to retain prominent shoulders, and some had a 'heavy stem', both faults which greatly detracted from the elegant, ideal shape. Plumage colour faults also crept in as fewer people were able to maintain separate cock-breeder and pullet-breeder strains.

However, the decline was not smooth; for example, there were no classes for large Moderns at all at the 1928 Crystal Palace Show (they had to go in AOV classes), but the 1930 Crystal Palace Show had four classes (cock, hen, cockerel, pullet: all colours together), with a total of 47 entries. The Brown-Red colour variety was only kept going by (father and son) Walter and George Firth. At the 1924 Birmingham Show there were 19 Brown-Reds, 11 of which were the Firths'.

Modern Game were exported to several countries in the early twentieth century, but were never particularly popular. They seem to have died out completely all over Europe, including the UK, during the Second World War. Horst Schmudde (author of the recent *Oriental Gamefowl*), who was born in Germany in 1934 and moved to America in 1964, sent some hatching eggs from one of the remaining flocks in the USA to Paul Hohmann in Germany to start their European revival. Initially it was mainly German fanciers, notably Edgar Pille, who multiplied them, and managed to remake some colour varieties, probably by crossing with Malays, Belgian Game and OEG. Some

very fine Birchen and Pile Moderns were being shown in Germany by the 1970s. British breeders obtained Moderns again from Pille, usually as eggs, during the 1970s.

All the pre-war Modern Game Clubs, including those for Bantams, had been suspended 'for the duration'. A new 'Modern Game Bantam Club' was formed in 1948, which was all that was necessary then as there were no large Moderns. Luckily, they were given some of the old clubs' cups in 1959. This Club, or some of its senior members at least, were not interested in large Moderns when they started to be entered in UK shows again in the mid-seventies, so large Moderns became a 'Rare Breed'. The Modern Game Bantam Club took over large Moderns from the RPS in 1979, taking a few more years to change the name to 'Modern Game Club'.

Since 1979 two classes have been provided for large Moderns (M and F), the highest entry being 21 (total of 2 classes) at the 1992 National Show at Stoneleigh. Very few show entry figures of major German shows were available when researching this chapter, but it is likely that 40 or more have been seen at some events since 1970.

Australian fanciers, who are not allowed to import anything, have made their own strains of large Moderns, mainly using large Australian Exhibition Game, a tall breed which is halfway between Moderns and Malays in terms of build and weight.

MODERN GAME BANTAM

'Partridge Bantams' have been bred in Europe since the sixteenth century, and are the ancestors of several breeds of bantams, including Black-Red Modern Game, OEG, Dutch, Pictaves and Belgische Kriel. As large Pit Game were transformed into Exhibition Game during the 1870s, other fanciers changed their bantams along similar lines. Partridge Bantams had never been a really popular exhibitor breed in the preceding years (say 1845 to 1870), although a few had appeared in shows. Large OEG rapidly became a popular

Modern Game Bantams. Originally a free gift with Feathered World *magazine, 2 December 1910. Artist: J.W. Ludlow*

show breed as soon as they became recognized as such in the 1880s, but OEG Bantams took longer to be established, so Modern type Game Bantams had a monopoly until the late 1890s. To illustrate how the relative popularity of the two breeds would change, compare entries at Crystal Palace in 1901 with 1929. There were 211 Modern Bantams and 78 OEG Bantams in 1901, but by 1929 there were still about 200 Moderns, but the number of OEG Bantams had risen to 302.

Very little information seems to have survived regarding the beginning of Modern type Game Bantams, in contrast to the full details of the creation of some other breeds. W.B. Tegetmeier mentioned Mr Monsey of Norwich in 1867; and W.F. Entwisle of Wakefield, the leading breeder of bantams generally in the late nineteenth century, credits his friend John Crosland, who also lived in Wakefield, as the pioneer in making the small but tall, tight-feathered, Modern type Game Bantam. Entwisle played a key role in refining Modern Game Bantams in shape and colour, though. He developed a strain of White Modern Game Bantams, from white chicks which hatched from Brown-Reds in 1862. The fashionable 'top colour' of Brown-Reds changed from orange to a lighter lemon-gold shade, which we now know was achieved by birds having a single recessive white gene, inevitably leading to a proportion of white chicks. Fred Smalley, who also has a place in poultry history for being the first to make Light Sussex Bantams, made considerable improvements in the type and style of Birchen Modern Game Bantams.

Drawings and photographs from the period show that the bantams were still evolving until after 1900, but were much the same as they are now by about 1910. Modern Game Bantams are tiny birds which can be kept in an ordinary sized garden or allotment and eat little. As a result, they did not decline very much during the difficult years from 1914 to 1945, and are more popular than ever today.

During the 'Golden Age' of the poultry fancy, say 1900 to 1939, there were specialist clubs for Birchens, Brown-Reds, Piles and Self Colours (Blacks, Blues and Whites), in addition to the main Modern Game Club, although the Brown-Red Club was rather short-lived. All the clubs still existing in 1939 suspended their activites for the war, to be replaced by a new Modern Game Bantam Club in 1948, later 'Modern Game Club' when it covered large Moderns as well.

EXAMPLE UK MODERN GAME BANTAM SHOW ENTRIES

> 1901 Crystal Palace, 211 (82 Black-Red, 23 Duckwing, 44 Pile, 35 Brown-Red, 27 AOC)
>
> 1911 Crystal Palace, 205 (48 Black-Red; 27 Duckwing, 42 Pile, 32 Brown-Red, 41 Birchen, 8 White, 7 Blue-Red/Lemon-Blue)
>
> Pile Game Bantam Club Shows, Kendal: 99 in 1911, 121 in 1912, 86 in 1913
>
> 1912 Crystal Palace, 261 (M Black-Red, 36 Duckwing, 63 Pile, 30 Brown-Red, 44 Birchen, 17 Black/Blue/White, 7 Blue-Red/Lemon-Blue)
>
> 1913 Kendal, 277 (49 Black-Red, 50 Duckwing, 86 Pile (mentioned above), 40 Brown-Red, 42 Birchen, 10 Wheaten females). It was unusual to provide classes for Wheaten Moderns in those days, most specialists just using them as 'cock-breeders' for Black-Red males. There were also Silver-Wheatens (for Duckwing males) and Pile-Wheatens (for Pile males).
>
> 1921 Kendal, 305

> Pile Game Bantam Club Shows, Bradford, 67 in 1922, 53 in 1924, 51 in 1925
>
> Birchen Game Bantam Club Shows, Bradford, 55 in 1922, 50 in 1924, 76 in 1925, 37 in 1934.

Entries of Modern Game Bantams at their major shows, Birmingham, Bradford, Crystal Palace and Kendal continued to fluctuate between 150 and 250 until 1939. Poultry showing was a much less popular hobby for many years after peace was restored in 1945, not reviving until a new generation joined our hobby in the 1970s. In the show records available when researching this chapter, no shows had above 100 Moderns until the 1978 National Show, when there were 113. The next milestone in their recovery was 208 Moderns at the 1987 National, and the highest entry since then was 281 at the 1994 National (81 Black-Red, 34 Duckwing, 34 Pile, 41 Brown-Red, 41 Birchen, 23 Standard AOC, 7 Non-Standard AOC, 17 Novice).

Modern Game Bantams are equally popular in the USA, all over Europe, and every other country where they have poultry shows.

MODERN GAME – TYPE DESCRIPTION

Clearly, the main characteristic of Modern Game, large and bantam, is their height. This is achieved by a combination of long legs, long neck, and tight plumage which emphasizes both features. Moderns can be trained to 'reach', by providing high food troughs and pen fronts solid to just below head height, so they get into the habit of standing well up to see out. The breed standard requires a 'short' back, but not as short on Moderns as OEG. Tight plumage is essential, especially lower neck (to emphasize prominent shoulders), tightly whipped tail, and around the abdomen (to emphasize length of legs).

Standard weights of large Moderns range from 5lb (2.25kg) pullets up to 9lb (4.10kg) adult cocks. A few of the very best birds are up

Pile Modern Game, bantam male. Photo: John Tarren

to this weight range; but not many. Bantams range from 16oz (450g) to 22oz (620g). Most are within this range.

Moderns can be described as being 'snaky' in general character, with a long beak and fine skull. Hens naturally have small wattles and comb. It is traditional to surgically remove the comb, wattles and ear lobes of males, an operation called 'dubbing'. This is now illegal in Germany, Sweden and the Netherlands. It was almost banned in the UK as well, but the Modern Game Club effectively lobbied enough influential polititians, and are still allowed to dub, subject to new regulations. Fanciers in countries where dubbing is banned have considered introducing pea or walnut combs to maintain original style, a controversial suggestion.

Facial skin colour, eye colour, beak colour and shank/feet colour are all divided into three groups, according to plumage colour variety.

Crele, Pile and White Moderns have red skin, red eyes, yellow beak, shanks and feet.

Black-Red/Partridge, Black-Red/Wheaten, Blue-Red, Gold Duckwing, Silver Duckwing and Blue Duckwing Moderns have red skin, red eyes, willow-green beak, shanks and feet.

Black, Blue, Brown-Red, Birchen, Lemon-Blue and Silver-Blue Moderns are all as dark as possible in these parts. Skin colour is 'mulberry', a dark purplish colour, eyes are black; beak, shanks and feet are black or dark bluish-grey.

PLUMAGE COLOUR VARIETIES

Blacks have black plumage with a green sheen throughout. Males might have a little silver or gold in hackles because most are fairly new strains made from Birchens or Brown-Reds.

Blues should be as even in colour as possible, a medium shade with little or no lacing. Hackles are glossy bluish-black.

Pile Modern Game, bantam female. Photo: John Tarren

Silver-Blue Modern Game, bantam female. Photo: John Tarren

Whites are pure white, which can be a problem with strains which are genetically very light Piles. It is now known that the barring gene is a very useful addition to Whites, as it is another gene which supresses pigment production, so a White × Crele mating, followed by some selective breeding, should eventually produce a good snow-white strain.

Black-Red/Partridge are the same pattern as Red Jungle Fowl, as are many standard breeds. However, exact shades, especially of females, differ from breed to breed. Closely examine live birds at shows to learn ideal colours and markings. This is a popular variety, so very good specimens will be needed to win at major shows. Males should have minimal neck hackle striping and well defined and coloured wing bays, which is why many Black-Red males in the shows are actually Wheaten-bred. Those who stick to Partridge females to breed Black-Red show males use Partridge hens with minimal neck-hackled striping and 'foxy wings' (clear light brown, without peppering). Pullet-breeder Black-Red males, those needed to produce winning Partridge females, have some brown in the breast (to give better salmon breasted females) and a stronger neck striping in neck and saddle hackles (to give better neck striping and back/wing peppering on females).

Black-Red/Wheaten males are similar to those above, and are shown together in all but the largest shows in the UK. They should be a shade lighter in 'top colour'. Females vary in shade, the lighter, creamy coloured hens being bred from males with some brown on breast.

Blue-Reds are the same pattern as Black-Red/Partridge, but with all black parts changed to bluish-grey. Blue-Red/Wheatens probably exist, but are not standardized in the UK. If double mating is applied to these, use the same principles as above.

Duckwings should officially be two separate varieties, Silver Duckwing and Gold Duckwing, but seem to have been effectively merged in Moderns as far as shows are concerned. They are the same pattern as Black-Red/Partridge, but with all gold/red parts on males changed to silvery white or shades of yellow to light orange on Silvers and Golds respectively. On females, the neck hackle is white with light black striping (on both) and the back and wings appear grey from a distance, but are actually fine black peppering on a greyish-white ground colour, slightly richer on Gold Duckwings. The breast is salmon on both types of Duckwings, again slightly richer on Gold Duckwings. Both varieties are genetically 'Silver' (as opposed to Black-Red/Partridge, which are genetically 'Gold'), but Gold Duckwings have some other minor genes to give them their relatively slight yellow/gold shades. The author does not know if anyone today uses double mating systems, so ask a specialist.

Blue-Duckwing are as Gold Duckwings and Silver Duckwings, with all black parts changed to bluish-grey.

Pile (Pyle in USA) derived their name from the heraldic term for an inverted V. It is almost the same as the Black-Red/Partridge pattern, but with black parts replaced by white. It is difficult to breed birds with rich colour and clear white, each in the correct places as seen in the pictures. Expert 'show preparation' is needed to win with Pile Moderns, some of which would be regarded as faking in other breeds, but have been accepted as normal practice within the showing community for well over a century. Ask an expert for details.

Crele are genetically Black-Red/Partridge, plus the barring gene. Males have pretty neck, shoulder and saddle plumage: rich and light-orange striped, with black streaks on the feather shafts in the dark orange stripes. Barring is usually clear on wing and tail feathers, but the weak part of the pattern on virtually all Crele Modern males is their breast, belly and thigh feathering, blurred shades of grey instead of the clear cuckoo-barring depicted on prints. Crele females have the same pretty neck hackle markings, and their back and wings are soft shades of brown and grey. Females have a salmon breast; with negligable barring effect. Barring is caused by a sex-linked gene, which means there is (genetically and visually) only one type of female, but two types of male. Those with only one barring gene are considered prettier by most people, the top colour being richer generally. This type will be preferred by most judges. Males with two barring genes are lighter in colour overall.

Birchens are mostly black, also with black shanks/feet and very dark facial skin. Neck feathers on both sexes, plus back and saddle of males, is silvery-white with black centre striping. Front of neck and upper breast feathers have delicate white lacing. There are many versions of 'Grey' in Old English Game, from very light 'Millers Grey' or 'Mealy Grey' to mostly black 'Dark Grey'. 'Birchen Grey' was originally a Dark Grey with brown shoulders in the eighteenth century, but the name 'Birchen Grey', shortened to 'Birchen', was adopted by 'Exhibition Game' fanciers *circa* 1870, and so

on to Modern Game breeders. *See* Chapter 23: Old English Game for more details of historic Game colours.

Double mating is used to an extent on Birchens in regard to this lacing: Over-laced males (lacing extending too far down breast) are used to obtain correctly laced females, and to avoid 'black-capped' hens. Correctly laced males are bred from females with very little lacing at all.

Silver-Blues are as Birchens, but the black is replaced by bluish-grey.

'Brown-Red' Pit Game also came in many shades, some of which were actually shades of brown and red, but again Exhibition Game (*circa* 1870) and Modern Game selected got things wrong. 'Brown-Red' Moderns were their own version of what had been called 'Streaky Breasted Orange Reds' before 1849. They are black and lemon, in the same pattern as Birchens. Double mating, if used, follows the same principles as Birchens. Most fanciers, and judges, prefer Brown-Red females, which win major prizes at shows more often than males.

Lemon-Blues are as Brown-Reds, but with the black replaced by bluish-grey.

SPECIAL REQUIREMENTS

Modern Game, large and bantam, are very much a breed for enthusiasts, although the tiny bantams are very sweet, always very tame, and make excellent pets. They will not damage your garden, unless you are a really obsessively perfectionist gardener!

All breeders should join the Modern Game Club (or its equivalent in other countries) and get to know as many existing members as possible for advice on breeding details. Advice is critical when the potentially difficult issue of dubbing has to be faced for the first time.

Large Moderns need plenty of exercise, so that means generous-sized grassy runs. They are susceptible to leg weakness if kept shut inside, especially in the latter stages of growing, from three to eight months of age.

New Hampshire Reds. Artist: C.S.Th. van Gink

CHAPTER 22

New Hampshire Red

New Hampshires are one of more recently made pure breeds – making this one of the shortest chapters in this book, as there is little history to record. Although there are two, very rare, other colour varieties (New Hampshire Whites and Blue-tailed New Hampshire Reds) it is a single colour variety breed in most countries. New Hampshires have achieved greatest popularity as a fanciers' exhibition breed in Germany and the Netherlands.

The main originator was Professor A.W. ('Red') Richardson, poultry lecturer and Director (1918–20) at the Department of Animal Sciences, University of New Hampshire, Durham, NH. As far as is known, New Hampshires were developed from Rhode Island Reds, with no other breeds being involved. Exhibition Rhode Island Reds and New Hampshire Reds today each have their recognized plumage colour, but Prof. Richardson's flocks included every shade in between. He was criticized by people who associated pure breeds with quality, even for layers and broilers; who said his flocks looked like a bunch of mongrels. Prof. Richardson made a memorable riposte, 'The bird is not producing colour for sale, but meat and eggs. What we like in New Hampshire is the colour of the money they make for us.'

Broiler chicken rearing, a major branch of agricultural production today, started on a very small scale about 1900 in the New England states of the USA. The target market was New York and other large cities on the east coast. Its rate of development was partly controlled by progress in technology, particularly very large incubators, refrigerated storage and transport (to get finished product to consumers), and improved chick and grower meals. Epidemics, especially pullorum disease, regularly killed 20 per cent of each batch of chicks, often as many as 50 per cent. Broiler farmers then led the way in bio-security measures to prevent infections, which are normal practice now.

Rhode Island Reds had been popular dual purpose birds since they were standardized in 1904, but by 1920 were failing to meet the increasing expectations of specialist broiler rearers. They were slow feathering and slow growing, and their dark colour left noticable feather stubs on oven-ready birds. Prof. Richardson selected for rapid growth, rapid feathering, better conformation and high hatchability. Plumage colour was initially ignored, but most of his birds were beginning to be noticably lighter than Rhodes. This change may have been connected with selection for rapid feather growth, which was essential for two reasons: body heat retention, which helped food conversion efficiency, and protection from breast blisters which cause downgrading.

Although not recognized by the American Poultry Association until 1935, New Hampshires were accepted by commercial producers in the twenties. Two commercial producers in the state, Fred Nichols and Andrew Christie, took up New Hampshires about 1922, which helped to transform them

New Hampshire Red, large male. Photo: John Tarren

from a professor's experiment into a commercial breed. Andrew Christie (1888–1964) was a leading promoter of New Hampshires, particularly in the APA standardization procedure. He was probably no more interested in plumage colour than Prof. Richardson, but was aware that many poultry farmers had traditional views about standard breeds.

NEW HAMPSHIRES IN THE UK

The main, possibly only, importer of New Hampshires to England before the Second World War was Mr C.C. Ernst of High Birch Poultry Farm, Clacton-on-Sea, Essex. Adverts in *Feathered World Yearbooks* in 1935 and 1936 were the only evidence found, so it is not known when he imported them, or how long he continued to breed and sell them after 1936.

Poultry farming in the UK was delayed in getting back to normal after the war by a Newcastle disease outbreak during 1947–8. By this time American poultry farming was well

on the way to being transformed into, at least the beginnings of, the modern poultry industry. Hybrid broilers such as 'Cobbs' had not yet appeared, so producers were using crosses between White Cornish males and either Barred Rock, White Rock, or New Hampshire females.

This is a significant date, because it was the date the British Government abandoned an embargo on the importation of American commercial breeding stock introduced in 1950, under the pretence of Newcastle disease precautions, although some American hatching eggs had been smuggled in. After 1963, the infant British broiler industry quickly switched to American hybrids.

Between 1950 and 1963, most British table chicken producers were still using cockerels from Rhode Island Red × Light Sussex crosses, some used North Holland Blues, and a very few used New Hampshire Reds or North Holland Blue × New Hampshire Red crosses. The two main breeders using (pure or crossed) New Hampshires were Kenneth L. Boothman, Swartha House Farm, Silsden, Keighley, Yorks, and A.J. Peppercorn, of Norton Lindsey, Warwickshire. The latter had housing capacity for a total of 13,500 growing broilers in 1956, a massive enterprise in those days.

There may have been an occasional specimen entered in British shows during the 1950s and 1960s, but New Hampshires were practically unknown among hobbyists until some were imported from Germany and/or the Netherlands about 1980. They were covered by the Rare Poultry Society until the (British) New Hampshire Red Club was formed in 1997.

NEW HAMPSHIRES IN EUROPE

They were introduced, about 1950, by the American Government, as part of post-war reconstruction efforts, to several European countries. On a commercial level, they were eventually replaced by hybrid broilers, but continued to be bred in large numbers by hobbyists, including show exhibitors.

New Hampshire Red, bantam male. Photo: John Tarren

White New Hampshires started to appear in German shows in 1956, made by crossing New Hampshire Reds with White Barnevelders. Dutch fanciers remained loyal to their (very similar) White Barnevelders, so would not accept White New Hampshires. They are not recognized in the UK or USA. Some time between 1986 and 1990, Blue-tailed New Hampshire Reds were made in the Netherlands. This is a very pretty new variety which although not yet (in 2008) seen in the UK, is likely to be popular when imported.

As an indication of their popularity among European fanciers, there were 215 large Reds, 31 large Whites and 128 Red bantams at the 1971 Hannover Show.

NEW HAMPSHIRE BANTAM

Little definite information could be found on the origin of New Hampshire Bantams, and that information was conflicting. There were probably several strains made, independently, by fanciers in Austria, East and West Germany, and the Netherlands during the 1950s and early 1960s. They have become very popular in Europe. Over 300 birds have been entered at German National Shows. New Hampshire Red Bantams have been bred in the UK since the 1980s.

They were made by crossing under-sized large New Hampshires with various bantam breeds, including Australorps, Barbu d'Anvers, Barnevelders, Bielefelders, Dresdners, Niederrheiners, Rhode Island Reds, Welsummers and Wyandottes. White New Hampshire Bantams were made, but were never popular, and Blue-tailed Reds also exist, but are too new to have reached their potential.

NEW HAMPSHIRE DESCRIPTION

New Hampshires are classed as a heavy breed in the UK, but are not massive, so are an active practical breed. Large fowl weights range from 2.5kg (5½lb) pullets up to 3.85kg (8½lb) adult cocks. Official bantam weights vary from country to country; but 1,000g (36oz) females and 1,100g (39oz) males are realistic.

General body shape is broad and well rounded, with a medium length back, a shape which could be described as halfway between Rhodes and Wyandottes. The tail is medium length, well spread, and looks well balanced with the neck when the birds are seen from the side.

The comb is single, medium sized, and straight on both sexes, although a slight tilt at the rear is normal on females. Lobes are red, eyes are orange-red; beak, shanks and feet are all yellow with brownish shading. They need access to grass and/or maize in their diet to mainain yellow pigmentation.

Plumage is mainly chestnut-red in several shades. Consult several experts to get a consensus of the ideal, as opinions may vary. Both sexes have black tail feathers and wing markings, with black markings on the lower neck feathers of females only.

Old English Game 'Fig-Pudding' hen and Yellow Birchen cock, two rare old colours. Originally a free gift with Feathered World *magazine, 13 July 1928. Artist: H. Atkinson*

Old English Game: Black-Red cock and Clay hen. This is the type promoted by John Brough which Herbert Atkinson and other Oxford supporters despised. Artist: J.W. Ludlow

CHAPTER 23

Old English Game, Carlisle and Oxford Types

This chapter concentrates on Old English Game (usually shortened to OEG) since they were established, with that name, in the 1880s. Before cockfighting was finally banned in the UK in 1849 they wery simply 'Game', although famous strains were individually named, such as Bailey's Muffs and Cheshire Piles. It will not go into detail about fights, but aspects of how they were organized are mentioned because they were the origin of plumage variety naming.

For those who are interested, there are a surprisingly large number of books about Game Fowl and cockfighting. Some very old and rare books, such as Robert Howlett's *Royal Pastime of Cockfighting* (1709) have been republished (1973) for those interested in historical aspects.

Cockfighting was a very popular entertainment in England for some 2,000 years until it was finally banned in 1849. There were many attempts to ban it long before then, but these were not concerned with animal welfare. King Edward III ordered the Sheriffs of London to forbid it, along with most other public entertainments, in 1365, to force able-bodied men to spend their little free time on archery practice. England was at war with France for most of his reign, and he needed more archers. Oliver Cromwell banned it in 1654, partly because he was a Puritan anyway, and partly because he suspected Royalist 'cockers' would plot against him between fights. The last acts

against cockfighting, in 1835 and 1849, were for animal welfare, however.

Game cocks had been bred in a range of sizes, from small 'Match cocks', which weighed about 3½lb (1.5kg), up to 'Shakebags', which were 7lb (3kg) or more. The latter were mainly kept by poorer people, who would hold informal fights outside, in a barn, or their local pub, with any two cocks which looked near enough the same size for everyone to accept it as a fair fight. Small to medium sized cocks, up to about 5½lb (2.5kg), were kept by the wealthy; a fight would only go ahead if there was less than an ounce difference in weights of the two cocks. There were organized 'Mains', contests of an agreed odd number of fights, traditionally twenty-one.

The smallest Match cocks are now represented by Spanish Game, some of which could be descendants of the many hundreds of cocks taken to Spain by British army officers during the Peninsular War against Napoleon, 1809–12. Although some Carlisle type large OEG are as heavy as Shakebags, these old strains are probably more accurately represented today by Belgian Game and French Combattant du Nord.

Organized Mains, with strict rules, were at their peak from about 1750 to 1820. Improved roads and coaches made travel easier, so making it possible for larger numbers of people to travel longer distances simply for entertainment. Sometimes the contests were between two very wealthy individuals, the 12th Earl of Derby (1752–1834) being the most significant. He is mainly known today as the founder of the Derby and Oaks horseraces, the latter named after his estate in Surrey. He had hundreds of cocks at any one time, and employed three men to look after them, a father and son called Roscoe (one was Thomas, not known which) for the general care and breeding, and a Mr Potter who did the pre-match conditioning and match handling. If a Main was arranged in which all cocks had to be, say, between 4lb and 4lb 6oz, the Earl's men could easily find twenty-one suitable birds. Men of modest means arranged Mains on a team basis, one town against another, finding enough cocks within weight limits from several flocks. There would normally be a primary bet between the two individuals or groups, say £50 per fight plus £100 'the Main'. Other spectators made private bets aside from this, and these people, unlike the leading participants, could not afford to lose. Some Mains degenerated into scenes similar to today's football related riots, hence some of the earlier laws suppressing cockfighting.

Cocks had to be weighed and listed by neutral referees a few days before a contest to sort out, by weight, which 'team A' cock would fight which 'team B' cock. Referees needed a plumage colour naming system which could be quickly written in a match list, and adaptable enough to cover even the most unconventially coloured birds. The colour variety names used by these eighteenth-century cockfight referees remain the basis of chicken plumage colour and pattern naming today. Their system was, of course, only concerned with cocks, but as most people involved were also breeders, they had names for female plumage patterns as well.

It has often been said that Game Fowl can be any colour, which is true up to a point; but some colours were generally preferred over others, and many breeders kept to closed strains, so that all their birds would be virtually identical. Earl Derby had three strains: Greys, Piles and, his main strain, white-legged, light-eyed, Light Black-Reds, many of which had a few white wing and/or tail feathers. The next Earl Derby's estate steward (after 1849) was Captain Hornby, who crossed the remaining birds to transform them into Exhibition Game, with willow-green legs, red eyes, standard Black-Reds, without white feathers. Some of the original strain was kept going by the Roscoe family after they left the Earl Derby estates. When listing a lot of similar birds, cockfight referees would record any distinguishing old scars, odd coloured claws, and so on. This was to ensure the same bird was brought back for the fight, not a big brother. Most people preferred 'Reds', including Black-Reds, Brown-Reds and Gingers, because they were natural colours for chickens, and were thought likely to be generally fitter than unusual colours.

There is not space here to fully describe every colour variety recognized by the old referees, so their five versions of Piles are given here as an example: 'Smock-breasted Bloodwing Pile' (smock = white), 'Streaky-breasted Ginger Pile', 'Streaky-breasted Custard Pile', 'Marble-breasted Spangled Pile' and 'Ginger-breasted Yellow Pile'. Show judges, whether assessing Game of other breeds with a Pile variety, such as Leghorns, only recognized one version of Piles, similar to the first-named above, but allowing some variation of top colour from orange to chestnut-red. When OEG breeders split into rival Carlisle and Oxford groups (*see* below) in the 1930s, the Oxford standard acknowledged all the old versions of Piles, although it did not give full descriptions of them. They applied the same historical approach to all other colour varieties.

By 1870 Game birds winning at the shows were noticeably taller and tighter-feathered, especially in neck and tail, than Pit Game had been before 1849. 'Exhibition Game' were gradually being transformed into a separate breed, Modern Game. Breeders who did not approve of these changes arranged for classes for 'Old English Game' in 1883 at Aspatria, Cleator Moor and Wigton Shows in the north of England. By 1888 there were also OEG classes at major shows, such as Birmingham

Ginger Oxford type Old English Game, large trio. Photo: John Tarren

and Liverpool. An Old English Game Club, based at Cumberland, was formed about 1887. This club held some excellent shows, but did not do all the functions of breed clubs today. This was not the only club, and even OEG specialists have had trouble researching this period of the breed's history. There was also the complication of two, briefly three, rival interpretations of OEG shape.

We now have Oxford and Carlisle types, effectively two separate breeds, but the process of divergence was gradual, and the two groups were not simply divided by geography. Tensions gradually developed regarding interpretations of breed standards, with no one saying too much in public, until Herbert Atkinson died in 1936. He was universally respected as the leading judge and Game Fowl artist. Sixteen of his paintings were reproduced as prints and

given with *Feathered World* magazine, 1912 to 1933, which were framed by hundreds of breeders. He did not keep great numbers of birds because he spent most winters in India, so could not impose too much on his housekeeper. Once he had died, Carlisle type supporters felt freer to express their opinions. Atkinson lived at Ewelme, Oxfordshire, and he dominated the Old English Game Fowl Club. Its name was changed to Oxford Old English Game Fowl Club in 1928. Various years have been given for when it started, 1887, 1889 and 1890. The Club's annual show was at Oxford until 1939, moving to a hall in Derbyshire some time later. It has never covered OEG Bantams. While still judging on type more than colour, the Oxford Club has done much more to preserve ancient colours and the rare Henny subvariety than Carlisle breeders. Until about

*Henny Partridge Oxford type
Old English Game, large cock.
Photo: John Tarren*

1920 or so, many birds entered at major OEG shows in the north, Aspatria, Carlisle, Cleator Moor, Cumberland and Wigton, had entries from both schools of thought, because they were not too different from each other at that stage.

The Cumberland OEG Club did continue, however, and gradually became dominated by northern breeders who preferred heavier, broader-bodied, tighter-feathered birds. A second club, the OEG and OEG Bantam Club was formed in 1901, with a succession of northern based secretaries, at Leeds, Carlisle, Northumberland, and Carlisle again. The present Old English Game (Carlisle) Club is probably an amalgamation of these clubs, but details are not clear. Oxford type supporters stopped going to these northern shows in 1936, when Atkinson died, and took some

of their specialist cups (such as 'Best Henny cock') back with them.

It was mentioned earlier that a short-lived third type of OEG appeared at the shows. These were regarded as crossbreds by both Carlisle and Oxford people (possibly the only matter they agreed on) but were grand, colourful looking birds which impressed general judges. Herbert Atkinson mentioned (contemptuously) John Brough as being the source of many of them. Mr Brough's father had been a respected Game cock breeder before 1849, when it was customary to 'walk' young cocks, which meant paying cottagers to keep a Game cock with their hens for a few months. The cottagers were not allowed to keep any other cocks, but could breed from the Game cock, and eat any cockerels they reared. John Brough modified this system after 1849, now buying part Game crossbreds from the cottagers his father knew for his table chicken dealing business. About 1890 he saw his chance to sell seven-eighths bred Game to exhibitors for significantly higher prices, selecting birds which happened to have standard plumage patterns, mostly Light Black-Reds, Blue-Reds, Spangles and Duckwings. Lighter colours, ideally with white shanks and feet, had been preferred for table birds, so were normal in these strains. These Black-Red cocks came with creamy Wheaten hens, which soon replaced Partridge and dark Wheaten hens in OEG classes at all shows except those effectively controlled by the Oxford Club. Comments elsewhere suggest Brown Leghorn × OEG crossbreds won under some judges. These pseudo-OEG were depicted in prints and postcards by A.F. Lydon and J.W. Ludlow, both of whom produced many wonderful pictures of soft-feather breeds, but were hopeless with Game breeds. Photos of OEG suggest this type was declining by 1920, although they seem to have been incorporated into Carlisle Black-Red/Wheaten strains. Lots of OEG were entered in shows everywhere, too many for it to be worth giving many entry figure examples. By 1901 OEG were getting more popular, but had not yet completely replaced large Moderns as a leading exhibition breed. At Crystal Palace there were 95 Moderns and 144 OEG, followed a few weeks later by Birmingham, with 325 Moderns and 135 OEG. Between 1912 and 1939 there were usually about 250–300 OEG at all the 'classic' shows, but it is interesting to note that they were all Oxfords at Birmingham, and all Carlisles at the London shows, Crystal Palace, Alexandra Palace, Dairy and Olympia (plus the flashy crossbred type up to 1920).

The Oxford Show, which was a private event, not part of a general poultry show, grew to 572 birds in December 1928, with similar numbers up to 1939. The annual Carlisle Show was the main event for northern OEG breeders, and did include bantams as well. The highest entry of large OEG known was 535 in 1926, but figures are not known for all years. They often had

Muffed Partridge Oxford type Old English Game, large hen. Photo: John Tarren

Oxford-supporting judges until 1930, before the differences became irreconcilable.

The 1929 Crystal Palace Show had 52 Black-Red/Wheatens (by then an amalgamation of the Carlisle and crossbred types), 19 Spangles (similar), 32 Brown-Reds and 23 Birchen-Greys (both pure Carlisle types), and 65 in four AOC classes, which were a real mixture of types and colours, including at least one Henny cock and an 'old fashioned type Brown-Red', both of which must have been Oxfords. Carlisle type Brown-Reds and Birchen-Greys were similar to these varieties in Moderns (perhaps a little darker), whereas the same varieties in Oxfords were still as variable as they had been before 1849. More colour details are given later in the chapter.

General judges and show organizers could not ignore these arguments, and seem to have tried several ways of coping with them at shows

other than those which were well known to be dominated by one side or the other. The 1933 *Feathered World Yearbook* noted that very light-coloured, soft-feathered Wheaten hens (crossbred influence) were not winning any more, prizes instead going to harder-feathered, darker-shaded Wheatens. Some shows had separate classes for 'Pit Game' (Oxfords) and 'Exhibition OEG' (Carlisles): controversial at the time, but essentially the situation at most UK shows today. The Oxford Club continues to hold its private annual show, typically with about 300–400 entries, now including a dozen or so 'Miniature Oxfords'. Oxford entries at Stoneleigh and Stafford have fluctuated from a meagre twenty to a reasonably impressive hundred. The Carlisle Club also holds its annual show on its own, and has had entries approaching 500 large and 800 bantams, so is a major event.

Crele Oxford type Old English Game, large female.
Photo: John Tarren

Golden Duckwing Oxford type
Old English Game, large male.
Photo: John Tarren

158

CLOCKWISE FROM TOP LEFT: *Brown-Red Carlisle type Old English Game, large male. Tasselled Grey Carlisle type Old English Game, large female. Splash Carlisle type Old English Game, large male. Duckwing Carlisle type Old English Game, large female. Photos: John Tarren*

OLD ENGLISH GAME BANTAM

OEG Bantams were not exhibited under that name until about 1896, but similar bantams had been bred all over western Europe since the sixteenth century. As the Black-Red/Partridge pattern is the colour of wild Red Jungle Fowl, the main ancestor of domestic chickens, it is reasonable to assume that many of the first bantams brought here then were this colour. They were eventually developed into different breeds in each country: Dutch Bantams in the Netherlands, Pictaves in France, Belgische Kriel in Belgium, plus Spangled Bantams into Doornikse/Tournais, also in Belgium. As has been said earlier in this chapter, cockfighting was a very popular form of entertainment,

and some of the birds used were rather small (1.5kg/3¼lb) 'Match Cocks'. Although Black-Red/Partridge was one of the most popular varieties, there were plenty of other colours as well, all of which were common in the English countryside. By the early nineteenth century we can also assume most common Game colours also existed in miniature form. When poultry shows started they were too common for their own good. Most bantam fanciers wanted something pretty and exotic, the 'designer pets' of their day – Pekins, Sultans, Yokohamas and other strange new imports were the main focus, especially for wealthier fanciers. A few 'Partridge Bantams' were shown during the 1850s, and at least one pair of Duckwing Bantams is known to have been

Spangled Old English Game Bantams. These, miniatures of the Oxford type, are now represented by US type Old English Game Bantams. Originally a free gift with Feathered World *magazine, 15 April 1932. By then this type had already died out in the UK. Artist: Herbert Atkinson*

entered in London's Metropolitan Exhibition in December 1852. By 1870, when large Game had already become 'Exhibition Game', the only 'Game Bantams' seen at the shows were, if anything, ahead of the large fowl in being transformed into Modern Game. It is quite possible that no OEG type Bantams were seen at a show in the UK in the thirty years from 1868 to 1898.

When they re-appeared they were initially in two colour varieties, Black-Reds and Spangles, and very much 'Miniature Oxfords' in shape. The prime movers in this revival were Dr Robert Kerr, of Corkicle, Whitehaven, and his neighbour Captain Thompson. They are believed to have tried crosses with White Rosecomb Bantams to reduce overall size and increase size of tail. They were soon joined by William Dickinson and Tom Garner, both from Carlisle, and Robert de Courcy Peele, from Ludlow.

Although the OEG Fowl Club never had classes for bantams at their Oxford shows, several Oxford members got involved with bantams for the first decade of their revival. Herbert Atkinson even judged OEG Bantams at the 1901 Birmingham Show. There were two classes for Spangles (20 males, 18 females) and two for AOC (11 males, 8 females), which included Black-Red/Partridge, Black-Red/ Wheaten, Duckwings and Blues.

As said earlier in this chapter, the Carlisle based Old English Game and Old English Game Bantam Club was formed in 1902. It supported OEG Bantam classes at several shows. A separate Old English Game Bantam Club was formed in 1926 by Oxford members, with an Oxford based standard, 'in so far as they can be adapted to the Bantams'. This remained the published standard for many decades, although the birds had changed beyond recognition by 1939.

OEG Bantams were rising in popularity before the OEG Bantam Club was formed in 1926, with about 150 birds at Bradford, Cleator Moor, Crystal Palace and Leeds 1909– 16. Kendal had 379 in 1920 (90 Black-Red, 89 Spangle, 41 Black, 20 Birch, 19 Brown-Red,

39 Blue, 53 AOC, 28 Selling). OEG Bantams as shown in the UK today are very different from the miniature Oxfords the founders of the OEG Bantam Club had in mind. They have a very rounded breast, very short back and very broad shoulders; wings are carried higher, the neck is shorter, and the tail is whipped and rather small. This type, initially only Spangles, won major awards in the 1927–28 show season. It was believed they were made by crossing previous, Oxford type, Spangles with Indian Game Bantams, but this was denied by their owners. OEG Bantam Club Secretary, M. Warriner, did not approve, as he made clear in the 1928 *Feathered World Yearbook*, 'Tails are, more often than not, mere wisps of short feathers tightly held together, devoid of side furnishings. This is more noticeable in old birds, and especially the Spangled variety.' His went on to criticize other aspects of this new type. Robert de Courcy Peele, Club President, made similar comments in the 1930 *Feathered World Yearbook*, 'Just at present, I consider shortness of body and width of shoulders are the fanciers' idols'. He pointed out that the new type walked awkwardly, were not very active at home in their runs, and he didn't like the short tails either. This yearbook also had an article by George Fitterer, Secretary of the American Bantam Association, titled 'The American Bantam Fancy'. 'Hundreds of Old English Game Bantams from England have found their way to American homes'; but this export trade might not continue, he warned: 'We are well aware of the fact that two types exist in England. However, the type wanted on this [USA] side of the pond is a duplicate of the large Old English in miniature' [not the] 'pot-breasted, stub-tailed and thick-legged Old English'.

When researching for *Old English Bantams as Bred and Shown in the United States* (1991), F.P. Jeffrey and William Richardson checked through hundreds of show results in America. The first Old English Game Bantam entries they found were in 1914: 6 at Boston and 39 at New York. Black-Red and Spangled varieties were admitted to the *APA Standard*

Spangled Carlisle type Old English Game, bantam pair. Photo: John Tarren

Silver Duckwing Carlisle type Old English Game, bantam male. Photo: John Tarren

Off-colour Carlisle type Old English Game, bantam male. Old English Game of any colour, however unconventional, can win 'Best OEG' awards, but would not be made 'Show Champion' over correctly marked birds of other breeds. Photo: John Tarren

Muffed Black-Red Carlisle type Old English Game, bantam male. Photo: John Tarren

Dark Black-Red/Partridge, 46 Duckwing, 111 Black, 67 Blue, 146 Brassy-Black/Brassy-Blue/Furnace/Polecat, 52 Blue-Red and Blue-Duckwing, 35 Crele and Cuckoo, 16 Brown-Red, 8 Dark Grey, 45 Pile, 48 AOC, 12 Muffs and Tassels, 17 Juveniles. Non-standard coloured birds in AOC do win 'Best of Breed', which is unlikely to happen in America.

The book on OEG Bantams in the USA mentioned above has a summary of the relative popularity of colour varieties there, including a few interesting changes that occurred between 1930 and 1990. For example, in 1930 Spangles were second most popular, with Blacks well down the list; but by 1990 Blacks were the most popular colour and Spangles had dropped well down. Popularity charts were collated from show reports in the *OEG Bantam Club of America Yearbooks*. A few colour varieties seem to be bred only in either the UK or USA, not both, but the relative popularity of most of them is fairly similar in both countries, with one glaring exception: Whites are the third most popular colour in the USA, but seldom seen in the UK.

OEG TYPE DESCRIPTION

British Poultry Standards has three standards for OEG: Carlisle, Oxford and Bantam. American standards are different again, and OEG standards are slightly different in other countries as well. There is not space to cover all of them here, and in any case the written Carlisle and UK Bantam standards are largely ignored by breeders and judges, who seldom even attempt to justify the current style, simply asserting 'This is the type that wins'. Looking at large OEG adult cock weights we see: USA 5lb (2.25kg), Oxford 4–5½lb (1.8–2.5kg), Carlisle 5½–6lb (2.5–2.7kg). In fact, most Carlisle cocks are well over 6lb (2.7kg). Anyone thinking of starting to breed OEG should not only study the standard of the version they prefer, but also get a rounded view by studying the other types as well. As much of the judging is on the basis of body shape, muscularity and fitness, beginners must discuss

of Perfection in 1925. Blacks, Whites, Gold Duckwings and Silver Duckwings were added in 1938, others following later. Fanciers, and their organizations in America have consistently placed much more emphasis on correct plumage colours and patterns than have their British counterparts.

It is most unlikely that UK and USA fanciers will ever move towards a common type, although some British fanciers would like more tail on their birds, and American fanciers would like the wings to be slightly shorter and held higher on theirs. Oxford type bantams (or 'Miniature Oxfords') are still rare, and are larger than USA type OEG Bantams.

Both forms of OEG Bantams are very popular; for example, there were 1,751 entered in the OEG Bantam Club of America's 1990 Annual Show. Since the 1970s, British OEG Bantam Club Shows have fluctuated from about 600 up to 802 (the highest found) in 1994 at Stafford. To indicate relative popularities of colour varieties of OEG Bantams in the UK, here are details of entries at Stafford: 120 Black-Red/Wheaten, 78 Spangled, 58

Furnace Carlisle type Old English Game, bantam female. Photo: John Tarren

Blue-Furnace Carlisle type Old English Game, bantam female. Photo: John Tarren

and handle birds with experts. All these standards refer to OEG having a broad breast, short back, shallow belly, all tapering towards the base of the tail. However, roughly similar words in all cases are interpreted very differently, perhaps seen most obviously when large Carlisle and Oxford pullets are compared. Carlisles are much broader-bodied and stand more horizontally than Oxford and USA type OEG.

OEG males have traditionally been 'dubbed', the surgical removal of wattles, loose ear lobe skin, and most of the comb. The amount and shape of remaining comb is slightly higher in Carlisles than Oxfords and USA type OEG. Some countries have either banned dubbing or introduced stricter rules regarding how it must be done and by whom. Novice breeders should check with experts well before they have their first group of maturing cockerels. Even if they are in a country with no relevant legislation, this is not a procedure anyone should do the first time on their own.

OLD ENGLISH GAME COLOURS

There is not space here to give much more than three lists, but they will at least indicate the differences between American, Oxford and Carlisle types, large and bantam in all cases. Most of the darker varieties (Black, Blue, Brown-Red and Grey) have dark facial skin, dark eyes and dark shanks and feet in all three types. Medium coloured varieties (Black-Red/Partridge and Duckwings) have red skin, red eyes and white shanks/feet in the USA, with yellow or willow shanks/feet also allowed in Oxfords and Carlisles.

Oxford Colours (following tradition from the eighteenth century)

Black-breasted Dark-Red (mostly black, with red hackles)

Black-breasted Red (with Partridge females)

Shady or Streaky-breasted Light-Red (with light or dark Wheaten females)

CLOCKWISE FROM TOP LEFT: *Black-Mottled American type Old English Game, bantam male. Blue-Red American type Old English Game, bantam male. Blue-Silver Duckwing American type Old English Game, bantam male. Blue-Silver Duckwing American type Old English Game, bantam female. Photos: John Tarren*

Black-breasted Silver Duckwing (name derived from glossy blue wing-bar on males)

Black-breasted Yellow Duckwing (usually called Gold Duckwing)

Black-breasted Birchen Duckwing (has maroon shoulders, not the same as Birchen Grey)

Black-breasted Dark Grey

Clear Mealy-breasted Mealy Grey ('mealy' = flour colour, so these are mostly white)

Brown-breasted Brown-Red ('Old fashioned Brown-Reds', and really are mostly dark brown)

Streaky-breasted Orange-Red (original colour version of USA and Carlisle 'Brown-Reds')

Ginger-breasted Ginger-Red ('Red Quill' in the USA; 'Gingers' in USA are different)

Dun-breasted Blue-Dun (eighteenth-century name still in standards, normally just called Blue)

Streaky-breasted Red-Dun (as Lemon-Blue in USA and Carlisle)

Yellow-Dun, Silver-Dun and Honey-Dun (Silver-Dun as Silver-Blue in USA and Carlisle)

Smock-breasted Blood-wing Pile (as, or slightly darker top colour than USA and Carlisle Piles; Eighteenth-century Pile sub-varieties, such as marbled breasted and custard Piles, are mentioned)

Spangled (must have white spots, but Oxford standard allows variety of ground pattern)

Black, Cuckoo and White (all as these varieties in other breeds)

Furness (or Furnace), Brassy-back (or Brassy-Black) and Polecat

Brown-breasted Yellow-Birchen (a rare old variety; males have brown breast and straw hackles; females grey hackle, 'robin breast', remainder brown)

Hennie/Henny (males with female plumage colours, pattern and formation; can be of any of the varieties above, but traditionally only a few, such as 'Grouse')

Muff (bearded) and Tassel (small feather crest behind comb); also could be on any colour, but only a few traditionally. 'Bailey's Muffs' were Black-Red/Partridge

Carlisle colours

Spangle (Bantams popular, large rare; ground pattern dark version of Black-Red/Partridge)

Black-Red/Partridge

Black-Red/Wheaten (females usually light, creamy shade; darker version called 'Clay')

Gold Duckwing

Silver Duckwing

Blue Duckwing

Blue-Red/Blue-Partridge

Blue-Red/Blue-tailed Wheaten

Pile

Crele (as Black-Red/Partridge + barring gene)

Cuckoo

Ginger-Red (very rare in Carlisles)

Brown-Red (Black and gold, as Moderns; large popular, bantams rare)

Lemon-Blue (Blue and gold, as Moderns; also large popular, bantams rare)

Birchen-Grey (Black and silver, as Moderns; also large popular, bantams rare)

Blue-Grey (Blue and silver, as Silver-Blue Moderns, large popular, bantams rare.)

Brassy-backed Black M/Polecat F (females brown breast, dark back, some with black lacing)

Brassy-backed Blue M/Blue-Polecat F (blue version of above)

Furness or Furnace (darker version of Brassy-Black; females with mainly black back/wings)

Blue-Furness/Blue-Furnace (Blue version of above)

Black, Blue, White (as other breeds in these colours)

Splash (by-product of breeding Blues: the only breed in which Splashes can be shown)

Muffed (bearded)

Tasselled (regularly seen on large; believed extinct on bantams, but was one flock pre-1980.) (Henny cocks not known in large or bantam Carlisles)

USA OLD ENGLISH GAME COLOURS

Black-Red/Partridge
Blue-Red/Blue-Partridge
Golden Duckwing
Blue-Golden Duckwing
Silver Duckwing
Blue-Silver Duckwing
Wheaten
Blue-Wheaten
Blue-Silver Wheaten
Red Pyle (USA spelling of UK Pile)
Spangled
Ginger-Red and Red Quill (USA Red Quills are the same as UK Oxford Gingers; males of these and USA Gingers all similar; USA Ginger females similar to UK Quail females)
Birchen, Silver-Blue, Brown-Red and Lemon-Blue all as UK Carlisles and Moderns
Crele (USA Crele OEG are far superior to UK Creles for clarity of markings)
Cuckoo (there have been attempts to produce Barreds, with sharper markings, as well)
Brassy-Back Black and Brassy-Back Blue
Self colours: Black, Blue, Buff, Lavender and White
Black-Tailed Buff, Black-Tailed Red, Black-Tailed White
Columbian, Buff-Columbian

The last two groups illustrate a significant difference of attitudes to colour varieties between American and British OEG fanciers. They have been made, presumably starting with crosses with other bantam breeds, and were recognized by the ABA because they were already

Black-Tailed Buff American type Old English Game, bantam female. Photo: John Tarren

recognized colour varieties in other breeds. For example, USA Standards only recognize one version of Greys, colour and markings as Birchen Modern Game. UK Oxford Standards include 'Mealy Greys' and other eighteenth-century varieties not currently recognized in other breeds, historical accuracy being their prime consideration.

SPECIAL MANAGEMENT REQUIREMENTS

Condition, fitness and muscle tone are prime considerations when judging OEG, so they need outside runs, ideally with swing perches. Large OEG were bred to fight for some 2,000 years, so solid pen divisions are essential. Bantams are less aggressive, so cockerels can be reared together, but they might start fighting when birds come home from a show. Hens sometimes fight as well, so only enter females who normally live together, ideally sisters, in trio classes.

White Orpingtons. Originally a free gift with Feathered World *magazine, 12 March 1909. Artist: A.F. Lydon*

Spangled and Jubilee Orpingtons. Originally a free gift with Feathered World *magazine, circa 1910. Artist: A.F. Lydon*

Blue Orpingtons. Originally a free gift with Feathered World *magazine, 15 November 1912 Artist: A.F. Lydon*

Cook's, in that he sold poultry feed, medicines, and appliances. Another strain was made in Germany, but neither lasted very long. Any still surviving by 1920 were probably renamed as Red Sussex.

Partridge Orpingtons have been bred most consistently in Germany, but a strain was also made by Mr A.P. Goodacre in California, *circa* 1912–21. Partridge Cochins and Partridge Wyandottes were probably crossed with Buff Orpingtons to make them.

Patterns never seem to be very clear on Orpingtons, perhaps it's something to do with their profuse and rather loose plumage. Partridge and Gold Laced Orpingtons are well behind their equivalents in Wyandottes in terms of clarity of markings. All the main varieties of Orpingtons are self colours (or nearly so, in the case of Blues), so it is surprising that a Lavender variety was not made many years ago. Kent-based fancier Priscilla Middleton had just established a strain at time of writing, 2008. She started from a cross between Black Orpingtons and some approximately Leghorn looking lavender birds bought by a friend at a poultry auction. It may be difficult to solve the normal straw hackle and feather quality problems of lavender chickens.

'OLD TYPE ORPINGTON'

Differences between exhibition based breeders and practical egg and table chicken producers became obvious by the 1920s, in this case highlighted when Australian Black Orpingtons, later Australorps, were imported in 1921 (*see* Chapter 4: Australorp for full details).

Farmers who had kept Buff and White Orpingtons for their original purposes were not happy about the way their breed was being developed, although these two varieties were seldom quite as feathery as show winning Blacks. Some of them formed the 'Old Type Orpington Club' to foster their interests, through supporting egg laying trials and a few selected shows. At this period some shows had 'Utility Sections', which reveals how deep the connection was then between the shows and poultry farming. They were not psychologically ready to make a complete break from the concept of pure breeds, although sex-linked crosses soon became the commercial norm. Hybrids did not appear in the UK until well into the 1950s. The Old Type Orpington Club concentrated on Buffs and Whites, as utility Blacks were now Australorps, with their own breed club, and the other colours were either extinct (Cuckoos), absorbed into Sussex (Jubilees and Reds), or essentially show birds (Blues).

It is not known how long the club remained active, but no references to it post-war have been found, although some Old Type Orpingtons were probably kept commercially until the 1950s. Old type Whites had effectively been replaced by White Sussex some time previously, and there were several other Buff and Buff-Columbian breeds available for fanciers.

ORPINGTON BANTAM

The miniature version of Orpingtons were first made shortly after large Orpingtons but, despite the efforts of fanciers in several countries, never really attracted much interest until about 1950. Large Orpingtons are massive in general appearance, indeed it is a vital characteristic of the breed. As with Faverolles, Indian Game and Malay Bantams, this has led to controversy about their size. What is the best balance between birds small

enough to be 'bantams', but big enough to represent their breeds?

Pringle Proud, in his book *Bantams as a Hobby*, said he first saw protoytpe Buff Orpington Bantams in May 1898. They had been made by John Wharton, also a leading Wyandotte breeder. He had made them from Buff Pekins and some unknown (probably Nankins) buff coloured bantams without feathered feet. Proud was impressed by their 'very level buff for a new breed'. Their only faults were remnants of foot feathering and a bluish shade on their shanks. He was considerably less impressed by the next Buff Orpington Bantams he saw. A class was put on for them at the November 1899 Carlisle Show. They were so variable in shape, size and colour that he said that 'they reminded him of the Boer Army', an irregular force of farmers who were doing very well against the British Army in South Africa at the time.

The next recorded strains of Orpington Bantams, Blacks and Whites, were made by Emil Kühn in Germany. He started, it is believed in 1907, by crossing (Black and White, as applicable) Pekins with Rosecombs. German Langshan Bantams were added later. He first exhibited them at the 1912 Leipzig Show. Other German fanciers made their own Buff Orpingtons shortly afterwards, probably using a similar method to John Wharton. These may have been remade between the wars and German fanciers certainly had to start again after 1945.

John Burdett made a strain of Black Orpington Bantams at Wingate, County Durham, in the 1920s. Others in the UK made Buffs and Whites in the 1920s and 1930s, and W.H. Silk imported some Buffs from Europe, possibly Germany or Denmark during the same period. None of these strains attracted much interest until after 1945.

Captain I. Brooks Clark made a strain of Buff Orpington Bantams in America during the 1910s, but Orpingtons of either size have never been really popular there.

Blue Orpington Bantams were first made by Jobst von Veltheim in the 1950s, and he also made a new strain of Buffs. German fanciers have led the way in making additional colours of Orpington Bantams, including Black Mottleds (as earlier 'Spangles'), Barreds, Birchens, Buff Columbians, Gold Laced and Partridge. Dr Clive Carefoot, the acknowledged leading expert on the genetics of poultry plumage colours and patterns, made Chocolate Orpington Bantams.

UK ORPINGTON CLUBS

As stated earlier in this chapter, each colour variety of Orpingtons was made from a different mixture of breeds; and each new colour seems to have been opposed by those keeping the previously existing colours. Therefore each colour had its own breed club until it either folded or circumstances eventually forced breeders to think about amalgamating. Blacks and Buffs were both very popular for a very long time, so did not need any other colours in their very successful Club Shows. Here is a summary of the clubs:

Black Orpington, large rose-combed female. Photo: John Tarren

White Orpington, large female. Photo: John Tarren

1887 'Orpington Club' formed; changed its name to Black Orpington Club in 1896 to make it clear it was not going to cover any other colours

1889? White Orpington Club; suspended 1939, and never revived

1898 Buff Orpington Club formed; still a very active club at time of writing (2008)

circa 1902–08? Jubilee Orpington Club formed; collapsed during 1914–18 war

circa 1902–08? Spangled Orpington Club formed; collapsed during 1914–18 war

circa 1902–08? Variety Orpington Club formed; collapsed during 1914–18 war

1909 Cuckoo and Blue Orpington Club formed (secretary was Arthur C. Gilbert, originator); Blue Orpington Club only after 1915; suspended 1918–22, revived 1922–39; suspended again

1912 Red Orpington Club; collapsed some time during 1914–18 war

There were also separate Scottish and Welsh Orpington Clubs, at least 1909–39

Buff Orpington, large male. Photo: John Tarren   *Buff Orpington, large female. Photo: John Tarren*

1929–39 Old Type Orpington Club; uncertain how long it existed during 1939–45 war, when there were no shows, but Old Type Orpingtons were kept in considerable numbers

1950 to 1975 Orpington Bantam Club. At some stage, Buff Club covered Buff Bantams, but the Black Orpington Club did not do so at this stage. This club covered Blue and White Bantams as well

1975 Orpington Club formed by merging of Black Orpington Club and Orpington Bantam Club; covered 'all colours except Buff', which then meant only Blacks, Blues and Whites. Large Blues (and nominally Whites, although none seen at the time) had been covered by the Rare Poultry Society 1969–75. As is shown in the summary of show entries below, since 2000 a few members have taken an interest in the 'minor' colours.

UK ORPINGTON CLUBS' SHOWS – EXAMPLE ENTRIES TO INDICATE POPULARITY

Orpington Club Show, 1901, at Alexandra Palace, London. All Blacks, but including some rose-combed Orpingtons, which soon died out, although Cook gave both combs prominence at the beginning: single comb, 4 classes/111 entries; rose comb, 2 classes/16 entries; selling, 2 classes/33 entries.

Buff Orpington Club Show, 1901, also at Alexandra Palace. A total of 313 birds in 11 classes, including one class of ten rose-combed Buffs. There were 110 in the four main classes, 89 in 2 novice classes and 104 in four 'limit' selling classes (5-guinea males, 5-guinea females, 2-guinea males, 2-guinea females). A lot of the birds in the open classes were probably sold as well, but at much higher prices.

The first ever classes for Cuckoo Orpingtons were at the 1908 London Dairy Show, and for Blues at the 1909 Crystal Palace Show, but numbers entered have not been found. The high point for the joint Cuckoo and Blue Orpington Club (before the Cuckoos were dropped) was their 1913 event at Crystal Palace, where there were four classes for each colour, with a total of 108 Blues and 18 Cuckoos entered.

Jubilee and Spangle Orpingtons reached their peak of show popularity, and it wasn't much of a peak, in 1912 and 1913. There were 34 Jubilees and 35 Spangles at their 1912 Club Shows at Ilford, followed in 1913 by 31 Jubilees and 37 Spangles at Crystal Palace. Red Orpingtons were even less successful, only having a single class for them at the 1911 and 1912 Crystal Palace Shows, with 11 and 13 entries respectively. Cuckoo, Jubilee, Red and Spangle Orpingtons were all effectively extinct in the UK by 1918, although they continued to be bred in small numbers in Germany, from where a few have been re-imported since 2000. Any Reds and Jubilees still in the UK by 1920 were probably absorbed into Red and Speckled Sussex.

White Orpingtons took some time to get established, no doubt because their type and size was so poor to begin with. Although Ludlow, Lydon and other poultry artists depicted them as the same shape as Blacks, Blues and Buff, photographs reveal the truth: most were more like White Sussex (not then a recognized variety). However, by 1910 the White Orpington Club was able to hold a very successful show at Sheffield with 151 birds in 10 classes. The club moved south to Camberwell in 1912 with 121 birds, and back up to York in 1913 where 115 birds appeared. The last big display of White Orpingtons was probably in 1921 at the Club's Show at High Wycombe, where there were 91 birds, said to have been of better quality than ever before, which compensated for the decline in numbers. Numbers rapidly declined from then onwards, with the last White Orpington Club Show entries found being 37 in 1930 at Crystal Palace.

The Great Depression of the 1920s and 1930s was not the ideal economic environment for Blue Orpingtons, a large fancy variety kept by the rapidly declining number of wealthy country gentlemen. However, they were so magnificent that even some normal commercial poultry farmers kept a pen going (including the author's grandfather), subsidized by more practical breeds and crosses. The Blue Orpington Club was suspended during the First World War, and re-activated in about 1922 or 1923. Its Club Shows at Crystal Palace in 1926 and 1927 had fifty birds both times, rising to sixty in 1931, later shows unknown. The Blue Club continued until 1939.

The Old Type Orpington Club, formed in 1928, held shows because that is what people did in those days. Some shows had utility sections, including classes for 'copper ring hens', which had proved their worth at a laying trial, where copper leg rings were 'awarded' to the best performers. Their December 1929 show at Tottenham had 33 Old Type Buffs and 22 Old Type Whites, some, no doubt, from the many enthusiastic domestic poultry keepers in the Greater London area. The Old Type Orpington Club gave their northern members a chance in 1930, holding their show at Clitheroe, where a total of 93 entries comprised 33 Buffs, 25 Whites, 11 AOC, 10 copper ring hens and 14 selling males.

Obviously the Second World War had a negative effect on all but the most practical breeds, which extended into continuing poultry food shortages and fowl pest outbreaks afterwards. Practical farmers were using crosses (normally Rhode Island Red × Light Sussex), eventually replacing them by hybrids. Poultry showing as a hobby did not become popular until the late 1960s. The 1954 National Show entry figures give an example of how Orpingtons were holding up during this difficult period. The Buff Orpington Club came through very strongly, with 58 large (6 classes) and 13 bantam (2 classes) entries; the other colours of large Orpingtons had declined dramatically to 19 (2 classes, probably almost all Blacks); and the new Orpington Bantam

Club was enjoying more support than the miniatures ever had before, with 27 Blacks (2 classes), 16 AOC (2 classes), 13 AC young stock and one class of 9 novice exhibitors' birds, the colours of the birds in the latter classes being unknown.

In more recent times the two most popular varieties of Orpingtons have been large Buffs and bantam Blacks, as indicated by the following examples of National and Stafford show entries:

Large Buffs, National: 1973–81, from 19 to 39; 1984–95, from 29 to 66; 1996–2004; from 42 to 94

Bantam Buffs, National: 1973–89, from 4 to 23; 1990–2004, from 25 to 58

Large Blacks, National and Stafford: 1976–81, usually 14–16; 1982–2007, 18–50, usually 25–35

Bantam Blacks, National and Stafford: 1976–80, 19–37; 1981–2001, 37–78, usually 55–65; 2002–07, 21–44.

Black chickens are not popular with newcomers to our hobby, which probably explains the rise in popularity of Buff bantams and the fall of Blacks'.

Large Blues: there were 17 at both the National and Stafford in 1988, 18 and 14 respectively in 2004, the highest entries in modern times

Bantam Blues: National and Stafford Shows 1976–2007 had between one (1997 Stafford) to 24 (1998 National)

Large Whites: these have only had separate classes since 1993, where nine have been seen at three shows, and eleven at the February 2007 National (show postponed from December 2006 because of bird flu)

Bantam Whites: there were 16 at the 1987 National Show, and nine other occasions where ten or more were entered. Oxfordshire based exhibitor, Dave Thorne, well known for his sense of humour, had several wins with a single-combed White

Black Orpington, bantam male. Photo: John Tarren

White Orpington, bantam female. Photo: John Tarren

Buff Orpington, bantam female Photo: John Tarren

Blue Orpington, bantam male. Photo: John Tarren

Wyandotte pullet which he managed to keep with very light shanks by controlled feeding (no maize!). He usually told the unfortunate judge its true parentage after the prize cards had gone up

Large and bantam other colours: these have been given a single class for both sizes/all colours since 1993, where up to nine birds, usually two, three or four, have been entered. It is not known what most of them were, but many were Clive Carefoot's bantam Chocolates.

ORPINGTON DESCRIPTION

William Cook's original type have now become Australorps in the case of Blacks and Blues, and effectively replaced by Lincolnshire Buffs and Red, Speckled and White Sussex for the other colours; so the original debate over 'true' Orpington type is redundant. There is still some scope for justifiable differences of opinion on the appropriate size of Orpington Bantams and the amount and structure of thigh feathering, which hangs down to cover the shanks and feet on many specimens,

particularly Blacks and Blues. Many leading Orpington enthusiasts like this 'feather duster type', while others, general judges and some Buff Orpington fanciers, think this amount of loose feather is untidy and suggests poor productivity.

British Poultry Standards gives different weights for each variety, no doubt a legacy from the multitiude of clubs, so here are the simpler German standards: 3kg (6½lb) pullets up to 5kg (11lb) cocks. Orpington Bantams should officially weigh 900g (31oz) females to 1000g (36oz) males, but those seen at shows in the UK are considerably heavier.

Orpingtons have small single combs, with small rose combs also being permitted on large Blacks only. Comb, lobes and facial skin are red, which can be a problem with Blacks and Blues as they have very dark eyes. Pullets often have very dark facial skin, but usually brighten after they have been laying for a few weeks. The shanks and feet of Buffs and Whites are white, and black or slate on Blacks and Blues, in this case ideally with white claws.

White Pekins. Originally a free gift with Feathered World *magazine, 16 November 1923. Artist: A.F. Lydon*

Pekin and Light Brahma Bantams. Artist: C.S.Th. van Gink

CHAPTER 25

Pekin and/or Cochin Bantam

The 'and/or' looks rather confused and out of place in the title of a book's chapter, but it is intentional, and reflects the breed's history. These bantams were 'discovered' by a British army officer in the British and French force, which attacked and looted the Emperor's Peking (Beijing) Palace in October 1860. The bantams were said to have been in the palace gardens. This attack effectively ended the 'Opium Wars', when the European powers forced the Chinese to open their ports for trade, particularly the opium trade. The British East India Company controlled the opium trade then, and while there were plenty of eager buyers in China, the Emperor resisted because he did not wish to see his people become a nation of drug addicts. The British media seldom mentioned this aspect of the wars, concentrating instead on the supposed benefits of bringing Christianity to China. It is not surprising that no information has been found on these bantams before 1860.

The officer (name and regiment not found, but probably the Royal Scots) sent the bantams to a friend in England (also unknown) who bred a few and then passed them on to a Mr Kerrick, of Dorking, Surrey. They were called 'Buff Pekins', but only the females could really be called buff; the males were rather darker, more a light reddish-brown. They were probably called 'Pekins', rather than 'Pekings', because the British upper classes seldom, if ever, pronounced the letter *g* (as in huntin', shootin' and fishin'). According to Harrison

Weir, they were first exhibited at a show in London in 1863, presumably, although this is not stated, by Mr Kerrick.

Mr Kerrick bred them for twenty years; which became more difficult as the ill-effects of inbreeding increased. During this period he sold spare birds to Henry Beldon, of Goitstock, Bingley, Yorkshire, a prominent fancier of the period, who sold his spare birds to local fanciers, including W.J. Cope (Barnsley, Yorkshire), John Newsome and J.S. Senior (both Batley, Yorks) and H.B. Smith (Preston, Lancashire). Messrs Cope and Smith crossed some of their Buff Pekins with Nankin Bantams to overcome the inbreeding problems. Other fanciers may have tried crossing with Booted Bantams, but no details were recorded. 'Buff' Pekins then were the same colour as Nankins (then and now), so although colour was not an issue, foot feathering, cobby body shape, emphasized by profuse plumage and the short, broad tail formation were all lost for several years. John Baily and Sons, of Mount Street, London, imported some about 1880 from Shanghai, proving they had not been unique to the Emperor's palaces.

Meanwhile, W.F. Entwisle had been working on a strain of Buff Cochin Bantams by selective breeding from undersized large Buff Cochins. By 1884 he had birds in this strain down to about 3lb (1.5kg), when further progress was made when he bought a dozen birds from a ship in London Docks. He also bought and sold stock with American fanciers working on similar lines.

Black Pekins were first brought to England from China some time during the 1870s. The hens were a sound black, but the cocks had white splashes here and there, plus gold or silver in their neck hackles. Fanciers here naturally started a programme of selective breeding to improve their colour, some of which may have tried crossing with Black Booted Bantams.

White chicks appeared among hatches of Buffs and Blacks, with crosses of White Booteds to establish strains of White Pekins in both the UK and USA. A.P. Groves obtained white chicks among his Buffs at his home at Chestnut Hill, Philadelphia, Pennsylvania, about 1890. They were vigorous enough to establish his strain without the need to cross with Booteds or anything else. Charles Jehl, of New Jersey, made another strain along similar lines, while J.D. Nevius, of Pennsylvania, imported Whites from England.

Matthew Leno, of Dunstable, Bedfordshire, obtained the only Cuckoo Pekin cock ever imported directly from China in 1883, which he crossed with Blacks to establish a strain. About the same time W.F. Entwisle bred a Cuckoo pullet from a Black Pekin × White Booted mating that he was trying to improve his Black Pekins and make White Pekins. He bred this pullet with a Cuckoo Pekin cockerel from Mr Leno.

Partridge Pekins were the only other colour variety for many years, and were also created by the Entwisle family. Some time during 1880s he mated a brassy-hackled Black cock to Buff hens, then mating the resulting birds with undersized large Partridge Cochins. He then bred from birds from these two matings, improving markings and reducing size by selection and the effects of inbreeding, as there were no further out-crosses.

Entwisle exported Partridge Pekins to the USA from about 1892 onwards, with Thomas F. McGrew, of New York (author of *The Bantam Fowl*, 1899) receiving some in 1895. This was a short-lived transatlantic trade as, by 1905, differences between UK and USA Standards made British strains useless in America in all breeds with the Asiatic Partridge pattern (Cochins, Wyandottes, and so on). American birds were several shades darker than their British equivalents.

PEKIN OR COCHIN BANTAM?

The Pekin Bantams brought by the army officer clearly came from Peking, but some later importations came from other areas, including Shanghai. Even if they had not become available to British and American fanciers, they would probably have made 'Cochin Bantams' anyway by crossing undersized large Cochins with Booted Bantams, a project which Entwisle and others seem to have already started.

Early Pekins/Cochin Bantams were quite upright, more like miniature Cochins. The crossing with Nankins and Booteds, needed to retain something when inbreeding became a problem (very few birds were imported), delayed progress in achieving the desired compact and very feathery general appearance. For several decades almost all of them had long stiff tail feathers and vulture hocks, which were pulled out for showing. Some judges complained that most birds at the shows, especially males, had no true tail feathers left at all, only saddle feathers. American fanciers seem to have made most progress in breeding birds with naturally soft tail feathers which could be exhibited with tails still attached – the rounded outline we see today. The dual name, 'Pekin or Cochin Bantam' was introduced by British fanciers to mollify both sides of the argument about 1912. American fanciers stuck to the name 'Cochin Bantam'.

By about 1927–30 some birds, on both sides of the Atlantic, were appearing at the shows which had lower carriage and more profuse body plumage (in proportion) than large Cochins. In the UK, we now define 'Pekin type' (in contrast to 'Cochin type') as being the very profuse feathered bantams which naturally stand with their head lower than the tip of their tail, this being called 'the Pekin tilt'.

'Cochin Bantams', as bred in America, Canada, Germany and elsewhere since the

Buff Pekin, male. Photo: John Tarren

Black Pekin, female. Photo: John Tarren

Lavender Pekin, male. Photo: John Tarren

Partridge Pekin, female. Photo: John Tarren

1970s may not be quite as low or 'tilted' as UK Pekins, but they are still lower and a different overall shape than large Cochins. There have been some imports and exports between the UK and these other countries, mainly of new colour varieties (*see* below), which further reduces any differences between 'Pekins' and 'Cochin Bantams'. A Cochin Bantam should, theoretically, be larger and more upright than a Pekin. Pekins are in the 'True Bantam' section at UK shows, the section for bantam breeds without a large fowl equivalent. Allowing for the fact that there are differences between strains and colour varieties

183

Cuckoo Pekin, female. Photo: John Tarren

Columbian Pekin, female. Photo: John Tarren

Black-Mottled Pekin, female. Photo: John Tarren

Blue-Mottled Pekin, female. Photo: John Tarren

in size and shape in several breeds, there is still scope for reasoned argument on the question of whether we are discussing two distinct breeds or one variable breed.

Many additional colour varieties have been added to the range since 1950, a lot of them made by German fanciers. Here is a summary of them and their creators:

Buff-Barred, Gertrud Bauer, Berlin, in New Breeds class, Hannover, 1954, standardized 1956

Lavender, K.J. Elderink, Enschede, shown 1938, standardized 1962

Silver Partridge, cock-breeders, Theo Appel, Offenbach/Main, *circa* 1962

Silver Partridge, pullet-breeders, Hugo Lorz, Offenbach, *circa* 1965–67

Birchen, H.-E. Knour, Bemühungen, 1963

Columbian, E. Fetzer started 1960, later also Hugo Lorz, standardized 1967

Buff Columbian, Paul Doll, Bad Winpfen, 1968, standardized 1971

Black-Red/Wheaten, D. Aschenbach, standardized 1969

Silver Duckwing/Silver Wheaten, unknown, the Netherlands, 1992

Blue marked Silver Columbian, 1992, Blue-Buff Columbian, 1993, both D. Aschenbach.

Yet more varieties were made during the 1990s, including: Crele; Millefleur, Porcelaine, cock-breeder and pullet-breeder Blue-Gold Partridge, Blue-Red/Blue-Wheaten, Blue-Birchen, Brown-Red, Lemon-Blue.

UK BREED CLUB

It was announced in the 10 May 1901 issue of *Poultry* magazine that the Pekin Club had been formed, with James Whitley, of Main Street, Bingley as secretary. Others present included Edwin Wright, J.F. Entwisle, J.W. Binns and T. Garrett. They held a very successful first Club Show at Kendal in November, one of the exhibitors being Queen Alexandra (wife of Edward VII), whose birds were too tall to win anything. There were four classes each (cock, hen, cockerel, pullet) for Buffs (45 entries), Whites (31) and AOC (27, those known being Black and Partridge), plus 16 in selling classes. A White cockerel owned by Messrs Hays was the first Show Champion.

In 1909 the club introduced a rule banning the removal of tail feathers for showing, which suggests fanciers must have made progress in breeding naturally shorter, softer tail feathers; if it had not been possible to exhibit Pekins with tail intact, it is unlikely its members would have voted for the rule change. Most Pekins today are left with their main tail feathers present, although main sickles are usually removed from males as they often stick out from the other tail and saddle feathers. Those Pekins with the most abundant foot feathering usually also had vulture hocks, which were also routinely removed. In 1912 the club's name was changed to 'Pekin or Cochin Club'.

Some Annual Club Show entries:

1910 Sheffield, 13 classes/71 entries
1911 Crystal Palace, 10 classes/105 entries
1913 Crystal Palace, 10 classes/101 entries
1919 Bradford Bantam Show (moved to Victoria Hall, Bingley), 27 Blacks, 17 Buffs, 11 AOC.

The 1920 *Feathered World Yearbook* listed a new 'United Pekin Club', in addition to the 'Pekin or Cochin Club'. Its secretary, A. Lindsay, lived at Kilmarnock, which indicates it was effectively a Scottish Pekin Club. Both clubs held shows in January 1921, with the new United Pekin Club attracting an impressive 104 entries at Kilmarnock, compared to the established Pekin/Cochin Club's 72 birds at Bradford. Blues and Black-Mottles started to be shown from about 1920. As with many other breeds, the Blues were from Herbert Whitley, of Paignton, Devon.

White Pekins were most popular in Scotland, with one fancier, G.L. Booth, importing birds from Canada, described as being of good type, feather and colour, but larger than British strains.

About 1927 some Blacks were imported from Canada, with good undercolour but dark eyes. It has always been difficult to combine sound black plumage, red eyes and yellow legs. Between 1923 and 1935 the annual show at Bradford usually had a total of about 100 to 130 entries, half of which were Blacks; a quarter each Buffs and Whites, with very few of the other colours.

Occasional importations from America and Canada, such as those mentioned above, made it obvious that the breed was diverging. British

Blue Pekin, female. Photo: John Tarren

Standard weights were quite high, allowing an adult cock to be 36oz (1kg). With the gradually increasing wealth of plumage bred here, a cock of that weight would have filled a normal bantam show cage, which would have been fine if the objective had been a true miniature Cochin, but was certainly not what fanciers here were aiming for. In 1933 the club reduced its standard weights to 24oz (680g) males, 20oz (570g) females, these weights to be regarded as the maximum allowed.

After the war, the first Pekin Club Show entry found was not until the 1973 National, but progress has been quite rapid since then, with 209 Pekins in 1984, 319 in 1989, and 367 in 2003, all at Stafford Show. The numbers of each colour in 2003 were: 80 Black, 74 White; 17 Blue, 31 Buff, 44 Black-Mottle, 38 Lavender, 33 Cuckoo, 17 Partridge, 5 Silver Partridge, 2 Barred, 5 Birchen, 7 Columbian and 2 Non-Standard. The remainder were juveniles, pairs and trios.

PEKIN DESCRIPTION

The British Pekin standard should be closely compared with the Cochin Bantam standard in other countries. British weights, 680g (24oz) males; 570g (20oz) females, are lower than elsewhere. They still look quite big because of their very profuse plumage. Ideal carriage is low, with the tail often higher than the head. This is called 'the Pekin tilt'.

Apart from their very profuse leg and foot feathering, a lot of their lower body plumage touches the ground. You should not be able to see any 'daylight' under a Pekin. All plumage should be soft and flexible; so although there is a lot of work needed to keep them clean, at least Pekin specialists are spared the broken feather problems encountered by Booted and Barbu d'Uccle breeders.

Pekins have a small, straight, single comb, red lobes, red or orange eyes, and the beak, shanks and feet are yellow, with some dark shading on Blacks.

The plumage colour varieties mentioned in the text above do not need further description as they are the same as on other breeds. There is, perhaps, one exception – the Partridge. Considering they have been in existence since about 1890, and Pekins are a popular exhibition breed, small and cheap to breed, Partridge Pekins are terrible. In the UK, Liz Player's are

White Pekin, male. Photo: John Tarren

easily the best, but even hers could have a lot clearer markings. Partridge Wyandotte and Partridge Plymouth Rock Bantams both have wonderfully fine pencilling, so it must be possible. There is clearly scope here for someone prepared to breed them in large numbers and select only the very best each season – twice – as separate cock-breeder and pullet-breeder strains will be essential.

SPECIAL MANAGEMENT REQUIREMENTS

They are a very 'high maintenance' breed, which must be kept inside, on very clean shavings, most of the time. They need a few days outside on the lawn sometimes, or their faces will get very pale. Visit, and keep in contact with, experts for continued advice.

Plymouth Rocks. Originally a free gift with Feathered World *magazine, 1911. Artist: J.W. Ludlow*

CHAPTER 26

Plymouth Rock

The 'Plymouth Rock' is a granite boulder on the shore of Plymouth Bay, the landing place of the Pilgrim Fathers in December 1620. The name has been used for two unrelated chicken breeds.

THE FIRST PLYMOUTH ROCKS

Dr John Bennett, who lived at nearby Plymouth City described a 'new breed' he had just made in his *Poultry Book* in 1850 which he called Plymouth Rocks. They were really still cross-breds, as he fully admitted he only started to make them in 1847. These birds probably died out by 1855, and had no connection to present day Plymouth Rocks. However, it is intended to make this book as complete as possible, so here are more details of Dr Bennett's birds. The first mating was in 1847: a 'Cochin China cock of Baylies importation' × 'a crossbred hen'. Dr Alfred Baylies, of Taunton, Massachusetts, imported some Cochin Chinas in July 1846. They weighed about 8 to 14lb, had light foot feathering, and were gingery-buff to red in colour. The hen had been bred by Dr Bennett, and was '½ Fawn Dorking, ¼ Great Malay and ¼ Wild Indian', the last-named apparently an Asil hen from his description.

The youngsters were bred together in 1848, and again in 1849. They were still a varied lot by 1850 when Dr Bennett launched them. They were large and rather tall birds, weights ranging from 6½lb (3kg) pullets to 10lb (4.5kg) cocks. Colours were variations of Red to Black-Red/Partridge, most had single combs and shortish tails, had either clean or slightly feathered shanks, and a few had a fifth toe from their Dorking ancestor.

BARRED PLYMOUTH ROCK ORIGIN

Several breeders had the same idea during the 1850s and 1860s, to make a larger, heavier version of the Dominique (*see* the companion volume *Rare Poultry Breeds*).

An unknown breeder started to develop a strain from crosses between Dominiques, White Cochin, Dark Brahmas and Light Brahmas in 1858. Some of these were bought by Mr A.H. Drake, of Stoughton, Massachusetts in 1866, who continued to refine them.

Joseph Spaulding, of Putnam, Connecticut crossed a single-combed Dominique cock with a black Asiatic (Cochin or Java, details unknown) hen about 1865. Some of these were bought by D.A. Upham, of Wilsonville, Massachusetts who exhibited them as 'Plymouth Rocks' in March 1869 at Worcester, Massachusetts.

Mark Pitman, of Beverly, Massachusetts developed his 'Essex County Strain', starting in 1856, mainly by selecting for increasing the size of existing single-combed Dominiques he bought from a Mr Lord who, in turn, had bought his first birds from Mr Upham.

H.B. May and I.K. Felch, both of Natick, Massachusetts, improved some of these strains in the 1870s. Many Dominiques had quite sharp barring, but the crosses with Asiatics

Barred Plymouth Rocks. Originally a free gift with Poultry *magazine, circa 1912. Artist: J.W. Ludlow*

(Brahmas, Cochins and Javas) to increase size would have resulted in fuzzy (Marans type) markings. Perfect barring was not achieved on Barred Rocks until 1900.

'The Grey strain' (perhaps made by a Mr Grey) started from a Dominique × (Spanish × Dorking) cross. An unknown breeder started with Dominique × (White Birmingham × Black Java) mating. Javas are still a recognized breed in the USA (*see* the companion volume *Rare Poultry Breeds*). White Birminghams were a forerunner of White Plymouth Rocks, used by D.A. Upham and I.K. Felch to make Barred Rocks.

Plymouth Rocks, initially only Barreds, were included in the first *American Standard of Excellence* published at Buffalo, New York on 15 January 1874.

With Brahmas being among the breeds used to make Plymouth Rocks, there were bound to be some pea-combed chicks. Mr H.S. Babcock

promoted pea-combed Plymouth Rocks, resulting in them being in the 1888 edition of the American Standards, but they were dropped by 1900.

Rose-combed Barred Plymouth Rocks were promoted by a few American and British breeders *circa* 1908–1918, but they were too similar to Dominiques to survive in the USA, and were replaced by (and probably absorbed into) Barred Wyandottes in the UK and Germany.

WHITE PLYMOUTH ROCK ORIGIN

These were recognized by the American Poultry Association in 1888. There was a lot of argument about this at the time, despite at least some White Rocks having been hatched from Barreds, because many breeders thought the name 'Plymouth Rock' should apply only

190

to the original variety. As White Cochins were one of the breeds used to make some strains of Barred Rocks, the recessive white gene was carried by some birds, and there were bound to be some matings between them which would produce 25 per cent Whites.

However, several other similar white plumaged breeds (or at least prototypes) had appeared in America since about 1850, and many of these were either crossed with White Rocks bred from Barreds, or just renamed by owners who thought they would sell better as 'White Plymouth Rocks'. These breeds included the following.

Danvers White, from the town of Danvers, Massachusetts, were bred from Dominique × White Cochin matings about 1850. Classes were provided for them in the New England states until about 1870. There were both single- and rose-combed versions, so any still surviving in 1888 were renamed 'White Plymouth Rock' or 'White Wyandotte' as applicable.

Albion/Bristol White, which came from Bristol County, Massachusetts. William E. Shedd of Waltham was a prominent breeder in the county who used the name 'Albion', but most of his neighbours used the other name since about 1850. They originated from White Dorking × White Cochin matings.

Birmingham White, of unknown origin, was a name used by D.A. Upham and I.K. Felch.

White Java belonged to the American Java breed which was eventually only standardized in Black and Black-Mottle varieties. They were used in the development of Jersey Giants before almost vanishing for many decades. White Jersey Giants are their nearest living descendants.

Sherwood Whites were developed by the Timberlake family at their Sherwood Plantation, Virginia in the 1850s, initially from White Georgia Pit Game × White Cochin (and possibly light Brahma) matings. Later, *circa* 1880–90, they were promoted by the Burpee Company (agricultural merchants). Sherwoods had lightly feathered feet, so may not have been widely used for Rock breeding.

White Wonder Fowl, from Maine, *circa* 1890 also had slightly feathered legs/feet, so again may not have been as useful for breeding birds which could be sold as 'White Rocks'.

Dirigo, from Maine, took their name from the state seal.

In addition, any single-combed chicks hatched from White Wyandottes were renamed!

All these breeds lost their identities as breeders crossed strains and selected for standard White Rock characteristics, but a few experts could identify ex-Danvers (smaller, but meaty and fine boned, so excellent quality) and ex-Bristols (larger, heavy boned) until 1900.

True White Plymouth Rocks started from some white chicks hatched from Barred Rock eggs bought by Oscar F. Frost, a miller from Monmouth, Maine in 1875. He exhibited them as White Plymouth Rocks at Bangor Show, Maine in 1876. These few chicks were to become the foundation of one of the most economically important (possibly the most important) chicken breed in the world as they are the basis of almost all female line broiler breeders. Oscar Frost's other hobby was writing poetry; his 'Brush Away the Tears, Nellie' being adapted into a popular song of the time.

The American Poultry Association meeting in January 1888 at Indianapolis had to deal with applications to standardize Oscar Frost's White Plymouth Rocks, Dirigos and White Javas, and decided to accept only one of them as they were so similar. Mr Frost won.

BUFF PLYMOUTH ROCK ORIGIN

Buff was the third variety to be accepted by the American Poultry Association, in 1892. As with Barreds and Whites, Buff Rocks were an amalgamation of unrelated, similar-looking breeds being made by several people, some of which were also prototype Rhode Island Reds. There were two main strains, and a possible third.

The 'Fall River Strain' was made by Mr R.G. Buffington and Dr N.B. Aldrich, both from Fall River, Massachusetts. They were also busy developing Rhode Island Reds, their lighter coloured strain being made by crossing prototype RI Reds with White Plymouth Rocks. Both men first exhibited these birds at Providence, Rhode Island, in December 1890, Mr Buffington entering his birds as Buff Plymouth Rocks, Dr Aldrich using the name Golden Buffs. At this stage they were Buff Columbians, with black neck striping, wing markings and tail.

Mr J.D. Wilson, of Worcester, New York made his ('Wilson') strain from Buff Cochin, Light Brahmas and Buff Leghorns. His birds were bigger and, although they varied in shades from light lemon-yellow to cinnamon, were a better colour than the Fell River strain. Wilson strain birds were first shown by another (unknown) exhibitor in 1893, with Mr Wilson first exhibiting in the poultry section of the 1893 World's Fair.

Another breeder was mentioned in an article by Mr J.H. Drew which was published in the (UK) Buff Plymouth Rock Club's 1955 *Yearbook*. He was Mr E.W. Brown, of Riverhead Farm, Old Mystic, Connecticut, who started making a strain in 1887. He may have been in contact with Dr Aldrich as he also used the name 'Golden Buffs' before switching to

Buff Plymouth Rocks. Originally a free gift with Feathered World *magazine, 23 October 1925, and again 8 June 1928. Artist: A.J. Simpson*

'Buff Plymouth Rocks'. His initial mating was 'Indian Doran' × 'Chinese Marsh'. Indian Dorans were a type of Calcutta Game (Asil), a sort of Crele/Wheaten/Pile, yellowish-buff with indistinct barring. Chinese Marsh were Buff Columbian Asiatics (Brahma or Cochin).

Breeders then spent the 1890s trying to remove the black markings, initially going for any shade from lemon to rich buff, as long as it was even. Buff Plymouth Rocks were standardized by the American Poultry Association in 1894.

PLYMOUTH ROCKS IN THE UK

Barred Rocks were imported by James Long, of Graveley Manor, Stevenage, Hertfordshire in 1870, with another lot being sent over by William Simpson Jr, of West Farms, New York to be exhibited in the AOV class at Birmingham Show as 'American Dominiques'. He did the same again in 1872. They were rather tall birds with single combs, and seemed more like Barred Rocks to J.W. Ludlow, the famous poultry artist, who bought some of them. More followed over the next few years. The 1889 Crystal Palace Show had an impressive entry of 164 Barred Rocks. British breeders placed more emphasis on markings than type, so they soon differed from USA birds.

There were to be several specialist clubs for Plymouth Rocks; the first, formed at the 1875 Crystal Palace Show was an unusual alliance, the Leghorn, Plymouth Rock and Andalusian Club. It was very successful up to 1914, but declined after 1918 and collapsed about 1925. By then it had been effectively replaced by an Andalusian Club, eleven Leghorn Clubs and six Plymouth Rock Clubs. These included, for both Leghorns and Rocks, separate Scottish and Welsh clubs, clubs for specific colour varieties, and some which reflected north–south or exhibition–utility arguments.

A straightforward Plymouth Rock Club was formed in 1895, the same year as the first Buff Plymouth Rocks arrived in Liverpool. They had been sent to Henry Digby, a duck breeder, by his brother who lived at Dover Plains, New

York State. Mr Digby took them straight from the ship to Liverpool Poultry Show, where they were bought by John Wharton, along with some Buff Wyandottes which had presumably arrived on the same ship. Mr Wharton decided to stick to Wyandottes (*see* further references to Mr Wharton in Chapter 35), so he sold them to James Bateman, of Longcroft, Milnthorpe, Westmorland, who had seen them at the show but didn't get to the sales office until after Mr Wharton. Mr Bateman was so enthusiatic about Buff Rocks he also imported some hatching eggs from Mr Buffington and some prizewinning birds from Mr J.D. Wilson.

Both American and British breeders worked hard by selective breeding to improve Plymouth Rocks, but by 1900 it was obvious they were working in different directions: so there was little point in further transatlantic shipments. Some American Barred Rocks were sent to the British Empire Exhibition's poultry section at Wembley in 1924, where our fanciers saw they had virtually become two separate breeds.

Early Barred Rocks (1870s) had rather blurred and crescent shaped bars, more like today's Cuckoo Marans. Both sets of breeders worked towards sharper, straighter barring, with the British going further in the direction of very sharp, very narrow bars, but at the expense of type and body size. Young Barred Rocks were very slow to feather at all (narrow barring comes with slow feather growth, barring being caused by a pigment 'switching on and off' mechanism) and had very long narrow feathers which eventually had a straggly appearance, with male tail and saddle feathers almost looking like dreadlocks. There was also a UK/USA difference in the exact colour of the barring; it was never exactly black and white. American fanciers decided to go for not quite white and not quite black bar of equal width on females and 60 per cent (nearly) black 40 per cent (nearly) white bars on males. British fanciers went for definite (greenish) glossy black bars with rather bluish or greyish light bars. Despite the published British standard describing equal width (black/off-white) bars; in reality the black bars

Barred Plymouth Rock cockerel. Extreme UK exhibition type, when breeders and judges seemed to be only interested in fine barring, ignoring breed type. This bird won prizes at several major shows in 1924, despite being taller and slimmer than the standard required and with not much of a tail. Photographer unknown

were usually wider. From a distance, British Barred Rocks looked generally darker than American Barred Rocks.

Differences between American and British Buff and White Rocks were not quite as extreme, although both varieties became taller in the UK, following (to an extent) the style of our Barreds. There was a considerable difference in the relative popularities of these two varieties in each country, however; Whites were very popular in America and fairly rare in Britain, the reverse situation applying to Buffs. The ideal colour of Buffs in the UK was described as 'the colour of a new gold sovereign', a familiar reference point for wealthy

fanciers, if not poorer country folk. Eventually Buff Rocks became a rather lighter, yellowish shade than Buff Orpingtons, the other popular buff breed here. American standards required Buffs of all breeds to be the same shade.

BLACK PLYMOUTH ROCK ORIGIN

Black pullets were regularly hatched among Barreds, particularly in the UK, where our Barred males were darker than American Barred males. A few black pullets had been bred in America as well of course, but breeders there never made them into a standard variety. They would have been almost identical to American Black Javas and (although smaller) Black Jersey Giants, so there was no point. Neither of these breeds existed in the UK then, and black breeds were more popular here then anyway. Black Orpingtons and Black Wyandottes were both much more popular in the UK than the USA, probably because a higher proportion of our poultry keepers lived in smoky cities. Only black chickens stayed looking smart in city backyards with all that air pollution. Black Plymouth Rocks started being entered in shows about 1905. They were never as popular as their Orpington or Wyandotte equivalents, but there was a short-lived Black and Blue Plymouth Rock Club, 1914–1924. There had been fair entries of Blacks in 1911 at Crystal Palace (9 male, 10 female) and Manchester (5 male, 19 female), but even this level of interest was never sustained. Most of the very few large Black Rocks seen at UK shows since 1924 have been pullets bred from Barreds. Some present-day beginners confuse exhibition Black Plymouth Rocks with commercial 'Black Rock' hybrid layers.

BLUE PLYMOUTH ROCK ORIGIN

Blue Plymouth Rocks (mentioned above with the Blacks) were recognized in both the UK and USA (recognized by the APA in 1920) but were never anything other than a rare novelty. The first known entry of large Blue Plymouth Rocks in the UK was at Crystal Palace in 1912, followed by a fine display of thirty of them in two classes at Liverpool in 1913. This variety seems to have been effectively killed off by the First World War. Herbert Whitley, who bred and exhibited blue varieties of many breeds, does not seem to have had Blue Rocks. There are currently (2008) a few very pretty Blue Rock Bantams being bred, but the large version has probably been extinct for many years. They could easily be remade by crossing a large Blue Wyandotte (rare, but can be found) with a large Black Plymouth Rock (possibly bred from Barreds). However, in view of their rarity, it would be more sensible to concentrate on the Blue Wyandottes or (also very rare now) existing colours of large Rocks.

GOLDEN BARRED PLYMOUTH ROCK ORIGIN

This is another colour variety of Plymouth Rocks which was made in England rather than America, the breed's general country of origin. They first appeared in public in 1914 at Crystal Palace and Otley Shows, and were a pastel pattern of buff and (nearly) white barring. Two classes were provided for them at Manchester Show in 1916, where 29 birds were entered. A separate Golden Barred Plymouth Rock Club was formed in 1924, which lasted until 1932. They were briefly (1946 to 1956) remade under a new name, the Brockbar, one of the autosexing breeds. There has recently been a revival in interest in autosexing breeds, so this breed might be remade, but will be called Brockbars, not Golden Barred Plymouth Rocks.

Barred Plymouth Rock, large male in UK. Photo: John Tarren

Barred Plymouth Rock, large female in UK. Photo: John Tarren

White Plymouth Rock, large male in US. Photo: John Tarren

SILVER PENCILLED PLYMOUTH ROCK

Silver Pencilled Plymouth Rocks were developed from single-combed chicks hatched among Silver Pencilled Wyandottes. They were recognized by the APA in 1907, and a Silver Pencilled Plymouth Rock Club was formed around the same time, but they were never very popular. The Madison Square Gardens Show, New York, of 31 December 1912 to 4 January 1913 had three trios and fourteen single bird entries of them, which may have been one of the best ever displays. Silver Pencilled Rocks were imported to the UK by Mr R.N. Palmer of Bristol in 1929 or 1930, and first appeared in public in 1930 at the Dairy and Crystal Palace Shows in London. The author is not sure if large Silver Pencilled Rocks still exist, but they could easily be made from Silver Pencilled Wyandottes.

PARTRIDGE PLYMOUTH ROCK

Two strains were made about 1900 by Sam Noftzger, of North Manchester, Indiana, and W.C. Crocker, of Foxboro', Massachusetts. They were accepted by the APA in 1908, the same year as an American Partridge Plymouth Rock Club was formed, which had attracted about 300 members by 1913. This variety was never used commercially in significant numbers, despite being as productive as Barreds, Buffs and Whites, but was a moderately popular exhibition variety up to the beginning of the Second World War.

As an indication of the peak of their popularity there were two shows held simultaneously, from 31 December 1912 to 4 January 1913. At Baltimore, Maryland, there was one trio and 44 single bird entries; and at Madison Square Gardens, New York, another two trios and 33 single birds.

British Plymouth Rock breeders were aware of their existence from the beginning, but none were imported until John Wharton (*see* Partridge Wyandottes) in 1927, buying stock from L.C. Allen, of Bean Site Farm, Sanford, Maine. Partridge Plymouth Rocks were accepted by the PCB in the darker form of the Partridge pattern which is normal in the USA, rather different from the lighter version of the pattern British fanciers are used to seeing on our Partridge Wyandottes. Although Partridge Plymouth Rock Bantams are (2008) bred in the UK, the author does not remember ever seeing a large fowl.

COLUMBIAN PLYMOUTH ROCK

These were accepted by the APA in 1910. Single-combed Columbian Wyandotte chicks and Light Brahmas were crossed with Barred and White Plymouth Rocks by a breeder in Ohio to make them. An American Columbian Plymouth Rock Club was formed in 1907, which had 115 members by 1913. Entries from 31 to 36 birds were seen at the major shows at Boston, New York and Philadelphia during the 1912/13 winter show season.

Columbian Rocks were first imported to the UK about 1928, with Captain A.G. Miller, of Hurstide Poultry Farm, West Molesey, Surrey, being one of the few to exhibit them here, with a John Taylor being mentioned as another importer. They probably died out in the UK during the Second World War here, but fresh stock has been imported by Tom Newbould since 2000.

UK UTILITY BUFF ROCK

A new Buff Plymouth Rock Club was formed in the UK in 1933 which tried to bridge the then diverging poultry farming and showing scenes. It provided classes for both 'Exhibition' and 'Utility' types. The official 'aims and objects of the club' included:

- To further the utility characteristics of the breed, and to encourage breeding of standard bred Buff Plymouth Rocks for utility purposes and laying trials.
- To work for one standard for exhibition and utility.

Although Buff Rocks were not as popular as Rhode Island Reds or Light Sussex, many flocks of them were still seen in the British countryside until 1900 or so, but they have now all gone.

AMROCK

Utility type American Barred Rocks were sent to Germany as part of post-war reconstruction programmes. They were standardized in Germany as a separate breed (from Plymouth Rocks) on 1 August 1958. Amrocks have shorter legs, a more compact general body shape and their barring is broader. A bantam version was standardized in 1983.

Barred Plymouth Rock, bantam female in UK. Photo: John Tarren

LARGE PLYMOUTH ROCK POPULARITY IN UK

Buff Rocks were probably more popular in the UK than their country of origin until the 1950s, but since then all colours of large Rocks have declined dramatically. Large Barreds

Barred Plymouth Rock, bantam female in US. Photo: John Tarren

Buff Plymouth Rock, bantam male in UK. Photo: John Tarren

Black Plymouth Rock, bantam female in UK. Photo: John Tarren

lost general support because the extremely tall UK exhibition type favoured by the enthusiasts had clearly lost all value as a commercial breed. Large Rocks have been rarer than many Rare Breeds in the UK for a very long time, the Plymouth Rock Club only continuing to thrive because the majority of its members keep the bantam version. Here are a few breed club show entry figures to demonstrate their rise and fall:

Buff Plymouth Rock Club Shows: 1909 Crystal Palace, 70 birds; 1915 Manchester, 100; 1925 Crystal Palace, 155; 1934 Birmingham, 103; 1938 Ashford, 56; 1962 Olympia, 11

Since 1964 (up to 2008) there have only been more than ten large Buffs at five UK shows, the best display being 22 at the 1981 National

Barred Plymouth Rock Club Shows: 1913 Crystal Palace, 180; 1915 Manchester, 168; 1925 Crystal Palace 140

Plymouth Rock Society Show, 1927 York, 243 large Rocks in total, including 115 Barreds

Plymouth Rock Society Show, 1930, total 'over 300', number of Barreds unknown. No further exact numbers of Barred Rocks at major shows during the 1930s found, but said to be falling

Plymouth Rock Club Show, 1954 Olympia, 15 large Barreds, plus 6 'Canadian Barreds'. Since 1971 (up to 2008) there have only been more than ten large Barreds at three UK shows

PLYMOUTH ROCK BANTAM

Several fanciers in the UK, USA and Germany started to make Plymouth Rock Bantams from about 1900. Many seem to have been single-combed chicks from Wyandotte Bantam breeding projects: Pekin/Cochin Bantams with poor foot feathering were also crossed with Scots Grey (for Barreds) and Nankin (for Buffs) and other suitable bantams, no doubt including farmyard crossbreds, to make Rock Bantams. They were slow to attract much interest, in the case of 'Barred Plymouth Rock Bantams' in the UK probably because they were little more than yellow-legged Scots Greys in general appearance.

Pringle Proud gave details of one early Buff Rock Bantam project in his book *Bantams as a Hobby*. He included a contribution from Mr F.W. Jones, of Middlewich, who was making Buff Rock Bantams and Buff Leghorn Bantams:

Blue Plymouth Rock, bantam female in UK. Photo: John Tarren

> In the year 1894 it occurred to me that, seeing it was possible to produce the large breeds of Buff Rocks and Buff Leghorns, it would be equally as easy to breed Bantams of these varieties. To this end I purchased a pair of Buff Pekins with as little leg feather as possible. From the produce of this pair I selected those chickens that were the nearest approach to clean-legged. The following year I inbred from these, and obtained two clean-legged pullets, and two or three fair cockerels. The best cockerel I mated to the two pullets in 1898, and was rewarded by thirty promising chickens, which ultimately turned out very satisfactory, in every way miniature Buff Rocks.

He went on to describe how, in 1897, he bred one of these cockerels with an undersized large Buff Leghorn pullet, to start his second project.

By 1914 a few Black and White Rock Bantams had been seen at the shows, but most of the still limited numbers were Barreds, with rather fewer Buffs. At the main shows, Birmingham, Crystal Palace and London Dairy (*circa* 1910–14), there were usually two classes for Rock Bantams with a combined entry of about twenty birds.

A Plymouth Rock Bantam Club was formed in December 1921 or January 1922. Its secretary was W. Ross, of Coley Hall, North Walbottle, Newburn on Tyne, one of the main clusters of Rock Bantam fanciers in the northeast of England. Its 1925 Club Show at Kendal had two classes for Barreds and one for Buffs,

with a total of forty birds entered. Photos of winners in the early 1930s show Rock Bantams were really looking like miniature Rocks by this time, although apparent breed type seems to have been achieved by removing the main tail feathers in some cases. Columbian Rock Bantams, first seen in 1932 at Crystal Palace, were probably single-combed Columbian Wyandotte Bantams. Plymouth Rock Bantam Club Annual Shows, at various venues in the north of England, continued to have about 35–45 entries up to 1939.

There were very few poultry shows until 1947, as the war was followed by a fowl pest outbreak. Very few of the 'other colours' seem to have survived this enforced break, but Barreds and Buffs seem to have prospered. They were good layers, and surplus cockerels were acceptable table birds in a time of rationing and extreme food shortages for back garden farmers.

White Plymouth Rock, bantam male in US. Photo: John Tarren

The 1954 Plymouth Rock Bantam Club Show, held as part of the National Poultry Show at Olympia, London, had a much more impressive entry of 8 trios, 65 Barreds, 69 Buffs, 9 AOC, 24 in two Novice classes. The PR Bantam Club amalgamated with the main club in 1964.

Barred PR Bantams entered: 1973 National 20; 1987 National 65; 2007 National 12. Entries were normally between 30 and 50, but have not been above this level since the 57 at the 1994 National Show, indicating a long term decline.

Buff PR Bantams entered: 1971 Birmingham 55; 1978 National 101; 1984 National 44; 1987 National 155; 1988 National 61; 2003 National 84; 2004 National 30. Entries were normally between 50 and 70, the two above were the only times there were over 100.

Black PR Bantams: there were only more than 20 twice: 2002 National 21; 2004 Stafford 21. Although still a long way behind Barreds and Buffs, Blacks are increasing.

White PR Bantams entered: usually about ten, with a surge 1984–86, when 24 to 26 were seen at the National and Stafford, and 20 again at the 2003 National.

Blue PR Bantams entered: only given classes since 1998 fewer than ten except for 17 at 2002 National and 11 at 2004 Stafford. The AOC classes since 1998 (that is, excluding Blues) have had fewer than ten except for 11 at 2003 National and 15 at 2006 Stafford Shows.

PLYMOUTH ROCK DESCRIPTION

Full descriptions are given in all standards books. Novice breeders are urged to closely study and compare American and British Standards as they are different, and the birds actually bred are even more different than the descriptions. British birds are much taller and with smaller tails than those in America. German Standard type Plymouth Rocks are somewhere between these extremes, with the addition of Amrocks (effectively utility type Barred Rocks) recognized as a separate breed.

British Rock enthusiasts have already 'improved to extinction' their version of large Barred Rocks. The large Barreds currently seen here in the UK are imported, so are much smarter than the weird looking creatures (almost like single-combed Barred Malays!) shown between the wars. The enthusiasts' bantam Barreds are not attracting many new fanciers at present, and are rather small and of poor type. Few judges are brave enough to give top prizes to imported (Dutch or German) Barred Rock Bantams.

British type Buff Plymouth Rock Bantams are sometimes rather too large, especially males, but are not as controversial as the Barreds. They are standardized in a lighter shade than Buffs of other breeds, which can

Columbian Plymouth Rock, bantam female in US. Photo: John Tarren

be difficult to maintain without light under-colour or white peppering in wing feathers.

The other colours are probably all from imported strains, and all are of a 'medium' type, acceptable to everyone. Whites need a lot of expert management and show prepa-ration. Blacks and Blues can be difficult to breed with bright yellow shanks and feet com-bined with sound undercolour. Partridge and Silver Pencilled Rocks will need to be double mated as for Wyandottes for best results. Most new Plymouth Rock fanciers since 2000 seem to have chosen these varieties rather than Barreds or Buffs.

Partridge Plymouth Rock, bantam male in US. Photo: John Tarren

Blue-Gold Laced Poland. This variety, as far as the author is aware, has never been seen in the UK. Artist: C.S.Th. van Gink

Frizzled Silver Laced Polands. Artist: C.S.Th. van Gink

CHAPTER 27

Poland or Polish

All colour varieties of this breed, bearded and non-bearded, are classed as one breed in the UK, USA and other English speaking countries, but are divided into two breeds in Germany, the Netherlands and other European countries. The bearded form, in self colours and several colour versions of the laced pattern, are called Paduaners in Germany and Nederlandse Baardkuifhoenders in the Netherlands. The non-bearded form, in White-Crested Blacks and related patterns, non-bearded selfs, and the now remade Black-Crested White variety is called Hollandische Haubenhuhn (Germany) or Hollandse Kuifhoender (Netherlands).

Crested chickens, some looking good enough to show today, have been depicted in European paintings since the Middle Ages. They were described and illustrated by Aldrovandi in 1600, Bechstein in 1793 (*Naturgeschichte Deutschlands*) and Blumenbach in 1805 (*Handbuch der vergleichenden Anatomie*). Although crested chickens have been recorded in many parts of Europe and the Middle East, most of the refinement into present colours, patterns and forms happened in the Low Countries, justifying the implied claims in the Dutch names of both types. It remains to be confirmed by DNA analysis, but all European crested breeds, including Sultans, probably started from crosses between normal hens and Silkies brought to the Middle East from China by Arab traders. Eric Parker, the leading British exhibitor of Polish 1950–2000, mentioned (in Ian Kay's *Stairway to the Breeds*,

1997) that chicken skulls with the distinctive domed formation of birds with large crests were found by archaeologists at a Roman dig in Gloucestershire, so they seem to be a very ancient breed indeed.

Although some of these birds may have been bred in Poland, the English name for the breed is generally thought to be derived from 'polled' (the dome shaped skull of hornless cattle) or 'pollarded', the spherical foliage of trees which has started to grow after being cut back. Willows and hazel were cut back regularly like this for centuries to provide suitable shoots for basketmaking. They were a common sight for some of our ancestors, willow growing being a major rural industry on the Somerset Levels and in the east of England from the Fens inland to Bedfordshire.

One of the ten classes at the first general poultry show ever held, in the grounds of London Zoo, 1845, was for 'Gold or Silver Spangled, Black or White Polish'. There had no doubt been a few birds imported to the UK long before this event, but the first person to bring them to England in large numbers was John Baily, who lived at 113 Mount Street in the fashionable part of London near Grosvenor Square and Park Lane. He presumably had another business premises, unless this area was very, very different in those days.

His experiences were included in early editions of Lewis Wright's *Book of Poultry*.

> I was, I believe, the first importer of fowls on a large scale from Holland; all our early

importations were from that country. The Polands were for some years confined to the Black and Blue with white top-knots. After a time we also received some Golden and Silver-spangled; all the early importations were destitute of beard, and had small combs in front of the top-knots, and ample gills [wattles]. Then came one or two pens of bearded birds (I speak of nearly thirty years ago) [*circa* 1845?], and they were much admired. Poultry shows were in their infancy, and it was a case of Montague and Capulet, Guelph and Ghibelline,* which should have the supremacy. The unbearded made a good fight, but the hirsute increased in numbers and influence. The originals made stout resistance, and tried at least for separate classes, but they lost ground, and gave up the contest. Still the bearded had combs and gills, but the fiat went forth [official ruling, in standards] and these were voted disqualifications; they have remained so to this day. The first Poland fowls I imported were in 1835. I believe the first bearded birds were imported some years later by Mr Baker. The first great breeder of them in this country was Mr Graham Vivian, MP, of Swansea, and one of the best pens ever shown belonged to Mrs Brunel.

White-Crested Black Poland, large female. Photo: John Tarren

[*Literary and historical references, to suggest fanciers argued a lot over spangling *versus* lacing. Most Polish had half moon spangles/poor lacing, ranging from OEPF to Brabanter markings. Montague and Capulet were the heads of the two rival families in Shakespeare's *Romeo and Juliet*. Guelphs and Ghibellines were warring factions in twelfth- and thirteenth-century Italy.]

Polish were a very popular show breed for some twenty years following 1845, as can be seen by the numbers entered in the 1855 Birmingham Show. In those days shows were essentially very up-market sales, and almost all exhibits were pens of a male and three females. Exact figures have not been found, but there were between 102 and 120 such pens of Polish at this show, divided into adult and young stock classes for White-Crested Black, Golden, Silver and AOC, which included Buff Laced/ Chamois, Blues and Whites. This display of over 400 birds has seldom, if ever, been bettered in the 150 years since. Among other colour varieties back then were self bearded Blacks, Cuckoos and Black-Mottleds (or these might be early Houdans).

Mr B.P. Brent, of Bessel's Green, near Sevenoaks, Kent contributed to Wingfield and Johnson's *The Poultry Book*, 1853, about Polish, most significantly about the (then) extinct Black-Crested White variety. He recalled the last hen of this colour he saw, at a canal boat builder's yard at St Omer, France, in 1845. He also made a (vague) reference to a fanciers' club where bearded and crested birds were prized. Both parts of his account indicate there had been groups of keen breeders for a very long time indeed before 1853. Black-Crested Whites were remade in the 1990s, and two more sightings have been recorded, in 1856 (W.B. Tegetmeier) and 1911 (C.A. House).

The earliest known flock of Black-Crested White Polish was owned by Peter Jasperz at Kennemerland, the Netherlands, in 1475. Moving on a couple of centuries, a white hen with a half white, half black crest was depicted in a painting by Monckhurst in 1657. Further

Chamois Poland, large male. Photo: John Tarren

Blue Poland, large female. Photo: John Tarren

mentions have been found in 1793, 1796 and 1813. After the hen in the boatyard story, W.B. Tegetmeier (poultry book author and friend of Charles Darwin) tried to make a new strain *circa* 1855–60, and C.A. House saw one in 1911. New strains have been made by European and American (Clark Kidder) fanciers in the 1990s. Breeds believed to have been used to make them include White-Crested Black Polish, Silver Laced Polish, Lakenvelders, and Black Headed White Dutch Owlbeards (Moorkop Nederlandse Uilebaarden). No perfectly marked specimens have been bred yet, and may never exist. They either have a good black crest, but with black extending down the neck and traces of lacing and other black markings elsewhere. Clear white bodied birds never have a solid black crest.

A Polish Club was formed in the UK in 1891, but was inactive for extended periods until reformed in 1912. The secretary 1912–19 was Fred Martin (initially at the Red Hart, Three Holes, Wisbech, and later Rectory Lodge, Upwell, Lincolnshire), who also kept Nankin Bantams alive through to the 1950s. Three more secretaries ran the club for short periods, until Major G.T. Williams (*see* Chapter 16: Japanese/Chabo) took over in 1924, continuing until 1939. Polish need much more care than most breeds, limiting the number of people ever likely to breed and show them. The club had 85 members in 1948, probably somewhere near its maximum. The first Club Show entry figures found were for 1913 at Crystal Palace, where four classes for large Polish (*see* later in chapter for bantams), with entries of five White-Crested males, nine White-Crested females, seven AOC males and nine AOC females.

Most Polish Club members seem to have kept bantams, the highest Club Show entry of large fowl found between 1914 and 1939 being twenty-three at Olympia in 1923. Moving on, there were ten large at Olympia in 1966, and eleven at Alexandra Palace in 1975, with Eric Parker winning first, second and third prizes both times, and many other years in between. Eric, who eventually had to give up because of ill health, was a hairdresser for many years, and no doubt transferred some of his skills to show chicken preparation. He continued to be UK's 'Mr Poland' until about 1994. When Eric stopped showing Polish, his place was taken by Terry and Claire Beebe, who also bred and

Chamois Poland, bantam female. Photo: John Tarren

White Poland, bantam female. Photo: John Tarren

exhibited every variety of Polish, both sizes, all colours, plain and frizzle feathered. At the time of writing, Mr and Mrs Beebe were planning to move to America. The breed was lucky to have such enthusiastic supporters, but it is a worrying situation when a breed is so dependent on so few people.

Frizzle feathered Polands had been known in the Netherlands, but were always very rare, for well over a century, but have only been regularly bred and shown in the UK since the 1990s. The highest UK Club Show entry since then was at Stafford in 2002, where there were thirty-two normal feathered, and twenty-two frizzle feathered large Polish.

Cornelis van Gink did paintings of Frizzled Polish, probably about the same time as the last recorded specimen of the old strains was seen: a Frizzled White-Crested Blue at the 1912 Utrecht Show, and there was a Frizzled White-Crested Black at the 1913 Crystal Palace Show. Van Gink's pictures and old descriptions of them inspired Dutch fancier Arie J. Boland to make them again. He started with the bantam version, by crossing normal Polish Bantams with Frizzle feathered Japanese Bantams in 1978. He had made Frizzled Polish Bantams of correct type and shank/feet colour by 1983, and in the full range of Polish colour varieties, and was starting on the large version, by 1992. Japanese Bantam genes slowed progress in getting full sized large Frizzled Polish; almost all were short in back and rather small by the time Arie died in 2002, so he never saw his project reach perfection in all varieties.

POLISH BANTAM

William Flamank Entwisle, of Calder Grove House, near Wakefield, Yorkshire, made the first Polish Bantams, as well as the first Brahma Bantams and other miniatures. He started this project about 1875 by mating an undersized large Gold Laced Polish with Gold Sebright hens. His Gold Laced Polish Bantams won cups during the 1880s. Entwisle repeated the process with Silver Laced Polish and Silver Sebrights, but these were less successful. Self Whites, Blacks and Blues, and White-Crested Blacks, Blues and Cuckoos followed,

Gold Laced Poland, bantam male. Photo: John Tarren

Gold Laced Poland, bantam female. Photo: John Tarren

using Rosecomb and Scots Grey Bantams. An outstanding White hen won many prizes: one reason why Whites were the most popular colour variety for many years.

The specialized care needed meant they were never really popular, but entries of twenty or so Polish Bantams were regularly seen at larger shows in the UK from 1890 until the revived club started to promote them at the 1913 Crystal Palace Show, where forty-five appeared (23 White, 22 AOC). AOC were an interesting assortment, not only standard White-Crested Blacks, self Blacks, Chamois (Buff Laced), Gold Laced and Silver Laced, but also unconvential Creams, self Buffs and Lavender Laced (laced pattern in colours of Porcelaine Barbu d'Uccle, perhaps).

During the twenty years between the wars, 1919 to 1939, club shows were held at a variety of places, including Birmingham, Bradford, Crystal Palace, Tavistock and York, to give all of their scattered members a fair share of travelling costs and inconvenience. Entry numbers have not been found for many of them, but one of the best known displays was in 1929 at York, where there were 31 large and 48 bantams. Polish have frequently won Large and Bantam mixed AOV classes, and are not very expensive to keep, so were useful for regular exhibitors.

Shows were suspended during the Second World War, not resuming until 1948 because of a fowl pest outbreak. In the sixty years since then, bantam entries at the annual Polish Club Show have fluctuated from a poor 20 birds in 1984 up to vintage years, such as 1987, when there were 95 at the National and 102 at Stafford. Whites have dropped from being the most popular variety of bantams to being a rarity; White-Crested Blacks and WC Blues have held steady; and the three laced varieties, especially Buff Laced/Chamois, have become most popular with the new generation of Polish breeders. Frizzled Polish Bantams have provided an extra range of varieties but their perceived difficulty has limited the number of people showing them.

POLISH DESCRIPTION

Full descriptions are given in the standards books published in all countries. Novice breeders should study the standard in their country, and then compare it with the birds actually winning at the shows. This breed is

White-Crested Black Poland, bantam male. Photo: John Tarren

White-Crested Cuckoo Poland, bantam male. Photo: John Tarren

much the same all over the world, with minor differences in the size of the bantams and the shape of the crests, particularly on males' crests. All except White-Crested Cuckoos and Bearded Cuckoos (very rare) have slate-blue shanks and feet, these two having white shanks/feet because the cuckoo/barring gene almost completely prevents dark pigmentation in scales.

The White-Crested varieties have coloured (black, blue or cuckoo, as applicable) feathers at the front of their crest, which is a standard requirement, but sometimes coloured feathers also grow in what should be the white part of

Frizzled Chamois Poland, bantam male. Photo: John Tarren

Frizzled White-Crested Blue Poland, bantam trio. Photo: John Tarren

the crest. If (gently) pulled out, the replacement feather will often be white or partly white. In the latter case, pull that out as well – third time lucky?

Gold Laced often have some white feathers in their crest – a fault which will only get worse if feathers are pulled out. Buff Laced/Chamois, on average, have rather better lacing than Golds or Silvers. Lacing has been required by breed standards (as opposed to spangling) for well over a century, so it is surprising that the lacing has not been improved as it has been on Sebrights and Wyandottes. The lack of progress has no doubt been because the breed's survival has relied on one or two leading fanciers at a time who kept all varieties. There is an obvious opportunity for considerable progress by specialists in one or two colours.

SPECIAL MANAGEMENT REQUIREMENTS

The crests of Polands need a lot of care, so novice breeders should only go to experts when buying their first birds, and arrange follow-up visits to learn all the techniques required. Birds ready for showing have reduced visibility, so their crests need attention during the breeding season. Some breeders trim crests back, others keep crests clear of their eyes with sticky tape or rubber bands. Crests are also susceptible to mite infestation, so all birds must be regularly handled, closely inspected and (if necessary) treated. Crests and beards can be soaked and ruined if (show ready) Polish are allowed to use normal open water bowls. Experts have ways of avoiding this problem, such as large size budgie drinkers for any individually housed birds such as reserve cockerels. Polish appreciate 'lawn time' as much as any other chickens, but should definitely not be out in all weather conditions. They are not suitable for beginners or for those with strong views on the benefits of natural, free range poultry keeping.

Rhode Island Reds. Note their bright red plumage colour, typical of early Rhodes. Originally a free gift with Poultry *magazine, 2 February 1912. Artist: J.W. Ludlow*

Rose-comb Rhode Island Reds. Originally a free gift with Feathered World *magazine, 7 July 1911, when the birds were depicted in the same bright colour as the* Poultry *print. These prints could be bought from the* Feathered World *office for many years after originally issued, this being a later printing, when they changed the colour to suit changed show fashions. Artist: A.F. Lydon*

CHAPTER 28

Rhode Island Red and Rhode Island White

Rhode Island Reds were not established as a proper breed until the 1890s, although they were gradually formed over the previous fifty years in Rhode Island, Massachusetts, possibly also parts of Connecticut, New York and New Jersey. Ports in these states were the bases of whaling ships which went as far as the Indian Ocean and south-west Pacific in search of their quarry. In addition to whale meat, they also brought back large Asiatic chickens, which were sold to local farmers to cross with farmyard hens. In the 1830s and early 1840s they were more or less Malay type, from 1845 to about 1860 replaced by Buff or Partridge Cochins/Shanghais. Farmers were encouraged to breed from Shanghai cocks by William ('Billy') Tripp and John Macomber, poultry dealers based at Little Compton, Rhode Island. They bought eggs and poultry from farmers to supply the market at New Bedford, and bought Asiatic chickens from ships to enable their farmers to produce better table birds. At this stage they were still variable crossbreds, although yellow shanks, feet and skin were already the preferred colour of plucked table chickens in America. Buff or red plumage colour would have given clean looking plucked table birds, yet were coloured chickens. White birds were considered delicate, and were more likely to be taken by predators on free range. John Macomber died a few years later, and Billy Tripp did not do any breeding until about 1880, when he tried crossing a

rose-combed Brown Leghorn cock with some 'old fashioned Buff Malay hens'.

John Tompkins, also from Little Compton, Rhode Island, started to produce similar birds about 1870, and went on to become a leading breeder and exhibitor when Rhode Island Reds became a recognized breed. He was followed by his son, Lester Tompkins, who moved to Concord, Massachusetts, and was still involved with Rhodes in the 1980s.

Birds were first shown as 'Rhode Island Reds' at Fall River Show, Massachusetts in 1879 and/or 1880, but their ancestors had been exhibited long before, under a variety of names, such as 'Golden Buffs'. The 'Bristol County Fowls' entered in the first American Poultry Show, at Boston in 1949, were also part of this type. After Plymouth Rocks and Wyandottes were standardized, any suitable Buff coloured birds were exhibited under these names, according to comb. Dr N.B. Aldrich, who lived at Fall River, so may have been the exhibitor there earlier, took Rhode Island Reds to the February 1892 Madison Square Garden Show, New York, but they did not attract much national interest. Richard V. Browning, of Natick, Rhode Island, entered some at the 1895 Rhode Island State Fair, held at Narragansett Park, Providence. He and Dr Aldrich combined to promote the breed through poultry magazines, which led to the Rhode Island Red Club of America being formed in 1898. A breed standard was adopted by the club at a meeting in 1903, leading to acceptance by the APA for single-combed Rhodes in 1904 and rose-combed Rhodes in 1905. There had also been a lot of pea-combed birds in the area, but they were not recognized by the club. A meatier, pea-combed bird of the same colour was promoted by Mrs Metcalf, of Warren, Ohio, which was recognized in 1905 as a separate breed, the Buckeye.

The first standard did not really describe exhibition Rhodes at they have been exhibited since the 1930s, but then the breed's pioneers did not know how they would develop. For example, female plumage colour was described as 'a rich, even shade of reddish buff, darker than the so-called "golden-buff". The female is not so brilliant in lustre as the male'.

By 1913 two more specialist clubs had been formed, one each for the single- and rose-combed versions, plus there was also the colourfully named 'National Red Feather Club', whose role has not been found by the author. There were also Rhode Island Red clubs in Canada, France and the UK by then. As an indication of their rapidly growing popularity at home, the Chicago Show, held in December 1912, with a total of 2,848 entries had 144 single birds and 18 trios of single-combed Rhodes and 133 single birds and 20 trios of rose-combed Rhodes. Lester Tompkins judged at Pittsburgh Show and won many prizes at Boston Show. This was an impressive first decade, and Rhode Island Reds went on to much greater popularity. A monument to the breed was erected in 1925 at Adamsville, Little Compton, which is still at the junction of Main Street, Adamsville Road and Westport Harbour Road. All the states of America have a symbolic state bird, and the Rhode Island Red chicken was adopted for this honour in 1954.

RHODE ISLAND WHITE

J. Alonzo Jocey, of Peacedale, RI (later of Towanda, Pennsylvania) started to make a strain of white table chickens in 1888, but did not use the name 'Rhode Island White' until after 1900.

He began by crossing a rose-combed White Leghorn cock with crossbred hens (¾ Buff Cochin, ¼ White Wyandotte). Mr Jocey started to advertise his Rhode Island Whites in 1904, eventually creating enough interest for a Rhode Island White Club to be formed in 1910 or 1911. At the December 1912 Chicago Show there were forty single birds and five trios entered.

Unfortunately for Mr Jocey, there were a lot of poor type White Wyandottes (some with single combs) and White Plymouth Rocks around then, some of which were then sold as 'Rhode Island Whites'. This caused the APA to delay standardizing Rhode Island Whites until their conference at Knoxville, Tennessee in 1922, and then they only recognized rose-combed Rhode Island Whites because there was enough difference between the type (especially visible back length and tail carriage) of Wyandottes and Rhodes to allow rose-combed Rhode Island Whites, but not enough difference between Rhodes and Rocks to risk single-combed Rhode Island Whites. Rhode Island Whites were never as popular as Rhode Island Reds. It was estimated that there were about 3,000 Rhode Island Whites in the USA in 2003.

RHODE ISLAND REDS IN THE UK

In 1903 Sidney Risden (possibly Risdon) brought three dozen Rhode Island Red eggs with him when he returned to his native Somerset after living in America for some years. He returned to America the following year, 1904, and left the twenty-five birds he had hatched and reared from the eggs with his brother Edward. Rhode Island Reds had been getting a lot of publicity in British poultry magazines at the time (they were standardized in the USA in 1904), so Edward entered fifteen of them in the 1905 Bridgwater Show. There were no doubt other importations, but these were the first, and the first time Rhode Island Reds were entered in a British poultry show.

The British Rhode Island Red Club (aka The Rhode Island Red Club of The British Empire) was formed in 1909 by Roger Smith, Rev. F.S. Banner, E. Banner and George Scott, the last-named being secretary until 1931. The club had 58 members in January 1910, 116 by December 1910, 240 by 1914, about 300 in 1920, and over 400 in 1935.

Rhode Island Reds were lighter and brighter in colour at this stage than they would become, when the very deep glossy chocolate shade became the exhibition norm. The club's first standard gives male plumage of 'bright cherry red, with back and wing-bows of darker red, the tail black or greenish-black', and 'the hen is of a lighter golden-red surface colour than the cock'. Early Rhodes did not have the long flat back, accentuated by almost horizontal tail carriage, but by 1920 the long rows of them seen at the shows were similar to present day birds, if not quite as dark.

There was a short-lived (1928–31) rival, the National Rhode Island Red Club. It was started by C.H. Horn and E.F. Benjamin, who accused the original club of covering up faking at the shows. This was refuted by George Scott and others, who pointed out that Mr Horn had been Vice-President and a club judge of the main club, and he had never disqualified anyone for faking or raised the matter at any of the many previous meetings he had attended, so had plenty of opportunities to reveal the widespread faking he now alleged. Peace was restored at a meeting in October 1931 at the London Dairy Show, and the clubs formally merged on 1 January 1932.

Here is a summary of major show entries, which indicate how rapidly Rhode Island Reds became one of the most important breeds in the UK, a dominance which extended from the show scene to practical producers. (sc = single-combed, rc = rose-combed.)

1909 (first) Club Show at York, 4 classes/75 birds

1910 Club Show at Sheffield, 4 classes/111 birds (sc males 41, sc females 36, rc males 18, rc females 15)

1911 Club Show at Brighton, 12 classes/153 birds (sc Cock 12, sc Hen 7, sc Cockerel

Rhode Island Red, large male. Photo: John Tarren

Rhode Island Red, large rose-combed. Photo: John Tarren

11, sc Pullet 25, rc Cock 4, rc Hen 3, rc Cockerel 22, rc Pullet 29, Novice Male 21, Novice Female 12, New Members Male 10, New Members Female 8)

1912 Club Show at Wolverhampton, 12 classes/227 birds

There was a controversy over chocolate coloured birds which won at the 1912 Dairy Show, which was debated at the AGM at Wolverharnpton. The meeting decided they wanted 'rich red' but not 'chocolate'.

1913 Club Show at York, 13 classes, 200 in single bird classes, plus 1 class of 5 trios

1914 Club Show at Leeds, 4 classes/200 birds (sc males 84, sc females 53, rc males 43, rc females 20)

1919 Club Show at York, 15 classes/392 entries, plus 31 selling

1920 Club Show at Croydon, 17 classes/494 entries

1920 London Dairy Show (only classes for young birds in all breeds) sc Cockerel 92, sc Pullet 119. These were two of the biggest classes in the show. Mr Cass won 1st and 3rd pullets with birds imported from America.

1921 London Dairy Show, sc Cockerel 199, sc Pullet 132.

The Great Depression caused a general reduction in show entries. Show entry numbers after 1950 are given later in this chapter, after Rhode Island Red Bantams.

RHODE ISLAND WHITES IN THE UK

There was a class of twelve Rhode Island Whites at the 1913 Crystal Palace Show, the first prize going to Mrs Lycett-Green of Darrington Hall, Pontefract, Yorkshire, who may have been the importer. Interest in the UK was always limited, but there were enough breeders to form a Rhode Island White Club late 1921/early 1922, initially with George Scott as secretary. This club collapsed and was replaced 1925/26, the new club only lasting until 1929. There may have been some commercial flocks, but no later show records have been found of Rhode Island Whites in the UK.

RHODE ISLAND RED BANTAM

Although the Rhode Island Red is an American breed, it is believed the bantam version was first made in the UK. The earliest mention of them found by the author when researching this chapter was in the 'other breeds' part of the Bantam section of the 1917 *Feathered World Yearbook*. Bradford Show, which specialized in bantams, was the first to provide a class for Rhode Island Red Bantams in 1920, increased to two classes in 1921. The International Show at Olympia also provided two classes from 1922, entries unknown, but followed by 16 cocks and 19 hens in 1923. The leading Rhode Island Red Bantam breeders in these first few years were Messrs E. Shelton & son, Mr Dixon, Mr J. Blades, Mrs Petrie and Miss M.H. Clay. No detailed 'how I made them' accounts have been found, but one can assume undersized large Rhodes were crossed with whatever suitable pure breed or cross-bred bantams were available.

The Rhode Island Red Bantam Club was formed in 1923, with Mr J. Voyce as secretary until George Scott took over this club as well in 1927, although the Bantam Club retained its separate identity. Numbers, size and quality gradually improved, in females more than males. It is still often the case that Rhode Island Red Bantam females are sweet little things, whereas their mates are frequently too large and untidy.

Some of the more successful RIR Bantam Club Shows before the Second World War were:

1925 at Bradford, 3 classes/56 entries
1926 at Birmingham, 4 classes/cocks + hens 14, cockerels + pullets 53
1933 at York, 5 classes/69 entries.

No details have been found to determine whether American fanciers imported Rhode Island Red Bantams from the UK or made their own strains; they probably did both. A few Rhode Island Red Bantams were imported to the UK from the USA about 2000, which gave fanciers here a rare opportunity to compare them in detail. They were similar in colour, but had significant differences in size, type and plumage quality. The American birds were smaller and did not have the poor plumage quality which sometimes prevents Rhodes from winning Show Champion awards in the UK, but they had higher tail carriage, which combined with their small size meant they did not seem to have a long flat back, an essential Rhode characteristic. The imported birds were crossed with British strains, producing excellent Rhode Island Red Bantams with the best features of both types.

The British Rhode Island Red Club amalgamated with the Rhode Island Red Bantam Club in 1984. It was said at the time that this was because the former had all the money, and the latter had all the members.

SUMMARY OF UK RHODE ISLAND RED SHOW ENTRIES POST-1950

National Show, 1954, Large: Cock 22, Hen 16, Cockerel 22, P 28, NovM 10, NovF 15, Trio 5. Bantam: Cock 15, Hen 8, Cockerel 25, P 34, NovM 11, NovF 17, Trio 9.

National Shows, 1973–79: Large fowl ranged from 11 to 30 entries, Bantams 23 to 59

National and Stafford Shows, 1980–86: Large 6 to 29, Bantams 17 to 51

National and Stafford Shows, 1987–90: Large 33 to 53, Bantams 43 to 55.

Rose-combed Rhodes, large and bantam, were given separate classes from 1991 onwards. Entries of them have been fairly consistent from then until the last figures available at time of writing, 2007. The highest entries, both at the 1998 National, were 19 large and 34 bantams.

Entries of large single-combed Rhodes between 1991 and 2007 have ranged from 19 (2001 Stafford) to 59 (1997 National), with their bantam equivalents ranging from 21 (1999 Stafford) to 88 (1997 National).

RHODE ISLAND DESCRIPTION

Full standards are given in American, British, Dutch, German and other Standards books. New fanciers should study birds at the shows to see how the standard descriptions are interpreted. Plumage colour, including undercolour and black wing markings are considered very important, so should be discussed with specialist breeders. Rose combs on Rhodes are compact and close to the skull. Poor feather quality, tatty tails and a tendency to slight frizzling are common problems in the UK. Eye colour should be red, and light eyes are another common fault which must be monitored.

Rhode Island Red, bantam male in UK. Photo: John Tarren

Black Rosecombs. Originally a free gift with Poultry *magazine, circa 1912. Artist: J.W. Ludlow*

Black Rosecombs. Originally a free gift with Geflügel-Börse *magazine, July 1942. Artist: W. Jennrich*

CHAPTER 29

Rosecomb (UK, USA)/Bantam (Germany)/Java (Netherlands)

Bantam is the name of a town and district in Java (part of Indonesia), the place where the first miniature chickens brought to Europe in the fifteenth century are supposed to have come from. They were a varied lot, of assorted colours, with single or rose combs, feathered or 'clean' feet. The Europeans who started to keep them began the long process which eventually led to the range of standardized breeds established when poultry showing started in the nineteenth century. Understandably, some of the first forms to be stabilized were miniature versions of the (then few) large breeds already established. Black and White bantams became the Rosecombs we know now, following the type of Hamburghs then known as 'Black Pheasants'. Until show standards fixed the names 'Rosecomb', 'Bantam' and 'Java' (as applicable in each country), they were often called 'Black Africans'. This name may have originated because Arab traders based on the east African coast brought them from southeast Asia to Europe.

The first Black Rosecombs recorded in England was the flock owned by John Buckton, owner of the Angel Inn at Grantham, Lincolnshire, in 1483, when King Richard s stayed there and took a liking to them. It was said that the flock had been at the inn since John Buckton's father's time, which might mean they were there well before 1450. Although the description given fits present-day Black Rosecomb Bantams, it is highly unlikely they were as small and perfectly formed as now. It is not known when the first White Rosecombs arrived in England.

Not much progress had been made since 1483, as noted in a report of them at the Birmingham Poultry Show held in December 1854, where, 'too many of the black ones lacked the white earlobes, which adds so greatly to their appearance'. However, 'The white bantams were neat and meritorious'. A leading breeder of Whites at this time was Rev. Granville F. Hodson from Somerset. He exhibited a much admired pen of them at Plymouth in 1853 (when he lived at Chew Magna), and at Birmingham in 1854 and 1855 (when he had moved to North Petherton). In those days shows consisted almost entirely of pens (trios or quartets) of birds, not single bird entries as now. Full details of the Rosecomb Bantams at these two Birmingham Shows have not been found, but there were about thirty trios at both events, with Blacks and Whites in about equal numbers (believed slightly more Whites).

Enoch Hutton, of Pudsey, Yorkshire, did a lot to improve the quality of Blacks, circa 1850–80. He crossed Blacks with Whites, followed by many years of selective breeding to fix the best qualites of both (he bred Whites as well, although he concentrated on Blacks), and made crosses with undersized Black Hamburgh males, which helped improve type, lobes and flow of feather (especially regarding tails), again followed by selective breeding to restore bantam size.

W.F. Entwisle (in *Bantams*, 1894) said that 'to his [Hutton's] yards can be traced the origin of nearly, if not quite, all the good Blacks now bred'. He said that Hutton had crossed Whites with Blacks because when he started Whites had good white lobes, whereas Blacks then had more or less red lobes. However, these crosses created new problems. Blacks should have black shanks/feet, Whites should have white shanks/feet, but after the crossing, both had slate-blue shanks/feet. The cross also spoiled the plumage colour of Blacks, especially cockerels, which started to have white feather tips here and there (especially wing tips) and gold in the hackles. The Black Hamburgh crosses eventually solved these problems.

G.H. Pickering, also from Yorkshire, also tried crossing with undersized Black Hamburghs, but in his case, only with White Rosecombs. Very few White Hamburghs have ever been bred in the UK, so presumably Mr Pickering couldn't find any Whites. Although

White Rosecombs were generally better than Blacks at this time, there was still plenty of scope for improvement.

The Rosecomb Club was not formed until 1908, although they had been promoted to an extent by the Variety Bantam Club. Rosecombs had declined somewhat, relative to other breeds, since their strong start in the showing scene in the 1850s. Nevertheless, there were usually some at most shows, and a fair display, if not outstanding, at major events such as the Crystal Palace in November 1901, where there were four classes of Blacks with a total of 47 entries, and four classes of Whites, total 36.

At its first few annual shows, 1909–1913, at Crystal Palace, there were between 114 and 172 entries in total. There were still roughly similar numbers of Blacks and Whites, but this had changed by the time the shows got going again after the war. The club had one more really good show, at Bingley, Yorkshire, in 1919, where 130 birds were entered, but from 1920 to 1939 they seldom had more than 70 entered, with no show at all some years.

Black Rosecomb, male. Photo: John Tarren

They lost a lot of money at some shows because the generous prize money given then had to be 'guaranteed' (paid by the club if there were not enough entry fees to cover the prizes) to the show organizers. Whites continued to decline more rapidly than Blacks, although they often won AOV classes at local shows. A really good Black would always look better than an equally good White because of the contrast of white lobes and black plumage.

Herbert Whitley of Primley Hill, Paignton, Devon, started showing a Blue Rosecomb cock in 1931, the only one until 1933, when a Mr Havard, from Gorseinon started showing some from a strain he made himself. Mr Whitley is mentioned in several other chapters of this book with blue varieties of as many breeds as he could find or make. Blues were eventually recognized by our Rosecomb Club, but the author has not discovered when it is believed both fanciers started with a Black Rosecomb × Blue Andalusian Bantam mating, as did an American fancier, Dr G. Irwin Royce, of California. He started about 1918–20, first showing his Blue Rosecombs at Los Angeles in 1927. Another fancier, name not found, was reported as starting the same time in Pennsylvania, in this case with Black Rosecombs, Blue OEG, and Blue Barbu d'Anvers Bantams. This strain was first exhibited at Madison Square Gardens Show, New York, in 1928. They were soon taken up by several fanciers in the eastern states.

No other colours were recognized by the British Rosecomb Club until very recently, although its members were aware that Mr Ostermann and other Dutch fanciers had Cuckoo and Black-Red/Partridge Rosecombs back in 1930. An Australian fancier, Arthur Brien, of Canterbury, NSW, also made a strain of Cuckoo Rosecombs, *circa* 1955–65, using Black Rosecombs and a Cuckoo OEG Bantam cockerel which was rather feathery and had partly white lobes.

Black Rosecomb, female. Photo: John Tarren

The British Rosecomb Club suspended activity during the Second World War, and was not reformed until 1959. Its first post-war Rosecomb Club Show at Northallerton in 1961 had about sixty birds entered. The 1993 Stafford Show, the last before the 'other colours' started to appear here, had a total of 93, including 13 Whites and 10 Blues. The highest entry since then was at 2001 Stafford

White Rosecomb, male. Photo: John Tarren

Blue Rosecomb, male. Photo: John Tarren

the tradition that these by-products of breeding Blues should be kept at home. Blacks remain the most popular colour, although not many newcomers to our hobby are taking them up, for two reasons: firstly, not many new fanciers are taking up Blacks of any breed, and secondly, they have a short show career, so fresh birds have constantly to be bred.

Rosecombs in the UK, especially Blacks, have much bigger ear lobes than Rosecombs in any other country, larger than British Standards require, but fashion has ruled over published standards. Only a very brave judge would go against this trend, and this is using the word 'brave' as applied in the world of politics, meaning foolhardy. Large lobes have made the short show career problem worse, especially on males. Facial skin, especially eyelids, soon turn white, and ear lobes droop out of shape and/or are blemished by horrible brown scabs. British type Rosecombs are considered out of proportion by Dutch and German fanciers, as can be seen by comparing them with the smaller lobed new colours, imported from these countries.

Show, with a total of 118, including 9 Whites, 12 Blues, 8 Columbian, 1 Black-Red, 1 Birchen and 9 in a non-standard class. Other colours which have been seen here include Black-Mottles, Buff Columbians, Furnaces and Millefleurs. Some Splashes have been shown, presumably by novices who are not aware of

Millefleur Rosecomb, female.
Photo: John Tarren

ROSECOMB BANTAM DESCRIPTION

New breeders should not only study the published breed standard in whichever country they live, but also photos of past winners in all countries and live birds at major shows. They should speak to experienced fanciers to fully appreciate every aspect of them. Rosecombs have won many Show Champion awards, but they have to be very good to do so. The Scale of Points for Rosecombs in *British Poultry Standards* gives thirty-five out of a hundred points for the head, and lobes must be 'spotlessly white' and ideal comb shape is clearly defined.

Their body should be small but 'cobby', not narrow and weedy. Their tail should be large and well spread, but not held too high. Viewed in profile there should be a smooth 'sweeping curve' down the neck, along the back, and up the tail. A sharp angle between back and tail, inevitable with high tail carriage, is a fault. Tail feathers should be very broad for the size of the birds, with rounded ends, quite unlike the painted tail feathers seen on Dutch Bantam males. Legs should be fairly short. Some long-legged males have won at shows in the UK, presumably by judges who were following the big lobe fashion and ignoring everything else.

DOUBLE MATING AND OTHER SPECIAL REQUIREMENTS

Rosecombs may look simple, with no complicated plumage patterns, feathered feet, beards or crests to worry about, but are in fact very difficult to breed to a high standard and keep in show-winning condition. All the birds in the large classes of Blacks seen at major shows probably look identical to outsiders, but close inspection reveal the differences between winners and 'also rans'. Fanciers need to hatch plenty each year to be sure of some in with a chance of winning, and young cockerels can ruin each other by a few pecks, never mind an all-out fight, so a lot of separate coops will be needed. They are clearly for specialists. Dutch Bantams (similar size, also with white lobes) are the only other breed which can reared with them by the many fanciers who are not so single-minded. Rosecombs and Dutch are two of the smallest breeds, but houses and pens for individually penned males must be big enough, with centrally placed perches, to avoid their long tail feathers being damaged. It is still possible to keep a flock of prize-winners in a normal garden.

Double mating has been used for Blacks to enable fanciers to achieve good lobes and glossy green-black plumage on both sexes. Winning females produce males with white in the face and red or yellow in the hackles (the type used as 'pullet-breeders'), whereas the daughters of winning males would have rather dull, matt-black plumage and small lobes (the type used as 'cock-breeders'). Dud birds are not necessarily 'cock-breeders' or 'pullet-breeders', they might just be duds. Rosecombs are best bought directly from established experts, who will be only too happy to advise anyone taking a serious interest in their favourite breed. Having said that, good trios of Black Rosecombs can be bought quite cheaply at poultry auctions because black chickens are not very fashionable with newcomers to our hobby. Anyone buying at auction needs to have done some research, especially regarding faulty comb shapes to be avoided, or they may find their purchase was not a bargain after all – however cheap they were!

Gold Sebrights. Originally a free gift with Poultry *magazine, circa 1912. Artist: J.W. Ludlow*

Silver Sebrights, 1899. Artist: J.W. Ludlow

CHAPTER 30

Sebright Bantam

These were made by Sir John Sebright, 7th Baronet of Besford. Before the development of his bantams is described, it is worth saying more about the man who made them. Besford in Worcestershire was the home of his ancestor, Sir Edward Sebright (born 1585, made Baronet 1626, died 1658), but the family had long since moved to its Beechwood Park estate at Markyate, near the Bedfordshire/ Hertfordshire county boundary. Sir John was born on 23 May 1767, inherited the Baronetcy 23 February 1797, and died 15 April 1846 at Turnham Green, which is now well inside London, but must have been fairly rural then, as he kept most of his bantams at this second home. He was (at times) Deputy Lieutenant of Hertfordshire, Sheriff of Hertfordshire and (Whig) Member of Parliament 1807–35. He was an MP in the House of Commons as a Baronetcy, an inherited knighthood, does not qualify as being a Lord. The Beechwood Park estate is now a private school, no longer owned by the Sebright family.

Some poultry authors disputed Sir John's claim to have made his laced bantams, probably on religious grounds, claiming that he had imported them (ready made) from India or somewhere else in Asia. They were still arguing in 1854, when the *Poultry Chronicle* settled the issue by publishing a statement by Mr Hobbs, who had worked for Sir John since about 1800. In those days many people believed domestic livestock breeds were as made by God as well as wild species, this being before Darwin's *Origin of Species* was published.

Mr Hobbs said, 'Sir John bought a very small buff bantam hen [Nankin?] at Norwich, and a reddish cockerel of the "henny" game type; at Watford he got a small hen resembling a Golden Hamburgh. By selecting, for five or six years, he gained the laced feather he sought, and fixed the type and pattern by in-and-in breeding for almost twenty years. Starting with a white cockerel he made the Silvers.'

Many, probably most, Spangled Hamburghs had crescent spangles, halfway to lacing then. The white cockerel was a White Rosecomb he bought from London Zoo, which he mated to 'prototype' Gold Sebrights some years after he started. Some accounts say Laced Polish were used in the development of Sebrights, which may have been the case for other fanciers, but Mr Hobbs denied Sir John ever used Polish. Black Rosecombs, as well as the White cockerel from London Zoo, were probably also used to help reduce size, and some early enthusiasts fanciers wanted white lobes on Sebrights, but this was abandoned as they realized they had more than enough problems trying to achieve the desired type, size and markings.

By about 1812 other gentleman fanciers were taking an interest, and Sir John had made enough progress, to form the Sebright Bantam Club (possibly called the Feather Club). It was a private club, with membership by invitation only. An annual show was held, initially somewhere in Brick Lane (presumably Brick Lane was much smarter then than it is now!), later at Gray's Inn Coffee House, Holborn, on the first Tuesday in February. Only birds under a year old were entered for competition, and most of the very high subscription fees, two guineas for each of the two colour varieties, was given as prizes. It has been claimed that this was the first specialist exhibition poultry breed club, but it might not have been. About the same time, possibly earlier, there were local clubs for the forerunners of Hamburghs in Lancashire and Yorkshire and for Spanish in Bristol and London. However these were for ordinary working men, probably ignored by Sir John and his friends, and few details of these clubs have been found.

According to W.F. Entwisle (*Bantams*, 1894) these private shows were still going in the 1880s, but a letter in the *Cottage Gardener* (4 December 1855) said they ended when Sir John died. The earliest mention found of the present Sebright Club was in the 1910 *Feathered World Yearbook*, when it was run

like all the other breed clubs. Sebrights were certainly entered in most 'normal' poultry shows from 1845 to 1909, but no mention of any of them hosting the 'Sebright Club Show' has been found. It is not known if Sir John's club changed into the later Sebright Club (and if so, when) or if the two clubs were unconnected. Sir John's son, Sir Thomas (1802–64), also bred Sebright Bantams, but may not have been as keen as his father. The 1855 Birmingham Show had between forty and fifty (exact number unknown) trios of Sebrights entered, this still being the era of all show entries being trios.

Specialist poultry artists have depicted perfectly laced Sebrights since their beginning, but it is most unlikely they really were that good in Sir John's day. Photography was in common use by 1860, but there are very few photos in poultry books before 1900. Poultry artist J.W. Ludlow wrote his reminiscences,

'Silver Sebright Bantams of Seventy Years Ago' (i.e. circa 1850), originally in Illustrated London News, reproduced in Poultry World 1920 Annual. *Artist: unknown*

Sixty Years of the Poultry Fancy in 1909, published in the 1917 *Feathered World Yearbook*, shortly after his death on Easter Sunday, 1916. He covered most breeds in a very useful 'before and after' way:

Sebrights, that is, the silver-laced, were upon the stage and going when I as a boy came on the scene over sixty years ago [*circa* 1848]. I remember them well as neat little patterns, and they then seemed to me to be smaller than they are now. This may not have been so as to the majority, but certainly many were so – smaller, neater, and less bulky – but the whole lot were of a creamy, or pale canary tint, instead of the absolutely pure white ground as seen today. The yellow was a characteristic which was apparent for very many years, and looked like being impossible of removal, but time and unity of purpose has seen its removal. Mind you, the canary tinge was very pretty and picturesque, but snowy whiteness was the decree, so they are thus purified up to the present gems of today.

Again, the original Sebrights had chiefly ruddy faces, combs, and wattles instead of the dark, gipsy, purply tint of the present generation. Again, the eyes were a little more colour then than now. The gipsy face and black eye is a fine feature, and appropriate as a pleasing contrast to the pure silvery lacing of today, and, further, in the old sort, the tails were occasionally very much speckled, and the wing coverts in the main rather sooty, smeary, and, further still, the cocks' tails were often a bit curved and spangly.

Wingfield and Johnson confirmed this (*The Poultry Book*, 1853), saying that tail feathers were often poorly marked, more spangled than laced. As late as 1900 the two central ('top') tail feathers of many males were curved, and often removed for showing. Judges passed them if they noticed.

The 'middle colour variety', Cream or Citron Sebrights were not recognized by the Sebright Club, although these pretty birds have persisted and have been recognized in some other

countries. Buff Laced or Chamois Sebrights have also been seen, but not recognized, here at times over the years, and are also established in other countries. A strain of Buff Laced was made in the UK by Sam Cadman (date he made them unknown, but he died before 1927) from Gold Sebright × Chamois Polish Bantam matings. J.F. Entwisle sold his flock (possibly on behalf of his family) to Miss Irene Osgood (a novelist), who sold them on to Mr T.G. Hough, the last known exhibitor before recently remade strains.

Sebright Club Shows from 1909 to 1913, part of Crystal Palace Show, had between 99 and 150 entries. A rival Sebright Society was formed in 1921 as a result of some arguments within the Sebright Club. No definite information on these arguments has been found, but the two most likely issues were subscriptions (the new Society only charged five shillings, plus an initial two-and-sixpence joining fee, compared to ten shillings and sixpence every year for the Sebright Club) and the loss of type which had occured in Sebrights, the result of everyone concentrating only on lacing. The secretary of the Society was Mr C.I. Young, of 8 Palmer Street, Frome, Somerset. The Sebright Society president was Sir Guy Sebright, 12th Bt. (born 1856, inherited title 1917, died 1933). The Club and Society settled their differences at the 1931 Crystal Palace Show, Sir Guy and Mr Young becoming president and secretary of the unified Sebright Club, with subscriptions cut to five shillings.

For a few years there had been the interesting spectacle of rival annual Sebright Shows:

1923: Club, Olympia 91 entries; Society, Crystal Palace 155.
1924: Club, Olympia 58; Society, Crystal Palace 158.
1925: Club, Crystal Palace 102; Society, Birmingham 105.
1930: Club, Crystal Palace approx. 65–70; Society, Oxford approx. 100.

The unified Club continued to hold its annual shows in London, Crystal Palace, then Olympia,

Gold Sebright, male. Photo: John Tarren

until all shows were suspended during the Second World War. Entries were between 70 and 100, with more Silvers than Golds (approx 60:40). There was a fowl pest epidemic in 1947, and the 1950s and 1960s were the low point of our hobby generally, so there was a long period of very poor Sebright Shows, with often fewer than forty birds in the years from 1946 to 1976. They did not exceed 100 entries again until 1985 Stafford Show, where there were 55 Golds and 64 Silvers. Entries have ranged from 54 to 123 at Stoneleigh (National) and Stafford (Federation) shows since then, up to the time of writing in 2008.

Sebrights are very pretty, so should be a lot more popular than they are. They are held back by their fertility problems. Even the experts are pleased if they get more than 10 per cent hatched of eggs incubated. Individually housed pairs give the best results, but this involves

Gold Sebright, female. Photo: John Tarren

more work and housing than most beginners are willing to put into their new hobby.

SEBRIGHT DESCRIPTION

The wording of Sebright standards is similar in all countries but, sad to say, seems to have been ignored here, in the breed's country of origin. Our breeders argue that the scale of points places more emphasis on colour and lacing than other points, and this is exactly what they have done. This is true, but the loss of type here has, in the author's opinion, been too great. Imported stock from Germany and the Netherlands has improved quality here since 2000.

British Poultry Standards requires:

> Carriage: Strutting and tremulous, on tip-toe, somewhat resembling a fantail pigeon. Type: Body compact, with broad and prominent breast. Back very short. Wings large and carried low. Tail square, well spread and carried high. Sebright males are hen feathered, without curved sickles or pointed neck and saddle hackles.

The rose combs on Sebrights are small on females, which they almost always are, but combs on males are often faulty. They should be low and compact and be 'square fronted'. Some are high, misshapen and are 'hollow-fronted', with a dent in the centre of the front surface.

All feathers should have narrow, but dense black, lacing all around. In this respect, British Sebright fanciers have excelled. There is a tendency for lacing to be sound, but with some centre peppering, especially on the underside of tail feathers. Clear centred tails are possible, but often at the cost of weak lacing. Breeders should try to steer a middle course, mating one extreme with the other if such birds are the only ones available. The ideal ground colour of Silvers is easily described, 'pure, clear silver-white', but not always so easily achieved. The exact shade of Golds has varied over the years, and from country to country. Concentrate on

Silver Sebright, female. Photo: John Tarren

achieving an even shade throughout (avoid light feather shafts) rather than a particular colour.

Facial skin and comb should be dark purple or dull red, although this is seldom achieved on males. Most of them do, at least, have dark pigmented skin around their eyes, which are black, or nearly so.

SPECIAL REQUIREMENTS

Infertility has been a persistent problem with Sebrights, often blamed on the hen-feathering of males. Other hen-feathered breeds, such as Campines and Henny Game, do not have such problems. It is more likely to be related to most breeders inbreeding for many years, although recently imported European stock has reduced this problem. Pair matings remain the best method, despite this improvement. Even in the best of times, Sebrights will never be very vigorous or fertile, so have enough incubator capacity to incubate as many eggs as possible. If you do manage to hatch and rear (they are also very susceptible to Marek's disease) more youngsters than needed, they sell well at the auctions.

Shamo. Originally a free gift with Geflügel-Börse. *1960. Artist: F.W. Perzlmayer*

Shamo. Originally a free gift with Deutscher Kleintier-Züchter. *1959. Artist: F.W. Perzlmayer*

CHAPTER 31

Shamo, Ko-Shamo and Relations

As far as the Victorian authors of poultry books were concerned, the only Oriental Game breeds were Asil, Malays and the smaller bodied long-tails, Sumatras and Yokohamas, some of which were used for cockfighting as well as being ornamental. A few clearly identified Shamo were imported directly from Japan, such as those bought by the Countess von Ulm-Erbach in Germany in March 1884. A few academic cockfighting enthusiasts in Europe and America knew about Japanese Shamo, but few others would have separated them from Malays.

There are many other Game breeds still bred for cockfighting in those countries in which it is either legal to do so, or only 'slightly illegal' (not a police priority). Some of these have been made from Shamo and other breeds to suit local requirements, the most notable being 'Brazilian Shamo'. These are slimmer and more elegant than Japanese Shamo, the result of crosses with Spanish Game: *see Oriental Gamefowl* by Horst Schmudde for more details.

Japanese fanciers developed their own tradition of poultry shows, based on native breeds only. Japanese/Chabo Bantams and the long-tails were the only ones regularly shown by fanciers in the rest of the world since Victorian times, the remainder being very recent arrivals, including the long-crowers and true Japanese long-tails. There are several small Shamo breeds, none of which are 'Shamo Bantams' in our normal sense. 'Shamo Bantams' were included in the 1979 edition of

American Bantam Association Standards (and possibly others), but were removed when it became clear they didn't exist, and American fanciers were starting to get details of the true small Shamo breeds from the Belgian, Dutch and German fanciers who established contacts with their Japanese counterparts. Little detailed historical information is available in English language sources, so this chapter mainly consists of descriptions of the breeds in this group: quite brief descriptions for those not kept in the UK or elsewhere in Europe.

SHAMO

The ancestors of Shamo were imported to Japan from Thailand (formerly Siam, probably the origin of 'Shamo'), perhaps from Indonesia and elsewhere in south-east Asia as well, in the sixteenth century. Japanese breeders then refined them into the form we see today. There are other theories that the ancestors of Shamo were imported much earlier, in the Heian Era (794–1192) from China with the ancestors of Shokoku, the most ancient Japanese long-tailed breed.

A group of scientists at the National Institute of Genetics at Mishima, Tomoyoshi Komiyama, Kazuho Ikeo, Takashi Gojobori and Yoshio Tateno, published papers in 2002 and 2004 on their work on mitochondrial DNA to help establish the origins of Japanese breeds. Samples were taken from Shamo in various parts of Japan, those from Okinawa seeming to be from a different ancestor from those on the main islands of Japan, Kyushu and Honshu. The Okinawa strain also appear to be the source of the ancestors of other Japanese breeds, including the long-crowers (and long-tails?). Their research suggests both places of origin, south-east Asia and China, were involved, although mixing since then has confused matters. Breed origin work based on DNA continues in several countries. Historians and palaeontologists could help too.

Shamos became available to German hobbyists when Friedrich ('Fritz') Wilhelm Perzlmayer obtained some young birds bred from a group imported in 1953 by Hagenbeck Zoo from Tokyo Zoo. He exhibited them at the 1955 Hannover Show, the beginning of Shamo as a recognized show bird in the west. Also in the early fifties, some American soldiers stationed in post-war occupied Japan took some back to the USA, but they went into the then legal cockfighting scene. Shamo were not recognized as a show breed by the APA until 1981, about the same time as the current generation of British fanciers started to take an interest. The number and quality of Shamo in the UK gradually increased and improved, a significant factor in this group of breeds leaving the Rare Poultry Society to the new Asian Hardfeather Club in 1999.

Several types of Shamo are recognized in Japan, some from specific regions of Japan, large and medium weights, some typically more upright than others in normal stance, and selected for specific fighting styles. The last aspect cannot legally be ascertained by breeders in Europe, probably not by those prepared to break the law either. Cockfighting in Japan (and elsewhere, where it is legal) is part of a rural tradition, and only makes historical and cultural sense in those societies, that is, where everyone has been brought up with the local rules and the local breed. European and American fanciers can only try to keep their Shamo somewhere near Japanese breeding traditions by recognizing large (O-Shamo) and medium (Chu-Shamo) types. For adult cocks, 4kg (9lb) is the dividing line, 3kg (6½lb) for adult hens. O-Shamo cocks can

weigh over 5.5kg (12lb), hens 4.8kg (10½lb). Although a map of regional types of Shamo appears in Horst Schmudde's book *Oriental Gamefowl*, it is not known if they still exist as distinct forms. C.A. Finsterbusch (in his book *Cockfighting all over the World*, 1928) used the terms Ainoku for large Shamo and Ashura for medium Shamo. These terms are no longer used, and he may have been mistaken.

SHAMO DESCRIPTION

As Shamos are quite similar to Malays, and fanciers are more familiar with Malays, it is probably most useful to describe Shamo in terms of its differences from Malays.

Both breeds have a powerful skull, short thick beak and prominent eyebrow bones, although Malay cocks' heads seem broader because they have walnut combs, which are wider than the pea comb of Shamos (walnut-combed Shamos exist, but are rare). On both breeds, wattles are very small, sometimes absent on males, always absent on females. Eyes are pearl white or yellow, darker on young birds. The neck is long, slightly curved, but straighter and more upright than on Malays. Neck hackle feathers are short and swept back to a point at the base of the neck. Horny tissue between beak and comb is one of their prehistoric characteristics.

The body is broad at the shoulders, carried almost upright, with a long, flat back (not curved as Malays). The tail is carried rather low, sometimes with the top line of the tail continuing in a straight line down the back. Sickle feathers, more sabre than sickle shaped, sometimes touch the ground on males. Other tail feathers are moderately whipped on males, tightly whipped on females. Wings are held slightly away from the body at the shoulders, which helps accentuate the apparent width of the shoulders. The tips of the wings should be held at the side of the body. The body is very muscular, scantily feathered, with the keel bone bare of feathers with bright red skin. The keel is not as deep and prominent as on Malays.

Black-Red Shamo, male. Photo: John Tarren

Partridge Shamo, female. Photo: John Tarren

Legs are long, with muscular thighs, but not as long as on the best exhibition Malays. O-Shamo can be as tall as Malays, but more of a Shamo's overall height comes from its more upright body carriage and straighter neck. Shanks and feet are yellow, shaded black on dark varieties.

Shamo are judged on head and body formation and carriage, not plumage colour; nevertheless there are recognized traditional varieties, mainly variations of the Black-Red pattern, the females ranging from wheaten, via a laced brown pattern, to black. Some other plumage colours are traditional, some more are not quite conventional, but often seen, while any attempt at making colours or patterns never known on Shamo would be unpopular to say the least.

Black and dark red-hackled black ('Abura') males are both usually with Black hens. Both sexes have dark shanks and feet (black epidermal pigmentation over yellow dermal tissue). The next shade lighter, 'Shojo' or Brown, overlaps to an extent. Brown hens have a brown ground colour with more or less black neck hackles, tail and wing markings. Back and wing feathers are laced with black, plus some fine black peppering in feather centres. Some breast feathers have small black spangles. There are also bright Black-Red males with wheaten females.

The silver gene is also found in Shamos, with the same range of shades from silver-hackled Blacks to Duckwings, with varying amounts of black hackle striping. In addition there are Yellow-hackled ('Kisasa') males. They are

231

probably genetically gold with dilution genes, but might be genetically silver with mahogany or autosomal red genes. Females follow the same spectrum, all in a slightly more silvery shade.

Other common colours are White ('Hakushoku'), Blue-Red and Blue ('Asagi'), and an irregular black and white mixture, only previously known in Europe on Exchequer Leghorns. They are called 'Goishi' in Japan, named after the bowl of black and white playing pieces (or 'stones') used in the popular Japanese board game of Go. Golden-Buffs (usually with some light lacing and other irregular black and/or bronze markings and/ or shading) are also recognized.

SMALL SHAMO BREEDS – SUMMARY

The most popular of this group is the Ko-Shamo. The most unusual is the Yamato Gunkei, a very heavily built breed with thick, wrinkled facial skin. Chibi and Tosa-Chibi are small, the same size or smaller than Ko-Shamo, but with as much Yamato Gunkei character as possible on a smaller scale. Nankin-Shamo and Echigo-Nankin-Shamo are also small, but finely built, the beak and head being more like normal bantams of the same body size. The remaining three breeds in this group are all rather larger, and are either mainly black or only exist with black plumage. They are Kinpa, Yakido and Tuzo. Little is known about the history of any of them. One suggestion is that one ancestor of all the small Shamo breeds was small Asil taken to Japan from India by Dutch traders in the seventeenth or eighteenth century. Between 1603 and 1867 the only contact between Japan and the rest of the world was a Dutch trading post on a small Japanese island. However, it has also been suggested that small fighting cocks were known in Japan as long ago as 800BC, but the author could not find further references about this theory.

KO-SHAMO

Ko-Shamo are not 'miniature Shamo' because they differ in several key respects, the two most obvious being their head and tail. Mature Ko-Shamo have some of the wrinkled skin characteristics of Yamato Gunkei, but not as well developed, whereas large Shamo are smooth-faced. The wrinkled skin feature would be a disaster on a cockfighting breed; it would swell up enough to completely block vision during a fight. This is enough evidence to confirm that none of the wrinkled skin breeds were ever anything other than show birds. Ko-Shamo have a short 'prawn tail', very different from the tails on both sexes of large Shamos.

They are bred and exhibited in noticeably different shapes and styles in certain regions of Japan, but no exact information about the types, or their home regions, has been available to European fanciers. Some Japanese experts consider Chibi-Shamo and Tosa-Chibi-Shamo to be sub-varieties of Ko-Shamo, rather than separate breeds. Communication with Japanese breeders remains difficult because few poultry fanciers are multilingual. It is believed Ko-Shamo and its sub-varieties were stabilized, recognized and standardized in Japan in the 1920s.

Ko-Shamo, Yamato Gunkei, Chibi-Shamo and Tosa-Chibi-Shamo share a characteristic which has been very controversial since they have been bred and exhibited in the west – split-wing. It has always been a disqualifying fault for all breeds in all poultry showing countries. Judges, especially older judges, were shocked when they were told by Oriental Game enthusiasts that split-wing is not regarded as a fault on these breeds. It is associated with the very scanty plumage all these breeds have, so birds with 'correct' wings (not split) are very likely to be too profusely feathered generally. Again because of communication difficulties we are not clear on this, but understand that some Japanese experts once regarded split-wing as a fault (but not a disqualification) on these breeds, but had to be accepted after 1945,

Black-Red Ko-Shamo, male. Photo: John Tarren

Wheaten Ko-Shamo, female. Photo: John Tarren

when very few birds had survived the war, and almost all the survivors had split-wing. German judges almost ruined Ko-Shamo in Europe by insisting split-wing was a disqualification, which resulted in German Ko-Shamo breeders crossing their first specimens (*circa* 1980?) with other breeds to eliminate split-wing. Fortunately they were 'put right' by Belgian, British and Dutch enthusiasts, all of which had more flexible governing bodies. All European poultry and fancy pigeon governing bodies now follow the general principle that each breed's standard should follow that of its country of origin.

The main general priority when breeding Ko-Shamo is to achieve as much breed character as possible, with a powerfully built head and body and thick shanks, while sticking to the standard weights: 600g (21oz) pullet, 800g (28oz) hen and cockerel, 1000g (36oz) cock.

'Mainstream Ko-Shamo' (that is, not including shorter Chibi- and Tosa-Chibi- types) are often said to be in three equal parts, a potentially confusing term which refers to their height proportions.

Of their total height: one-third is top of head down to shoulder, one-third is shoulder down to belly, and one-third is belly down to ground.

They do not achieve proper head character until over two years old, when the prominent eyebrow bone and thick beak are fully developed. Wattles are small or absent, but there is a dewlap of red skin (not as big on normal Ko-Shamo as on Chibi-Shamo and Tosa-Chibi-

Shamo). Eye colour is yellow or pearl white on adults, darker on youngsters. The beak is yellow, horn colour, or either of these with black shading on darker plumage colour varieties. Three comb types are allowed: pea, walnut and 'chrysanthemum' (wrinkled surface variant of walnut), all of which are small and compact.

The neck is long (one-third of the whole, *see* above), well muscled, and as erect as possible. Neck hackle feathers finish at a point on the back of the neck, above the shoulders.

The body is held upright, with the wings held away from the body to give the effect of prominent shoulders. The wing tips should ideally be held high on the side of the body, perhaps almost on the back, but certainly not so high that the wing tips touch each other on the back. Study as many Ko-Shamo as possible, live birds and photos, to fully understand ideal posture. Plumage is scanty, showing bare red skin along the keel bone, around the vent, and on the 'elbow joints' of the wings.

Legs are the correct length (on mainstream Ko-Shamo) to give the 'one-third/one-third/one-third' effect, the thighs being muscular and the shanks thick. Ko-Shamo, Chibi-Shamo, Tosa-Chibi-Shamo and Yamato Gunkei all have an unusual formation of four or five rows of small scales down the front of the shanks. Compare them with the shanks of other breeds to appreciate the difference.

The 'prawn' tail is very short, the centre feathers pointing down and round (between the legs), and the outer feathers pointing sideways. Again, see some good birds at the shows to fully understand this aspect.

The main plumage colour varieties are (various shades of) Black-Red males with wheaten or brown (with some black lacing on back) hens. There are also Duckwings (females silvery shaded versions of wheaten or brown), Buffs/Gingers (with some black markings), Blacks, Whites, Blues, Cuckoos and Creles, and various mixtures of black and white from

conventional Black-Mottles to Goishis as seen on large Shamos. Whites, Cuckoos, Creles, and the lighter coloured Black-Red/Wheatens are often too feathery.

YAMATO GUNKEI

These are probably the most extreme, most infertile, worst laying, (to most people) ugliest chicken breed in the world, yet they are the rarest and most expensive. They were first brought to Europe about 1980 by Belgian fanciers Willy and Geert Coppens (father and son), of Aalst. Several trips to Japan were needed, and even then the Japanese breeders charged the proverbial 'arm and a leg' for the birds. Since then they have been spread around Europe, but are still rare. They were developed in the Hiroshima region of Japan in the 1920s.

Yamato are not much taller than Ko-Shamo, but are twice the weight, from 1.3kg (2¾lb) pullets up to 2kg (4½lb) adult cocks. General characteristics are similar to Ko-Shamo, only much more so. The wrinkled skin on the face and neck of top quality mature birds is weird but incredible – usually stimulating an instant love or hate reaction when people first see them. They have, after all, come from the same country as sumo wrestlers, bonsai trees, koi carp and peculiar breeds of goldfish. They are not suitable for, or likely to be sold to, beginners.

CHIBI-SHAMO AND TOSA-CHIBI-SHAMO

These are Ko-Shamo-sized birds with as much Yamato Gunkei character as possible in miniature. Chibi cocks weigh 1000g (36oz), Tosa-Chibi cocks only 750g (26oz). Both are very rare, even in Japan. It is believed both of these were, like Yamato Gunkei, developed in the Hiroshima area.

NANKIN-SHAMO AND ECHIGO-NANKIN-SHAMO

These are very similar to each other, the latter being slightly taller and slimmer, and they have no connection to the buff coloured Nankin Bantam breed. Nankin-Shamo do not have wrinkled facial skin, and generally look more like Asil Bantams than other breeds in this group. Although they have tight body plumage, still with bare red skin along the breastbone, they have a longer tail than Ko-Shamo, and are not split-winged. It is rare in Japan, and none are known in the UK.

KINPA

These were created in the Akita region of Japan, probably *circa* 1820–50, but not brought to Europe until 1984 by Willy and Geert Coppens in Belgium, but remain very rare. Kinpa are quite small, weights ranging from 1000g to 1500g (36–43oz), and stand very upright. Their head is typical Oriental Game type, pea comb, minimal wattles, but with a throat dewlap. Kinpa males are hen-feathered, their most obvious breed characteristic. The main colour variety is Black, but Whites are also standardized, and other colours have existed.

YAKIDO

These were first made, about 1850, at the village of Yakido, in the Taki-gun district in Mie province, east of Osaka on the main island of Honshu. They were also first brought to Europe by Willy Coppens in Belgium. Yakido are much bigger than the other small Shamo breeds, weights ranging from 1.65kg (3½lb) pullets, up to 2.6kg (5¾lb) adult cocks. They are similar to large Shamo in general appearance. The only recognized plumage colour variety is Black.

TUZO

These are included in this chapter despite the fact that it is now known they are not recognized as a breed in Japan. C.A. Finsterbusch featured Tuzo in his 1928 book, *Cockfighting all over the World*, which despite this and some other mistakes, is still one of the most respected reference books on Game breeds. This reference no doubt led American servicemen in post-war Japan to think they had found the long-lost Tuzo breed, when in fact the birds they sent home to America were most likely crossbred pit game, perhaps a mixture of Kinpa, Yakido and Nankin-Shamo. Over the following twenty years 1945–65, they were stabilized into a standard breed. They are like a small Asil in general shape, at weights ranging from 1.5kg (3¼lb) to 1.8kg (3¾lb). The main colour variety is Black, sometimes with a little dark red in the hackles of males. Tuzo are stylish little birds, so are becoming quite popular despite their dubious pedigree.

SPECIAL MANAGEMENT REQUIREMENTS

All of these breeds will fight, including the hens and the most extreme exhibition Yamatos. A lot of separate houses and runs are needed, with solid pen divisions and run fences, at least up to above cocks' head height. These breeds are often bred in pairs, certainly no more than four pullets together. Bearing this in mind, it is no surprise to learn that fanciers seldom have large flocks of them; in fact the few birds kept often become very tame, and much-loved pets. Horst Schmudde (in *Oriental Gamefowl*) mentions a friend of his with a Shamo cock that enjoyed riding with him on the passenger seat of his pickup truck. Many other breeders have had favourite birds which followed them around like a pet dog.

White Silkies. Originally a free gift with Poultry *magazine, circa 1912. Artist: J.W. Ludlow*

Black and White Silkies. Originally a free gift with Feathered World *magazine, circa 1928.*
Artist: A.J. Simpson

CHAPTER 32

Silkie

This is an ancient breed; they were described as 'the wool bearing hen' by Aldrovandi in 1600, and by Marco Polo (*circa* 1300). Wandelt and Wolters have found references to Silkies from the Tang Dynasty (618–907) and an ancient Greek who heard of them in China well over 2,000 years ago (*circa* 350BC). Perhaps even more ancient descriptions are known in China. Silkies have several very unusual characteristics: Silkie plumage, head crest, unique comb, five toes, feathered feet and very dark pigmented skin and internal tissues. Several scientists are studying the DNA of many breeds of domestic chickens, and are hoping to establish some historical and relationship details from this information. The story of how and when such an unusual breed was created such a long time ago will be fascinating when finally discovered.

Silkies imported to the Middle East and Europe during the medieval period were probably crossed with ordinary chickens, eventually leading to the creation of Sultans, Polands and other crested breeds. Silkies are one of the most popular fancy breeds all over the world now, and their broodiness and gentle mothering abilities make them (pure or crossed) vital for anyone with eggs which have to be incubated naturally. Bearing all this in mind, it is surprising to find, when studying old poultry books, that Silkies were very rare indeed in the USA, UK and Western Europe when poultry keeping became fashionable and the shows started around 1845–55.

About this time another silkie feathered breed, the Emu Fowl, appeared briefly. Some Black Emu Fowls were entered in a Baker Street, London, show some time about 1850–55. They were probably made by crossing Silkies with Cochins/Shanghais and/or Langshans, and looked like what you would imagine such a cross to look like. No reports of any attempts to remake Emu Fowls have been found.

Silkies seem to have been imported to both the UK and USA about 1850. The earliest show entries known were at Boston, Massachusetts and an unknown UK show in 1852, and at Cheltenham, Gloucestershire, in June 1853. Wingfield and Johnson (*The Poultry Book*, 1853) said some had been imported from India which did well in south-west England but sickened when tried in the colder, wetter, climate of Lancashire. Rev. R.S. Woodgate, of Pembury Hall, Kent was an early British Silkie fancier, and was quoted by Lewis Wright. He had been given some when a child by Captain Finch, who brought them on a ship from China, about 1860. Some years later, in 1869, he added to his flock by buying some from Miss Hawker, whose brother, an officer in the Royal Navy, had brought her first Silkies from Japan (1867?). Harrison Weir mentioned a Mr Cross who had Black Silkies in 1860, and the 1913 *Feathered World Yearbook* mentioned that the Countess of Dartmouth had some Blacks in about 1874.

Despite being very cute and a suitable subject for expert exhibitors, Silkies remained rare in the UK until the Silkie Club was

White Silkies, large and bantam females. Photo: John Tarren

Gold Silkie, large female. Photo: John Tarren   *Partridge Silkie, large female. Photo: John Tarren*

formed in 1898. Mr H. Harwood was secretary for the first few years, followed by Dr Arthur Campbell, who ran the club until he resigned due to ill health at the 1932 AGM. His wife, Adele, was Silkie Club President until her death on 17 November 1930. Dr and Mrs Campbell also kept Sultans and created Campbell ducks. They lived at Rose Villa, Uley, Gloucestershire, where Arthur was the GP, until he retired and they moved to Cambridge Villa, St Ives, Ringwood, Hampshire in 1924. After his wife's death, Dr Campbell moved again, to Suncliffe, Steyning Avenue, Peacehaven, Sussex until he died, aged 94 in 1949 (or 1950).

The Silkie Club's Annual Shows, usually part of the Crystal Palace Show, did not attract huge entries, ranging from 40 to 59 between 1909 and 1916. Most of the Silkies shown were Whites. 'Buff or 'Gold' Silkies were believed to have been made by French fanciers, starting from a White Silkie × Buff Pekin mating. A British fancier, W.A. Jukes, developed Partridge Silkies, but no details of how he did it are known. Most Black Silkie males have brassy neck hackles, so he may have crossed a very brassy specimen with a Partridge coloured hen of some kind.

Annual Show entries gradually increased during Dr Campbell's remaining years as secretary, up to 1932. Entries have not been found for every year, but those known range from 43 in 1921 to 89 in 1927. The new secretary, Mrs E.S. Fentiman (186 Whitworth Road, Swindon) reported that the Club had 24 members in 1933. Dr and Mrs Campbell did a lot to improve the quality of Silkies, but they may have been responsible for their lack of popularity. Subscriptions were doubled in 1921, from five to ten shillings, to rebuild the Club's finances after the First World War. This was a lot of money in those days, too much for working-class fanciers, and it has been said that Mrs Campbell was not the friendliest or most approachable of women, which didn't help.

Mrs Campbell's efforts to improve Silkies must be recognized, however. She contributed to the last (1919) edition of *Wright's Book of*

Bearded Buff Silkie, bantam female in US. Photo: John Tarren

Poultry, on the changes made between 1898 and 1911, commenting,

> It is now quite the usual thing to see Silkie cocks with ragged wings and tails without hard feathers or sickles, whereas it used to be the exception. The hens, too, have much improved in wing – the hen I won the cup with at the [Crystal] Palace nine years ago [1902?] would not have a chance in the show pen today [1911?] – and cocks also used to be of a much coarser type, hard feathered not only in wings and tail, but also in the legs and feet.

Mrs Fentiman died while still secretary in 1960, to be followed by Mrs Doris Bryer, of Mackworth, Derbyshire until she retired in 1994. Over the sixty years in which the Silkie Club was run by these two ladies, membership rose from 24 in 1932, about 32 in 1935, 40 in 1975 (having dipped 1939–45) to about 60 in

1994. Like Mrs Campbell, Mrs Bryer was not liked by everyone, and deterred some fanciers from joining. Mrs Sue Flude took over in 1994, and saw membership rapidly rise to over 200 when she resigned in 2003, and there are even more now.

The rise in Silkie Club membership was reflected in annual show entries and an increase in the number of varieties, especially after 1990, when tiny Silkie Bantams first arrived in the UK from the Netherlands. Previously, Silkies had been halfway in size between most breeds of large fowl and bantams. These were crossed with Barbu du Watermaal to make Silkie Bantams. Original Silkies were then bred bigger, so there would be a clear difference between large and bantam Silkies. Bearded versions of both sizes also appeared about 1990.

Looking at the colour varieties, Gold and Partridge Silkies have gradually improved during the twentieth century, but many still have lighter skin than Blacks and Whites, maroon instead of dark blue. Blues were included as a recognized variety in the 1926 edition of *British Standards*, but very few were seen until many years later. Mr A.H. Draper, of St John's Wood, London, made a strain in the 1930s, starting from a cross between Black Silkies and Blue Wyandotte Bantams. Since 2000, American, Dutch, German and Swiss fanciers have made Barred, Red, Lavender and several other colours and patterns of the breed, not all of which really work with Silkie plumage. Of these, Lavenders are likely to be most popular.

Examples of Silkie Club of Great Britain Annual Show entries since 1946:

   1948: 12 birds (10 White, 2 AOC)
   1954: 49 birds (37 White, 5 Black/Blue, 7 Gold/Partridge)
   1962: 47 birds (32 White, 15 AOC)
   1982: 67 birds (46 White, 11 Black/Blue, 10 Gold/Partridge)
   1989: 111 birds (55 White, 22 Black, 7 Blue, 10 Gold, 4 Partridge, 7 Bearded, 6 Bantams).

Entries at the National (Stoneleigh) and Federation (Stafford) Shows have been very similar since then, regardless of which of the two was officially the annual club show.

   1993 to 2007: Large White, 24–95 (1997 Stoneleigh, an exceptional entry, usually 45–65)
   1993 to 2007: Large Black, 11–32
   1993 to 2007: Large Blue, 4–14
   1993 to 2007: Large Gold, 8–20
   1993 to 2007: Large Partridge, 2–12
   1993 to 2007: Large Bearded (AC), 2 –14

Bearded Silkie Bantams of all colours, and other colours of non-bearded Silkie Bantams were very rare before 2000, and will certainly become much more popular than past show entries would suggest. They were often together in AOC classes, so no records of each colour are available.

SILKIE DESCRIPTION

Full descriptions can be found in American, British, Dutch, German, Japanese and other standards books published around the world. Silkies are much the same everywhere, except possibly for weights. Silkies were once all halfway in size between most large fowl and bantam breed: males 3lb (1.5kg) females 2lb (1kg). They were officially classed as large fowl in the UK and as bantams in the USA. Not all countries have changed to the current situation, with larger large Silkies and very small Silkie Bantams, weighing 500g to 600g (17–21oz).

Despite the general improvements made by Mrs Campbell and others by 1914, some Silkies are still seen at shows with almost red faces, poor crests, over-sized irregular shaped combs, hard wing and tail feathers (as normal chickens) and lacking proper fifth toes. Novice breeders should be aware that young Silkies often look rather tall and thin, but they usually 'fill out' to become excellent birds in their second year.

White Silkies have to be pure white for showing, and need all the usual expertise for success. Black males still often have brassy hackles, although females are usually of excellent colour. As with Blues of all breeds, only a small proportion of those bred will be a good, even colour. Golds should be as even in colour as possible. Males have almost black tails.

Partridge Silkies should have markings as clear as is possible with Silkie plumage. Other self colours, Reds and Lavenders, should be as even as possible.

Other patterns, if bred, have the same problem as the Partridge variety: clear markings are difficult to obtain on Silkie plumage.

SPECIAL MANAGEMENT REQUIREMENTS

Silkies need houses large enough for them to be kept comfortably inside in bad weather. They are susceptible to scaly leg mite infestation and Marek's disease, so need to be regularly checked (and treated when necessary) for the former and vaccinated against the latter. Some breeders adopt a 'survival of the fittest' policy instead of vaccination regarding Marek's. Surplus Silkies, even those with serious breed faults (such as poor combs and lack of fifth toe), are very saleable as pets. For the sake of their future welfare with non-expert pet owners, breeders must explain these needs, especially regarding scaly leg mite, to buyers. Gold and Partridge Silkie males with breed faults can be useful for crossing with genetically silver hens of other breeds (such as Light Sussex or Silver Laced Wyandottes) for breeding sex-linked broodies.

Large Black Silkie female. Photo: John Tarren

Large Blue Silkie female. Photo: John Tarren

Sussex, Brown, Light, Speckled and Red. Originally a free gift with Feathered World *magazine, 11 October 1912. Artist: A.F. Lydon*

CHAPTER 33

Sussex

Table chickens had been reared in Kent, Sussex and Surrey for the London markets for two thousand years, as mentioned in the Dorking chapter. For most of this period it would not have been a major part of the rural economy of those counties because London was much smaller then, but it started to expand, with a rapidly increasing population, during the eighteenth century. 'Dorking Fowls' were recognized as a specific breed by the Romans all those centuries ago because they had their distinctive extra toes, but not all table chickens in these counties were five-toed. Poulterers did not care how many toes they had, they only wanted quick growing, plump birds, preferably with white skin, and white shanks and feet were a clearly visible indication of this on live birds.

Instead of a simple Dorking chapter, in his *Our Poultry, and all about them* (1902), Harrison Weir had a long and detailed 'Kent; Sussex, Surrey, and Dorking Fowls' chapter, which is not surprising as he lived his entire life in the three counties. He was born in 1824, and started to write *Our Poultry* about 1884. The Dorking breed had been changed quite a lot between 1845 and 1884, and Harrison Weir did not approve of any of the changes. He considered the bigger looking exhibition Dorking was 'a useless bunch of feathers' compared to the type he had known as a young man, circa 1845–50. The bird he remembered may not have looked as large, but they were actually much meatier because they had tighter plumage and finer bones. Both four- and five-

toed birds were bred in all three counties, so he thought they could have been named after any of the market towns in the area, a point he made again in 1903 regarding 'Sussex'. His drawings indicate that many of the birds looked similar to long-legged Scots Dimples (that is, those without the creeper gene). As far as plumage colour is concerned, some farmers bred Cuckoos and Whites, but most had a mixture of cinnamons, reds, spangles and speckles, with an assortment of markings. Although there was a lot of variation over the whole area, and no one cared about feather colour or pattern, some farmers selected for a particular pattern so their birds would be recognizable, in nearby villages at least, if stolen.

Some of the farmers who took a greater than normal interest in their poultry flock selected five-toed birds because they were aware of their history. In contrast to them, a lot of tenant cottagers and smallholders were more or less obliged to 'walk' young Game cocks if their landlord was a cockfighting enthusiast. A Game cock would be much fitter and more confident for its first fight if it had been allowed to run free with a group of hens and had never seen another cock (of any kind) for a few months before it was entered in a cockpit. The tenants were allowed to keep any chicks they bred from it, as long as all their hens were heavy table breed types – tenants were not allowed to have Game hens in case pure Game chickens found their way into the breeding pens of a rival 'cocker' (cockfighting enthusiast). Thus many

Red Sussex. Originally a free gift with Poultry *magazine, 6 September 1912. Artist: J.W. Ludlow*

of the ancestors of the Sussex breed were half-Game/half-Dorking(ish) crossbreds.

As was the case in the history of many other breeds, imported Brahmas/Cochins/Shanghais played a significant part of their development during the 1850s and 1960s. As far as the Sussex breed is concerned, Light Brahmas were most important. They were much bigger, or at least looked much bigger, than any chickens the country people of Kent, Sussex and Surrey had ever seen, so cockerels were bought from the first importers and breeders and bred with their general flocks, resulting in what would later be called Light Sussex. Poultry keepers in this area would have been better placed than those in other parts of the country to buy them as they were surrounded by ports, from the south coast,

along the Thames estuary, and in London, where they could meet sailors arriving from China and America (*see* Chapter 9: Brahma). It is no doubt a Light Brahma crossing which took place then that has resulted in exhibition strains of Light Sussex, which are much bigger and fluffier than utility strains of Light Sussex or other colour varieties of Sussex (which do not have separate exhibition and utility strains).

Early in 1903, Edward Brown (one of the world's leading poultry experts *circa* 1880–1930) was giving a lecture to farmers at Lewes, Sussex, where he said that while the table chicken producers in the county were still famous for their production techniques, they had almost allowed their traditional local breeds to die out. By 1903 many other breeds

Speckled Sussex. Originally a free gift with Feathered World *magazine, 25 October 1929. Artist: A.J. Simpson*

had been introduced, such as Faverolles, Orpingtons and Wyandottes, plus many table bird producers were using half-Indian Game (Cornish) crosses. One of the farmers present, Mr E.J. Wadman, said that he had a fine flock of uniform fowls, which had been there for several decades, which he would call 'Red Sussex'. Mr Wadman was not the only person trying to get Sussex accepted as a breed, as a Mr John Cole had entered some (Speckled) 'Sussex' in the AOV class at Lewes Show as far back as 1890. There may have been others at this event before 1903.

A meeting was arranged at the Elephant and Castle Hotel, Lewes, on the 23 July 1903, when it was decided to form a Sussex Poultry Club. Thirteen people attended, with Alderman John Miles acting as chairman, although only two

present actually kept chickens. Messrs A.J. Cox and A.J. Langridge became joint secretaries, handing over to Mr S.C. Sharpe, who also lived in Lewes, at a meeting on 21 December 1905, and remained secretary until 1923. Harrison Weir was offered the honorary position of Vice-President, but he refused because he feared that having a breed club, and a show standard, would do more harm than good.

Returning to the initial few weeks of the Sussex Poultry Club's history, there were further meetings on 30 July, 5 August, 1 and 8 September 1903, at which a committee was formed and a breed standard produced. The Club was affiliated to the PCGB, and the breed standard was recognized by the PCGB. There were three colour varieties at first: Light, Speckled and 'Red or Brown', all of which were still very variable at this early stage of trying to make standard varieties out of an assortment of flocks in the area which had not even been 'a proper breed' only three months previously. There were classes for Sussex in November 1903 at Lewes Fanciers' Show, at which Mr Wadman won the medal for best Red/Brown, E. and H. Russell the medal for best Light, and G.J. Lenny the medal for best Speckled. Lewes Show in November 1904 had a very impressive entry of 163 Sussex, making it clear that the breed was here to stay.

It soon became apparent that the 'Red or Brown' variety could not stay as it was because breeders and judges did not know which of the two plumage patterns and numerous variations in shade should take precedence. Reds were almost completely rich-red, with black neck striping, wing markings and tail (the same pattern, if less obvious, as Light Sussex). Brown Sussex were a darker variant of the common Black-Red/Partridge pattern. Hailsham Fanciers Association wrote to the Sussex Club on 29 June 1906, suggesting that only Red Sussex be recognized, an idea which the Club adopted at its 1906 AGM. As the Sussex cattle breed is rich red, there was probably local sentiment in favour of this colour.

All was not lost for Brown Sussex, however; the variety was promoted by Mr John T. Ade, of Grove Hill Farm, Hellingly, Sussex. But having made a decision to concentrate on Reds at the expense of Browns, the Sussex Club was not going to accept them again immediately. Mr Ade raised the matter with the Sussex Club in 1909, and when he was refused he formed a separate Brown Sussex Club. Browns were accepted by the main Sussex Club in 1913, and the Brown Club was closed down.

From being only recognized as a breed by a handful of farmers in Sussex before 1903, the 'new' breed rapidly attracted a lot of interest, if Sussex Club membership was an indicator: in 1905 there were over 90 members; in 1906, 170+ members; 1911, 300 members; 1928, 500+ members.

It remained one of the biggest UK breed clubs until 1939, and the Light variety was one of the most important commercial breeds until all pure breeds were replaced by hybrids.

At the shows, all four colour varieties were seen in roughly equal numbers up to the beginning of the First World War, as indicated by entries at the 1911 Crystal Palace Show: 27 Lights, 22 Reds, 27 Speckleds and 21 Browns. During the war, and into the early 1920s, the annual club show was held at Lewes, with classes for plucked cockerels as well as live birds. The 1920 show had an amazing 477 entries in 39 classes. The London Dairy Show, with its strong links between farmers and the meat trade, was a popular event with commercial Sussex breeders. Live bird classes were only provided for birds bred in the current year. In 1923 there were 360 (live) Sussex in eight classes; Lights, 75 cockerels and 121 pullets; plus 56 Reds, 74 Speckleds and 34 Browns (split between two classes in each case). Plumage markings were being stabilized, although neck hackle striping on Lights and the mahogany ground colour of Speckleds were still a long way short of the clarity which would be achieved by 1939.

The principle of sex-linkage was first brought to the attention of poultry breeders in a major way by Professor William Bateson (who coined the word 'genetics') of Cambridge University who put on a display of Gold × Silver matings and the resulting youngsters at the 1922 London Dairy Show. A few breeders, including some in Belgium and the Netherlands, had known Gold × Silver matings worked, although they didn't understand how or why, at least as far back as 1905.

Divisions between commercial producers and those who continued to believe in the superiority of pure breeds (and regarded shows as a form of breed quality control) suddenly became a lot sharper. Edward Brown, the man whose comments led to the effective birth of the Sussex breed, was one of the experts who did not foresee how poultry farming would develop, or the value of sex-linked crosses. He thought it a waste to kill all those day-old cockerel chicks, even if they were light breeds, and because this would mean the best-laying

Buff Sussex. Originally a free gift with Feathered World *magazine, 12 July 1929. Artist: A.J. Simpson*

individual hens could not be used for breeding stock because they would be crossbreds.

But others did see the shape of things to come, even with medium or heavy breed sex-linked crosses, where cockerel chicks could now be reared separately, perhaps being sold to the forerunners of the broiler chicken industry. Rhode Island Reds had recieved a lot of publicity since 1904, which led many UK producers to follow one of Prof. Bateson's suggestions, the Rhode Island Red × Light Sussex mating. Sussex Club members had an alternative idea: Red Sussex × Light Sussex. Pullets from this cross had been seen in local Sussex markets before 1914, with no one at this time understanding why there were no cockerels the same colour. The cockerels from this mating were similar to Light Sussex, but with gold neck hackles and shoulders. Some Sussex

fanciers, having seen the buff pullets with black markings like Lights, tried to make Buff Sussex as a true breeding variety, but there were no correctly coloured cockerels until Mr Knight exhibited one at Tunbridge Wells Show in July 1922, and even this one was not that good. Even now, in 2008, there is still more to learn about the inheritance of buff plumage, so it is not surprising that it took a long time before good specimens of both sexes could be bred reliably. The situation was not improved by some unscrupulous people selling pullets from the simple Red Sussex × Light Sussex cross for some years after Buff Sussex had been recognized, which did not happen overnight. John Raine had first entered Buff Sussex, pullets presumably, at the National Utility Poultry Show, Horticultural Hall, Westminster, in 1920. His strain had started

Speckled Sussex, large female. Photo: John Tarren

Brown Sussex, large male. Photo: John Tarren

in 1918 from a Buff Orpington cockerel and some Light Sussex hens with particularly heavy neck striping.

Mr Knight, along with Mr Howard and John and Mrs Raine were the main promoters of the new variety, who tried and failed to get the Sussex Club to accept Buffs at the 1921 AGM at Lewes. The Buff enthusiasts held an initial meeting at the 1923 London Dairy Show, rapidly followed by an inaugural meeting of a new Buff Sussex Club at the International Show at Olympia, which obtained formal recognition for Buffs by the PCGB Council in January 1925. Buff Sussex were adopted by the main Sussex Club in 1926.

A separate Utility Red Sussex Club existed from 26 March 1924 until some time during 1928. Its chairman was P.B. Adams, and its secretary B. Birkhead, of Whitehouse Poultry Farm, Bernehurst, Pexley Heath, Kent. They tried and failed to promote Red Sussex as a

credible alternative commercial breed to Rhode Island Reds.

Another tried and failed colour variety with its own short-lived separate club was the Cuckoo. It was made and promoted by Richard Terrot, who is better known to poultry historians for being the main UK breeder of Cuckoo Malines fowls. He started to make Cuckoo Sussex with a Cuckoo Malines × Light Sussex mating, followed by several years of backcrosses to Light Sussex. The Cuckoo Sussex Club continued to appear in lists of UK poultry breed clubs until 1939, but seems not to have been active for long after it was formed in 1927. A class was provided for Cuckoo Sussex at Barnstaple Show, Devon, in December 1926. Seven birds were entered, but only five appeared, and they didn't attract much interest.

Mr G.E. Howard had been breeding Brown Sussex for several years, some of which were so dark in plumage colour they seemed almost black from a distance. He thought, about 1924, he could make Black Sussex, while retaining white skin, shanks and feet. Such a colour combination might have been possible (black plumage and yellow shanks/feet exist on Black

Red Sussex, large female. Photo: John Tarren

Plymouth Rocks and Black Wyandottes), but never happened.

White Sussex were more successful, and had it not been for the small matters of the Second World War and the rise of the American broiler industry, they might have become one of the world's most commercially important breeds. Similar white birds had been made before; William Cook's first attempts at White Orpingtons were more Sussex shape than Orpington. Real White Sussex appeared about 1925, with Mr A.J. Falkenstein (Marston's Croft, Rotherfield, Sussex), already a prominent breeder of other colours of Sussex, exhibiting them. A class for White Sussex was provided in the 1926 Crystal Palace Show, in which 14 birds appeared from several exhibitors. Arthur Amey and James ('Big Jim') Smith were also involved with developing Whites, so it is not clear if a single person can be credited with being 'the originator' of this colour variety.

Partridge Sussex, with the same colour and pattern as Partridge Wyandottes, were created by Mr G.D. Richardson, of 7 The Close, Hanworth, Middlesex, in the early 1930s. Despite winning a first prize in the AOV class at the 1934 Olympia Show, this variety does not seem to have been taken up by anyone else, and soon died out. Mr Richardson started with a Brown Sussex × Partridge Wyandotte mating, later adding Buff Orpingtons and Partridge Plymouth Rocks.

Coronation Sussex, the same pattern as Light Sussex, but with blue markings instead of black, were made in time for the coronation (which never happened) of King Edward VIII in 1936. It is not known if any large Coronation Sussex survived up to the outbreak of the Second World War, but if so, they didn't survive much longer. Coronation Sussex Bantams appeared in the 1980s, but at the time of writing (2008) the author had not seen a remade strain of large Coronation Sussex.

Silver Sussex, a variation of the Birchen pattern seen on Modern Game, were made by Captain Ellis Duckworth, of Merriewood, New Dome Wood, Copthorne, Sussex, and were recognized by the PCGB Council in 1948. It is believed he started with a Light Sussex × Silver Pencilled Wyandotte mating, but no details have been found to clarify why he made them, or if their eventual pattern was the pattern he intended.

UTILITY SUSSEX

Poultry showing and poultry farming were clearly parting company during the 1930s, a process which was completed when pure breeds and first crosses were replaced by hybrids. This division was most visible with Sussex and the Rhode Island Reds. There were soon clearly different exhibition and utility types of both, with the utility types being considerably smaller than the exhibition types, and their colour and markings were well below the quality exhibitors were used to. These strains had, of course, been developed by farmers for producing sex-linked crossbred laying pullets. It was becoming known that you didn't need large birds to get large eggs. Indeed smaller

Light Sussex, bantam female. Photo: John Tarren

birds were more economical because less food was needed for body maintenance. One can understand why Edward Brown did not foresee how the industry would develop back in 1929 but, amazingly, some stalwarts in the Sussex Club still didn't understand what was going on in the 1950s. At the AGM in October 1951, Mr G.W. Barker 'deplored the types that he had seen at laying trials and he considered that the Sussex standards were correct'. Club secretary L.F. Outram (also author of two books about Sussex) wrote in the 1952 *Yearbook*, 'I would like, however, to see the Sussex that are entrants at these trials a little more substantial in frame, they seem to impress me with narrowness across shoulder, after all breadth and depth of body is an essential characteristic of a true Sussex'. Two other contributors to the yearbook, K.J.G. Hawkey and E.W. Tresidder were more in touch with the emerging realities of breeding for commercial egg production, but even they do not seem to have foreseen the complete separation of the egg

Buff Sussex, bantam female.
Photo: John Tarren

CHAPTER 34

Welsummer/Welsumer

The name Welsummer has been adopted in English speaking countries, although its original name, Welsumer, is still used in the Netherlands, Belgium, Germany and all other countries in mainland Europe. It has probably grown since then, but when breed was established, Welsum was a small village consisting of a church, a school and a few houses and farms. It is near the town of Deventer, to the east of Barneveld (*see* Chapter 8). Breeders in the nearby villages of Olst, Twello and Wijhe were also involved. The 'Welsumer' spelling is used in this chapter where the text refers to events in Germany or the Netherlands.

Welsumers gradually developed from cross-bred chickens bred to lay dark brown eggs, no one caring much what the birds looked like for the first twenty years from 1880 to 1900. Dark brown egg genes came from Langshans imported from China by Major Croad in Sussex in 1872, so it would have been a few years before they reached the Netherlands. Langshans laid particularly dark brown eggs, but Brahmas, Cochins and Malays were used as well. Poultry keepers in this area were fond of buying any novel cockerel to run with their assorted farmyard hens if they thought it would improve their flock. The poultry of the area were still a varied lot in 1900, some showing Malay ancestry by their long legs and neck, some with Asiatic Partridge markings (as Partridge Cochin females), and quite a lot carried the blue gene (Blue-Partridge, Blue-Wheatens, and so on). Protoype Barnevelders were also added to the mix. The only consistent factor was the large dark brown eggs the hens laid, which almost proved to be their downfall. Few, if any, of these breeders had incubators, so they had to wait until hens went broody. By mid-spring, the hens which had started to lay earlier in the season, those which laid most in the year as whole, were laying lighter coloured eggs. The hens laying dark brown eggs in April/May had only just started laying. Average egg numbers per bird per year was rapidly declining.

Between 1910 and 1913 the breed seems to have been rescued by two breeders, Mr Krudde, an egg dealer from Deventer, and A. Voorhorst, a farmer's son who was training to be a teacher, from Welsum. Mr Krudde crossed 'prototype Welsumers' with imported Rhode Island Reds, which improved egg numbers and uniformity of appearance (thereby establishing them as distinctly different from Barnevelders), but temporarily ruined eggshell colour. Brown Leghorns had also been used by someone (not recorded) in the area, which helped to establish their plumage colour and pattern, reduce size (to make them food-efficient layers), but also at the expense of egg colour. A. Voorhorst seems to have concentrated on the two aspects of eggshell colour and uniformity of plumage colour and pattern.

Then came the First World War. The part Rhode type of Mr Krudde probably survived fairly well, their increased egg production being useful during times of food shortages. A. Voorhorst only had a dozen or so birds left in 1918, so had to hatch as many as he could in 1919 and 1920. The new breed, if it was uniform enough to qualify as such, was due to be launched at the first World Poultry Congress at The Hague/Den Haag in 1921. Birds were exhibited there, followed by the first attempts to produce a breed standard in 1922–3, and then by the formation of a breed club in 1927. They started to be spread around Europe, to Germany in 1925 and England in 1927.

WELSUMMERS IN THE UK

It is not known for sure when they were first imported into the UK, or why the extra *m* was added to the name, but they were launched onto the British poultry scene in 1928. Several British breeders imported stock, with J. Mantel, of Soesterburg, advertising in *Poultry World* magazine from The Netherlands. Lytham Show, Lancashire, was the first to provide classes for Welsummers, and the British Welsummer Society was formed there. Its Secretary was W. Ward, of 37 Lorne Street, Lytham, and the Vice-President was Mrs Audrey M. Pape, initially of 6 Connaught Court, Connaught Street, London W2 and Heath Lodge, Newmarket, Suffolk, later moving to Shrewton House, Shrewton,

Wiltshire. Mrs Pape was Australian, and the daughter of George Chirnside, Werribee Park, Werribee, Victoria, Australia, a leading figure in the development of Australorps. It is believed she moved to England about 1925.

The small group of initial members did their best to promote Welsummers, following their display in Lancashire with another display, six males and ten females, at South Molton Show in Devon in early November of 1928. Later in the same month, two classes were provided for Welsummers at the Crystal Palace Show, where W. Powell-Owen had to judge eleven cockerels and seventeen pullets. He complained that the 'standard' he was provided with to judge these classes was too vague, essentially telling him to look for a darker coloured, red lobed, plumper version of Brown Leghorns. The breast colour of males ranged from completely black, via various mixtures, to completely red-brown.

If there was any agreement at all, it was to avoid solid black breasts, as these would encourage breeders to cross with Brown Leghorns, which would obviously ruin their egg colour. Dutch breeders had not already produced a detailed standard – they were not interested in showing. This attitude would not do in the UK, where even commercial poultry farmers still expected their stock to look like 'proper pure breeds'. Powell-Owen helped to write a more detailed standard, which was accepted by the Welsummer Society at a meeting at the Crystal Palace Show in November 1929.

In 1930 the Welsummer Society was replaced by the Welsummer Club. It is not clear if it was a completely new organization, or a simple change of name, or something in between. Former Vice-President, Mrs Pape, became the new secretary, so there was obviously not a complete change of personnel. However, there had been a lot of criticism about the vague breed standard (even the revised version) and the continuing considerable variation in the birds bred and shown. Despite all this, the club (or clubs) continued to attract members:

Welsummer, large male. Photo: John Tarren

Welsummer, large female. Photo: John Tarren

Barnevelders were classified, but the PCGB only offered two choices, light or heavy. Most of the birds brought over to the UK in 1927–29 were relatively modest in size, evidence of the Brown Leghorns also used to make them, which partially explains why the Society chose 'light'. However, they did not really stay light breeds. They have been at least the same size as Barnevelders and Marans, both officially heavy breeds, since the 1950s.

Despite their many qualities, Welsummers suffered a long period of neglect by poultry keepers generally for several decades. The Club had about 200 members in 1932, and it had 200 members again in 2000, but in 1972 it was down to just nine paid-up members. The Welsummer Club's Annual Shows at Olympia in 1954 had 47 large and 25 bantams (*see* below), down to 25 large and 15 bantams in 1962.

Welsummers are now (2008) one of the most popular pure breeds among hobbyists. They are still officially light breeds, despite many Welsummers now being bigger and heavier than most Barnevelders and Marans.

WELSUMMER/WELSUMER BANTAM

Although the large breed originated in the Netherlands, Welsummer Bantams were first made in England, with another strain, made independently, rapidly following in Germany. Dutch fanciers took them up about 1950, presumably by importing English and German strains. The first recorded Welsummer Bantam, a pullet (exhibitor's name not found), was entered in the 1930 Bradford Bantam Show.

Welsummer Bantams did not lay brown eggs at first, an inevitable result when undersized large Welsummers are crossed with other bantams, in this case Black-Red/Partridge OEG, Rhode Island Red and Partridge Wyandotte. Various combinations of these breeds would easily produce birds which looked like miniature Welsummers, but

50+ in January 1929, 135 in January 1930 and over 200 by November 1931.

Criticism about the show standard did not stop, so the Welsummer Club held another meeting at Crystal Palace in July 1930, during the World Poultry Congress. After everyone voiced their grievances, a sub-committee was formed, which produced another breed standard, which was provisionally accepted at the Crystal Palace Show in November. The Welsumer standard in the Netherlands standard still allowed at lot of colour variation, so wasn't much help. After allowing a year for everyone to study the standard in detail, resulting in a change in the female neck hackle description, the standard was finally adopted in 1932.

The original Welsummer Society had requested that the PCGB put their new breed in the light breeds section, which has been a matter of debate ever since. For most of their history, Welsummers have been roughly the same size as their close relations, Barnevelders, and not very different in size from Marans, both of which are in the heavy breed section. The Dutch National Poultry Club also had a medium section, in which Welsumers and recovering the dark brown eggs would take a lot of selective breeding.

Classes for bantams were included in the Welsummer Club's annual show at Crystal Palace for the first time in 1933, where five males and six females were entered. The exhibitors were Mr Belbin, Mr Bines, F.E. Entwisle and the partnership of Messrs Thompson and Athen. Mr Belbin won both classes, probably because of the birds' small size, as the male was criticized for looking too much like a single-combed Partridge Wyandotte Bantam, and his female showed obvious OEG ancestry. Mr Entwisle's and Mr Bines' birds looked more like Welsummers, but were rather too big to be credible bantams. They were gradually improved, but did not become really good, or popular, until the late 1960s.

Paul Wagner, of Altenburg im Ostzipfel Thüringens, started his breeding programme about 1930, but was stopped by the Second World War. New strains were made in the 1950s, mostly using undersized large fowl and Rhode Island Red Bantams. They rapidly became extraordinarily popular in both East and West Germany during the 1950s and 1960s. Welsumer Bantams, and other utility bantam breeds, fitted perfectly into the allotments rented by millions of city-dwelling Germans, East and West, in the post-war period. Entries of 200 or more Welsumer Bantams regularly appeared at major shows in both parts of Germany then, numbers that are still seen today. The record number of Welsumer Bantams at a show was an amazing 510 at the 1995 National Poultry Show at Nürnberg.

Welsummer Bantams have never achieved this level of popularity in the UK, but about fifty have been on display at the major shows.

WELSUMMER/WELSUMER DESCRIPTION

The British Welsummer Club has not revised its standard since 1932, which is unfortunate as the breed was still in its infancy then, both in the UK and in the Netherlands. Since the breed has stabilized, several details have not

Welsummer, bantam female. Photo: John Tarren

Duckwing Welsummer, bantam male. Photo: John Tarren

turned out as the pioneers expected. W. Powell-Owen admitted in his book *The Welsummer* (1932) that there were still many differences of opinion and a lot of variation in the birds existing then. He was on the club's committee and helped write the standard.

It is assumed that readers will have a copy of *British Poultry Standards* (if not, buy one!), so this part of the chapter will simply highlight differences between the 1932 standard and the 2008 reality.

Carriage, it says, should be 'upright, alert and active'; alert and active – yes, upright – no. When standing normally, the back should be approximately horizontal.

As for type, this part is still accurate. To explain the apparent length of back (in most breeds more defined by the formation of neck and lower back/tail plumage than the actual length of the back), remember that two of the breeds involved in creating them were prototype Barnevelders and Rhode Island Reds. The back of a Welsummer should be fairly long and flat (as Rhode Island Reds), although slightly shorter, and with higher tail carriage, from the Barnevelders.

The comb should be single, straight and upright, perhaps slightly over at the rear on laying females. It remains important for the comb to be not more than 'medium size', as there should be no tendency to Leghorn type heads.

The main plumage colour variety is sometimes called 'Red-Partridge', to indicate that while being roughly a Black-Red/Partridge, there are differences from other breeds.

Red-Partridge Males have the following colour: the neck hackle, back, shoulders and saddle hackle are various shades of golden-brown and red-brown – *see* the photos. There is some indistinct black neck striping in the lower neck feathers, mostly out of sight near the roots. The breast, belly and thighs should be predominantly black with irregular red-brown markings. 'Irregular' markings were considered important in the 1930s because Welsummer Club officials did not want show judges and exhibitors to select for specific

markings or start double mating. Welsummers were to remain a utility breed.

British Standards state that Red-Partridge females have 'Hackle golden-brown or copper, the lower feathers with black striping and golden shaft'. Today the striping goes well up the neck, but is very indistinct, still with a bright gold shaft. There is a band of darker feathers around the edge of the facial skin, down the front of the neck, which then merges into the rich chestnut-red breast. The back, wings and two top/central tail feathers are warm brown with very fine black peppering and bright, light gold shafts. Common faults to be avoided include:

- ground colour yellow or olive-green tinge instead of warm brown
- peppering tending to form a pattern, as Asiatic Partridge
- gold lacing on feather edges.

The standard says, 'Wing bar chestnut-brown', which implies part of the wing should be this colour, without peppering or golden shafts. In reality, some wing feathers this colour are tolerated rather than required. If there are no plain chestnut wing feathers at all, the peppered wing markings usually spread down to the breast and belly, which should be clear chestnut-red.

Silver Welsummer is a very rare silver version of the above pattern.

Golden Welsumer are only bred in Germany (hence 'Welsumer'), and are rare there. Males have bright yellow-gold neck and saddle hackles. Females of Silvers and Golds are similar, a darker shaded version of the Silver Duckwing pattern as seen on OEG.

Crele Welsummers effectively exist, but are standardized as a separate breed, the Welbar, one of the autosexing breeds; *see* the companion volume *Rare Poultry Breeds*.

The eye colour is 'red'; orange is acceptable, yellow is not.

The legs and feet are 'yellow'. They usually (especially females) have some darker shading.

'Ideal Silver Wyandottes'. Originally a free gift with Feathered World *magazine, 15 November 1895. Artist: A.F. Lydon*

CHAPTER 35

Wyandotte

The first variety of Wyandotte, large Silver Laced, was recognized by the American Poultry Association in 1883. Several breeders had roughly the same idea, to create a practical dual-purpose breed with the pretty laced pattern which then only existed on Sebright Bantams and Laced Polands. Spangled Hamburghs were also used, as many had half-moon spangles, tending towards lacing, as now seen on Derbyshire Redcaps. There were plenty of wealthy 'gentlemen farmers' in nineteenth-century America, in the eastern states at least, and they would appreciate a flock of ornamental chickens running out on the lawn in front of their grand houses as do their twenty-first-century equivalents today.

These breeders were all working independently, however, so all these 'prototypes' differed in details such as comb type and whether they had feathered feet or not. They all agreed on the laced plumage pattern, medium/large size and yellow skin/shanks – already established as the preferred colour of plucked table chickens in America. A lot of names had been invented for these broadly similar 'new breeds', either by individuals or small groups working together.

AMERICAN SEABRIGHT

This was the spelling of Sebright used. Mr L.W. Whittaker, of North Adams, Michigan, developed these. They had rose combs and clean (not feathered) legs, so were essentially the same as the eventual Wyandottes. He had an engraving made of the type and pattern he was aiming for in 1872, although such birds probably did not exist then. This picture was useful in the long term, as all the other breeders eventually agreed on it.

EUREKA

Mr Kidder, of Northampton (NY?) had a strain of silver laced birds with pea combs and feathered shanks/feet bred from an initial Dark Brahma × Spangled Hamburgh mating.

HAMBLETONIAN

Isaac K. Felch, of Natick, Massachusetts made this prototype Wyandotte. They may have had rose combs and clean legs as Mr Felch was involved in writing a provisional standard.

ONEIDA COUNTY FOWL

Mr Payne, of Binghampton, New York, had his prototype laced fowls as early as 1866, so may have started to breed them before the Civil War.

SEABRIGHT COCHIN

Again, this was the spelling of Sebright used. A.S. Baker, Rev. Benson and John P. Ray, all of New York State, co-operated to produce this strain, possibly starting as early as 1864. Details of which breeds and matings, and who did what and when, are confused, as the three breeders seem to have argued later. The 1905, American edition of Harrison Weir's *Poultry Book* has a completely revised Wyandotte chapter by T.E. Orr, of Pennsylvania. Mr Orr was also involved in the development of the breed, and his chapter includes extensive coverage of the arguments between rival breeders.

Hambrights, Excelsiors, Columbians and Sebright Brahmas were also mentioned by Mr Orr in his Wyandotte chapter, but no further details of these strains have been found.

The American Poultry Association held a meeting at Buffalo in 1877, at which Mr Kidder, Mr Payne and Mr Whittaker and their rival groups of supporters all applied for their respective breeds to be recognized. Mr Felch also attended this meeting, but it is not certain if he brought any of his birds to the meeting. The APA wisely told them all to go away and sort themselves out – they were only going to accept one large laced breed.

All of these breeders lived in the north-western states, where winters are long and very cold. This fact helped them to agree on the compact form of rose comb. Clean shanks were more practical than feathered shanks. The name was suggested by Fred A. Houdlette, of Waltham, Massachusetts. They were said to be named after the Wyandotte/Wendot Native Americans. (This was the name Hurons actually called themselves. The Huron name was invented by French settlers in Canada, which the tribe was perfectly aware was based on an insult.) It was also the name of a ship owned by Fred Houdlette's father. The new breed, with its new compromise name, was finally accepted by the AFA in February 1883.

At this stage, they still did not match up to the picture. The breast feathering of males was mostly black, their 'lacing' being little more than small white centres to each feather. Females had much better breast lacing, but the centres of most feathers on their back and wings had a lot of fine black peppering.

As soon as they were standardized, some Silver Laced Wyandottes were sent to England,

to Mr J. Pilling, of Woodside Farm, Ashton, near Chester to be exact. He bred and sold some, the first known UK exhibitor being Tom C. Heath at the 1884 Staffordshire Show, then the 1885 Birmingham and Crystal Palace Shows. Mr Heath lived at Keele Home Farm, Keele, Stafford, now part of the University grounds.

Brothers W. Allen Spencer (1858–1929) and Richard F. Spencer (1864–1937) of Chelmscote, Warwickshire started with Wyandottes in 1886, and concentrated on breeding perfectly marked birds, especially males. They realized that double mating, with separate 'cock-breeder' and 'pullet-breeder' strains would be needed for consistent success. They were followed by Arthur J. Spencer (1901–1988), and then by his daughter, now Mrs Margot Haines, who still breeds Laced Wyandottes. Some time later (*circa* 1910?) Fred Houdlette visited the Spencer family on a trip to England, and was said to greatly admire their stock, but other American breeders were not so complimentary. In his 1908 book, *Wyandottes in Colors*, Theo. Hewes said,

> While the breed is American in origin, it was the English breeders who first got the open centers fixed, [that is, mostly white feathers with fine black lacing, not mostly black feathers with small white centres] but what they did to shape in getting the color was awful. The open-center birds imported from England resembled a cross between a crane and an ostrich.

Apparently stock from England, probably the Spencers', had been shipped back to America about 1900, where they were crossed with local strains in an effort to produce birds with the size and type of the best American strains and the clear lacing of English stock. Writing in the 1915 *Feathered World Yearbook*, J.H. Brooksbank agreed that British breeders of Wyandottes, especially the Laced varieties, had produced birds with excellent markings, but 'are far too long on leg'. American breeders would have imported British strains

Silver Laced Wyandottes, pullet-breeders and cockerel-breeders. Originally a free gift with Feathered World *magazine, 20 November 1908. Artist: A.F. Lydon*

for their superior lacing, but didn't because of their poor type.

Silver Laced Wyandotte males had been standardized with a clear white back and shoulders, which was genetically inconsistent with perfect lacing on the back and wings of females. The Spencer family was the first to discover that exhibition males came from hens with imperfect back and wing markings, whereas perfect laced hens came from males with laced shoulders, some of which were actually hen-feathered.

GOLD LACED WYANDOTTE

There were others, but the main pioneer strain of Gold Laced Wyandottes were originally called Winnebago Fowl, and were developed in Winnebago County, Wisconsin, an area which had previously been the home of the Winnebago tribe of Native Americans before they had been killed or driven west by white settlers. Joseph McKeen, of Winnebago Poultry Farm, Omro, was the main, but not only, breeder of the variety. Winnebago Fowls were kept by many farms in the county and surrounding areas, including part of Illinois. They had been bred from Buff Cochins, Partridge Cochins, rose-

Gold Laced Wyandottes, pullet-breeders and cockerel-breeders. Originally a free gift with Feathered World *magazine, 19 November 1909. Artist: A.F. Lydon*

combed Brown Leghorns and other unknown chickens. The resulting birds were not very uniform, although most were generally some shade from buff to brown, with variable, laced or pencilled markings. Mr McKeen crossed his Winnebagos with American Sebrights he bought from Mr Whittaker as hatching eggs in 1879 to improve their lacing. When Silver Laced Wyandottes were standardized in 1883, and were getting a lot of publicity in poultry magazines, it was obvious that Winnebagos only needed a change of name to achieve similar instant fame. He first exhibited his new Gold Laced Wyandottes at the 1886 Chicago Show, where he sold a trio for $75, plus others for high prices.

Other breeders working along the same idea about 1880 included G.L. Buskirk, of Odell, Illinois; Jacob Ryder, of Waynesboro, Pennsylvania; and Mr W.E. Shedd, of Waltham, Massachusetts. Gold Laced Wyandottes were accepted by the APA in January 1888. Some were soon sent to England, Mr A. Geffcken of Southampton being the importer.

BLUE LACED WYANDOTTE AND BUFF LACED WYANDOTTE

These two varieties were first made by Ira C. Keller of Ohio, the Blue Laced originally being called Violet Laced or 'Violettes'. He started,

Buff Laced Wyandottes. Artist: Kurt Zander

probably about 1886, by crossing Gold Laced Wyandottes/Winnebagos with some white chicks which had appeared in hatches of Silver Laced Wyandottes. Mr Keller first showed his Buff Laced Wyandottes in New York in 1895. Charles Pond and a Mr Brackenbury also made these varieties, Mr Pond by matings similar to Mr Keller's, with Mr Brackenbury using White Wyandottes, Buff Cochins and a (as Andalusian) blue hen. Neither variety attracted interest in the USA, and were never standardized there.

Rev. John Crombleholme, of St Mary's, Clayton-le-Moors, Accrington, Lancashire imported stock from Mr Keller in 1897, which attracted a brief flurry of interest here, with

a separate Blue Laced Wyandotte Club for a few years (1905–1910?), with T.R. Grant, of Moseley, Birmingham as secretary, but both Blue Laced and Buff Laced soon became rare. A few of both varieties were shown in the UK during the 1920s and 1930s, which may have been Dutch or German imports, as are strains bred here since the 1960s.

WHITE-LACED BLACK WYANDOTTE

This was intended to be a reversed version of the Silver Laced pattern, but in reality they were over-laced Birchens, roughly similar to

Silver Sussex. They were made in England by Rev. J.W.A. Mackenzie, of Whitwick, near Leicester about 1905, with a second strain made independently in the Netherlands about 1920. F.J.S. Chatterton did an idealized painting of the intended variety, which never became a reality. The last mentions of them found at shows in the UK were in 1926 at Crystal Palace and 1927 at York.

WHITE WYANDOTTE

White chicks occasionally appeared among hatches of Silver Laced chicks throughout the 1870s, when Wyandottes were still at the prototype stage. Many breeders kept quiet about them because they detracted from the status of 'pure breed' which they were trying to promote. Others saw the potential of Whites as a new variety, especially as table birds, so began to promote and exhibit them. Prominent among these breeders were George W. Towle and B.M. Biggs, both of New York State, and Fred Houdlette and George Wooley, of Massachusetts. White Wyandottes were recognized by the APA at a meeting at Indianapolis in 1888.

For many years after 1888 comparatively few White Wyandottes were really pure snow-white, most having a few black specks and males were usually brassy. But at least there was no pattern to worry about, so breeders could concentrate on type, producing shorter-backed, shorter-legged, plumper-breasted and

White Wyandottes. Originally a free gift with Poultry *magazine, circa 1912. Artist: J.W. Ludlow*

generally more rounded Wyandottes than Laced or any of the later patterns. They were bred in large numbers in the eastern states as small/medium table birds – early broilers. Although layer type strains of White Wyandottes were developed in the UK during the 1920s and 1930s, they were never bred for laying (only as broiler-breeders in today's terms) in the USA. Commercial egg producers concentrated on White Leghorns, and anyway White Wyandotte pullets laid rather small eggs, and eggs from old Wyandotte hens were too round to fit in the egg cartons and trays of the time. The National White Wyandotte Club was formed in 1899, and had over 1,000 members by 1904.

No records have been found of exports of White Wyandottes from the USA to the UK, but they were exhibited at shows here from about 1890 onwards. They were almost certainly made here by crossing Silver Laced Wyandottes with White Dorkings, White Cochins or any other suitable white chickens. Despite their dubious origin, they attracted enough interest for a separate (from the United Wyandotte Club) White Wyandotte Club to be formed on 23 July 1903 at Tunbridge Wells. The club still exists today (2008). There were separate clubs for specific colour varieties of several breeds in the UK before 1940, but most have since cut down to a single club. There are still five clubs for colours of Wyandottes, however.

With no patterns to worry about, and White Orpingtons never really catching up with Blacks, Blues and Buffs for size, British fanciers adopted White Wyandottes as their favoured medium to compete in the 'who can breed and prepare the biggest, fluffiest, whitest chicken' stakes. Egg production, fertility and general usefulness as a practical breed suffered, although there were still enough competitors to fill classes at the major shows until the 1960s, when fewer people had the time or inclination to compete. At smaller local shows, the winning White Wyandotte would always be a contender for 'Best in Show', and the prize money and kudos which went with winning. This is still the case in 2008, but there are even fewer people with the time and expertise to exhibit them to perfection.

Poultry showing and poultry farming started to diverge in the 1920s, a division which was particularly evident with White Wyandottes, where very different 'exhibition type' and 'utility type' birds were developed. Utility type Whites were smaller, much tighter feathered, much better layers, and appeared to have a much longer back. Crosses with White Leghorns were said to have been involved. Despite some public appeals for both camps of breeders to return to an intermediate type, exhibiton and utility Whites continued along their differing paths until the 1950s, with the utility strains eventually being replaced by hybrid layers. Clem Shaw preserved his strain through to the 1990s, and a few other breeders are keeping it going. It is not known if the current breeders are continuing Mr Shaw's meticulous production recording methods.

PARTRIDGE AND SILVER PENCILLED WYANDOTTES

These two varieties have to be considered together as, despite their different names, they are gold and silver versions of the same pattern, the latter also being the same colour and markings as Dark Brahmas. Just as the original Wyandottes were made to have a practical farm chicken with the pretty lacing previously only seen on Sebrights or Polands, so Partridge and Silver Pencilled Wyandottes were made with the idea of having their pretty patterns without the troublesome feathered feet of Partridge Cochins or Dark Brahmas.

Joseph McKeen, the originator of Gold Laced Wyandottes, stated to work on a new Partridge variety about 1880. He was joined in this project by a neighbour, Mr E.O. Thiem, who later moved to Denison, Iowa. Mr McKeen died in 1896, and left his best birds to Mr Thiem in his will, the remainder being sold by his widow to Mr W.A. Doolittle, of Sabetha, Kansas. Mr Doolittle continued to work with Mr Thiem to improve this, the

Partridge Wyandottes. Originally a free gift with Feathered World *magazine, circa 1910. Artist: A.F. Lydon*

'western strain'. Mr Thiem had first exhibited the new 'Partridge Wyandottes' at the 1894 Midcontinental Show at Kansas City. Here he learnt, to his great surprise, that George H. Brackenbury and Ezra Cornell, both of New York State, had been working on identical 'Golden Pencilled Wyandottes' since 1889, later known as the 'eastern strain'.

Both strains had mainly been developed from Gold Laced Wyandotte (still in early stages, many having elements of partridge pattern instead of clear lacing) × Partridge Cochin matings, but other birds had been tried as well, in the case of McKeen/Thiem/Doolittle, including Dark Cornish. For a few years, perhaps until about 1900, the western strain was meatier and heavier than the fluffier, but better marked eastern strain (Brackenbury/

Cornell), but these differences gradually disappeared as stock was distributed and bred by others.

They were standardized as 'Partridge Wyandottes' (not 'Golden Pencilled') by the American Poultry Association at its meeting at Chicago in 1901, and a Partridge Wyandotte Club of America was formed about the same time.

Silver Pencilled Wyandottes were also made by Brackenbury and Cornell, which is no doubt why they were named as such. They would probably have been called 'Silver Partridge' if McKeen/Thiem/Doolittle had been involved. Brackenbury and Cornell had both kept both varieties, but Brackenbury had concentrated on Partridge (or 'Golden Pencilled' as he would have preferred) and Cornell concentrated on Silver Pencilleds. This was a slightly later project, so they started from half-made Partridge Wyandotte × Dark Brahma matings. Silver Laced Wyandottes and Silver Pencilled Hamburghs are believed to have been used at some stage as well. They were standardized by the AFA in 1902, and a National Silver Pencilled Wyandotte Club was formed in 1905, but still had only twenty-five members by 1912.

Partridge Wyandottes were bred in generally darker shades in America than later strains in the UK and most other countries. The darker American birds could be bred from a single strain, whereas very different cock- and pullet-breeder strains were essential elsewhere. Any brown/red in the breast of males would be much less noticeable in America, as would minor faults in the markings of females. Similar faults would be all too obvious on British strains.

John Wharton, of Honeycott Farm, Hawes, Yorkshire, read about Partridge Wyandottes in an American poultry magazine in 1894, probably the first birds shown by Mr Thiem at Kansas City. He wrote to all the original breeders, finally importing three males and eight females from Mr Thiem in December 1896. Mr Wharton's investment soon paid dividends; at the 1901 Crystal Palace Show he sold his class winning cockerel for £100 and three hens (one of which had won its class) for 100 guineas (£105) the lot. There were not many more transatlantic shipments of Partridge Wyandottes because of colour differences. Another British fancier, Mr Pettipher, of Banbury, Oxfordshire, made a strain of Partridge Wyandottes from scratch, not using any American birds. It is not known what he made them from, although Partridge Cochins must have been the main ingredient.

A Partridge Wyandotte Club was formed here in 1902 or 1903. It was successful at first, but declined during the 1930s, was suspended in 1939, and not re-activated until 1964. Progress was slow until Dr Clive Carefoot's period as secretary, 1967–75, when membership rose from 30 to 100. Most members by

White Wyandotte, large female. Photo: John Tarren

Blue Laced Wyandotte, large female. Photo: John Tarren

Silver Pencilled Wyandotte, large female. Photo: John Tarren

then kept bantams, so there are still (in 2008) few keeping large fowl, and they have a lot of work to do to restore their former quality. Their high point was probably York Show in 1912, with 130 large Partridge and 60 large Silver Pencilled Wyandottes.

Silver Pencilled Wyandottes wers also first imported by Mr Wharton, no doubt encouraged by all the money he was making out of his Partridge Wyandottes, in January 1901. A separate Silver Pencilled Wyandotte Club was formed (*circa* 1905?), but only lasted until 1914. Very few were seen at shows from 1920 until very recently, when fresh stock has been imported from Germany and the Netherlands.

Double mating is essential for Partridge and Silver Pencilled Wyandottes because correct to standard patterned females are a few genes different from correct to standard solid black breasted males. Spotted breasted males ('pullet-breeders') are needed to breed well marked females and very dark ('cock-breeder') females, almost devoid of markings, are needed to

produce black breasted males. The standards were written before genetics was understood, so no one realized that they were demanding the impossible from a single strain. Leading fanciers soon learnt how to breed winners, even though they didn't understand why, but they kept their knowledge secret. German fanciers were more open about all this, and in 1926 they divided cock- and pullet-breeders into separate varieties:

cock-breeder Partridge became Rebhuhnfarbig
pullet-breeder Partridge became Braungebändert
cock-breeder Silver Pencilled became Silberhalsig
pullet-breeder Silver Pencilled became Dunkel.

This change has helped their popularity, as the previous cock-breeder hens and pullet-breeder cocks can now be shown (there are standards for them) instead of having to be kept at home.

BLACK WYANDOTTE

Like the Whites, black chicks appeared in hatches of Silver Laced, plus, in this case, some hatches of Golds. These had been seen since the earliest stages of the breed's creation, but did not seem to have the same potential as Whites as a new standard variety. Two breeders who decided to do something with them were Mr F.M. Clements Jr of Ohio and Mr F.J. Marshall, initially also of Ohio, later moving to Georgia, both starting in 1885. Their first problem was that 'Black Wyandottes' were not completely black, having white in hackles and wings. They gradually improved their stock, exchanging cockerels to help each other. Black Wyandottes were standardized by the APA in 1893. Initially American fanciers concentrated on plumage colour, glossy greenish-black down to the skin, and accepted dark shading on their shanks. About 1930 there was a change of emphasis, more concentration on yellow shanks and an acceptance, on males at least, of some white undercolour. This appalled some purists, but made for a more attractive bird in general appearance, and the white undercolour made surplus cockerels better looking plucked table birds. Black Wyandottes were never popular with American farmers, but were kept by domestic poultry keepers in city suburbs. In the era of coal and steam black chickens stayed good looking, whereas white hens soon looked grubby.

Black Wyandottes were first seen in the UK about 1900. There may have been imports from the USA, but no details have been found. Arthur E. Ellett, of Waterfall Poultry Farm, Southgate, on the northern outskirts of London, made his own strain from an almost black chick hatched from Gold Laced bred with other overly dark Gold Laced. Another pioneer with the variety was Tom H. Furness, of Carlton House, Chesterfield, whose pair of winning birds was depicted in a *Feathered World* colour plate given with the issue of 15 November 1907.

As in America, Black Wyandottes were most popular with urban poultry keepers, but these were a much more significant group in crowded Britain. Although there was the disadvantage of double mating being necessary to produce solid black feathered birds with yellow shanks, there was only ever one type of Black Wyandotte, no separate 'exhibition' and 'utility' forms. Males with white undercolour were used as pullet-breeders and matt-black females with dark shanks were used as cock-breeders.

In 1909 six specialist Wyandotte clubs held a joint annual show at Cambridge. The entries give an indication of the relative popularities of the varieties then: Black 201, White 200, Gold and Silver Laced 124, Partridge 111, Columbian 87, Silver Pencilled 50: an amazing total of 773. This level of interest in Black Wyandottes could not continue, but the club's annual show still attracted between 80 and 100 birds during the 1920s and 1930s.

There are now (2008) very few UK fanciers with large Blacks, the Black Wyandotte Club

being kept going by bantam breeders. There are two very different types, neither of which are entirely satisfactory. German stock, which seem rather narrow bodied but do have nice bright yellow shanks and feet, and a much bigger (too fluffy?) strain which usually have rather dark shanks, probably part Black Orpington. A cross might produce birds with the best features of both. This allows some latitude on undercolour of males.

BUFF WYANDOTTE

Mr E.O. Thiem of Iowa, one of the Partridge Wyandotte originators, was also involved with making Buffs. Prototype Partridge and Gold Laced Wyandottes, Buff Cochins and prototype Rhode Island Reds (then 'Golden Buffs') were used to make them. Buff Plymouth Rocks were being made at the same time from a similar mix. Some Buff Wyandottes and Buff Rocks may have been siblings, named according to comb type. The main problem was obtaining an even buff colour, most being either too dark with black markings or too light with white peppering. Despite these problems, Buff Wyandottes were standardized by the APA in 1893. The American Buff Wyandotte Club was formed in 1898, and had about 400 members by 1912. It did not last, however, and they had dramatically declined by the 1930s.

Some American Buff Wyandottes were exported to the UK and entered in the 1893 Liverpool Show. No one here thought they were very good, and some British fanciers were already making their own strains from scratch, which were a better colour. John Wharton, the Partridge and Silver Pencilled importer, had started to make some from a Silver Laced Wyandotte × Buff Cochin mating because he thought the American birds too red. A pair owned by John Moore was depicted in a *Feathered World* print in 1898. Michael Harrison, of Shaw House, Head's Neck, Carlisle tried to form a Buff Wyandotte Club in 1914, but the First World War delayed its formation until 1920. Unfortunately he died shortly afterwards, the club's administration being continued by his widow and son Edward until 1939. The first club show at Newburn on Tyne in 1920 had forty birds entered, but it was downhill from there. The Club may have been listed until 1939, but does not appear to have been active after 1927. A fancier in Yorkshire made some Buff Wyandottes in the 1970s, but they soon died out. There are only two significant breeders of them in the Netherlands, who have helped Grant Brereton and others revive them in the UK since 2000.

COLUMBIAN WYANDOTTE

This plumage pattern, called 'Light' in Brahmas and Sussex, gained its name from the first display of 'Columbian Wyandottes' at the Columbian Exposition, or World's Trade Fair at Chicago in 1893, held to celebrate the 400th Anniversary of the Discovery of America by Christopher Columbus. It has been adopted as the scientific name for the pattern, the gene responsible being assigned the notation Co.

The first were bred, probably by accident, by Rev. B.M. Briggs, of New York State from a cross between White Wyandottes and Barred Plymouth Rocks. Mr W.B. Richardson, of Knightsville, Rhode Island, worked to improve their markings using Light Brahma crosses. Theo. Hewes (author of *Wyandottes in Colors*, USA, 1908) and E.O. Thiem helped to improve them. They were very popular for a few years; the National Columbian Wyandotte Club formed in 1906 and had about 400 members by 1912, but the interest didn't last, and they were already declining by 1920.

They were soon exported to the UK, with a Columbian Wyandotte Club being well established here as well by 1909. Its 1910 show at Cambridge had an impressive entry of 87 birds. Colour and markings took a few years to stabilize, initially ranging from almost white birds, with poor neck striping, to over-marked birds with dark undercolour which showed on the surface. Grey undercolour had to stay to ensure correct markings, but didn't show on show winners. When White Wyandottes diverged into fluffy exhibition and tight feathered utility types, the Columbian enthusiasts were determined not to allow a similar division to happen in their favourites, so stuck to an ideal type which was smaller and more halfway between these extremes.

The Columbian Wyandotte Club had a run of very successful annual shows, declining during the 1930s: 1911 Leeds, 83 birds; 1912 Leeds, 109; 1919 Manchester, 148; 1920 Bristol, 273; 1921 Birmingham, 241; 1927 Mansfield, 171; 1933 Birmingham, 46; 1934 York, 52.

There may not have been a single large Columbian Wyandotte exhibited at a UK show from 1950 to 2000, but a few are appearing again, as a result of imports from Germany and the Netherlands and some creative breeding by a few young enthusiasts.

BLUE WYANDOTTE

Blue Wyandottes were not made in America, instead being created by British and German fanciers. They first appeared at UK shows about 1905, possibly made by H.C. Ardron, of The Fosse, Syston, Leicester, the first secretary of the Blue Wyandotte Club in 1906.

They held a few impressive shows, the entries found being: 1910 Leeds, 54; 1911 Leeds, 83; 1912 Wolverhampton, 80; 1913 Liverpool, 93; 1914 Leeds, 104; 1915/16 (31 Dec and 1 Jan) Mossley, 74; 1920 High Wycombe, 76.

The club collapsed in 1921, for reasons unknown. Since then a few have been seen at UK shows from time to time, but it is difficult to breed good Blues. They should not have Andalusian type lacing, the females ideally being very evenly coloured, as are males, apart from their glossy blue-black neck, back and saddle plumage.

SPANGLED (BLACK-MOTTLE) WYANDOTTE

A few Black-Mottles, then called Spangles, were shown at Crystal Palace and elsewhere *circa* 1908–14; Rev. Mackenzie, Mr Archer and Miss Murrey were the known exhibitors. Since then, this colour variety has only been represented by bantams, although a few large Black-Mottles may have been shown in Germany. A class of eleven birds at the 1913 London Dairy Show was probably their highpoint at shows here.

BARRED WYANDOTTE

A pair of Cuckoo (coarsely barred) Wyandottes were entered in the 1897 London Dairy Show, but no more was heard of them in the UK until 1925. Barred Wyandottes were never bred in America. Barred Wyandottes were made in Germany, circa 1900–08, from Black Wyandottes, Barred Rocks and Dominiques, where they became the third most popular variety, after Blacks and Whites. There was a brief flurry of interest in the UK from 1925 to 1933, with a short-lived Barred Wyandotte Club being formed in 1930. They were standardized by the PCGB on 14 January 1927, but they probably died out by 1939. There were new imports *circa* 2000. These are difficult to breed with both good sharp barring and good rounded type and large size; they tend to be either well barred and small or big but fuzzy.

RED WYANDOTTE

Many early Rhode Island Reds had rose combs, and some of these were almost certainly entered in American shows as 'Red Wyandottes' between 1883 (when Laced Wyandottes were standardized) and 1904 (when Rhode Island Reds were standardized). After then, any similar birds were called rose-combed Rhode Island Reds in America. A few British fanciers, including the Rev. Mackenzie, bred and exhibited Red Wyandottes *circa* 1910–14, which then died out. Red Wyandotte Bantams exist now in the UK, Germany and the Netherlands, but no large ones.

PILE WYANDOTTE

Arthur E. Ellett, of Waterfall Poultry Farm, Southgate, then on the northern outskirts of

London, made Pile Wyandottes *circa* 1900–10 from Partridge × White crosses, with Gold Laced added later. He intended Pile females to be a similar colour to Pile Game, with a yellow neck, salmon breast and white back and wings. This was genetically impossible from the Wyandottes he used, and a cross of Pile Game, or Pile anything else with the required female pattern would have ruined breed type as all potential breeds have the wrong type. They died out by 1918. Grant Brereton started to make a strain about 2002 with Partridge Wyandotte × Pile Leghorn matings. By 2008 he had made excellent progress, particularly with males, but still has a way to go. Big bodied females with the desired pattern will be difficult, perhaps impossible to breed.

WYANDOTTE BANTAM

J.F. Entwisle continued his father's tradition of making bantam versions of large breeds by producing the world's first Wyandotte Bantams in Yorkshire, although they started by accident. A Partridge Modern Game Bantam hen flew over a ten foot high garden wall, and was mated in the adjoining stable yard by a Dark Brahma Bantam cock. This resulted in two pullets with pea combs, of roughly Duckwing colour and pattern, and near enough to Wyandotte shape to give Mr Entwisle the idea using them to start a new project. Exact dates are not known, but this probably happened in 1895 or 1896. Mr Wharton and Mr Moore (see large Partridge, Silver Pencilled and Buff Wyandotte histories) were consulted, with both sending their smallest (large fowl) Partridge and Silver Pencilleds for the next stage. He was successfully showing both varieties of Wyandotte Bantams in AOV Bantam classes in local shows by 1902. In the same year he also won first prize in the AOV Bantam female class at Crystal Palace Show, with a White pullet which appeared in a batch of Partridge chicks (many carry the recessive white gene). Another friend, Mr Sugden of Kildwick, gave him a suitable crossbred (White Japanese × White Silkie) cockerel for him to start a strain. He started making Blacks from

Wyandotte Bantams. Originally a free gift with Feathered World *magazine, circa 1913. Artist: A.F. Lydon*

Black Pekin × Black Rosecomb crossbreds, and Columbians from a Black-tailed White Japanese × Silver Pencilled Wyandotte Bantam (which were established by then) mating. Black-Mottles (then usually called Spangles) and Cuckoos/Barreds (name dependent on clarity of barring) came by accident as he was refining Blacks and Whites. Entwisle referred to a Mr Grant who made all four Laced colour varieties, he thought by crossing Indian Game Bantams with various crossbreds, coloured as required for each project. Other fanciers in the UK, USA and Germany then followed independently, adopting one of two basic methods. Some started with undersized large Wyandottes of whichever colour variety was applicable, and then looked around for suitable bantams to cross them with. Others just used a mixture of

bantams, usually including some Brahmas or Cochins/Pekins to get the general body shape, and something with a rose comb and clean (not feathered) legs. Pringle Proud reported a new, improved strain of Black Wyandotte Bantams had appeared at the shows in 1907, which had been made from Silver Pencilled Wyandotte Bantams and Black Plymouth Rock Bantams bred from Barreds.

Wyandotte Bantams, edited by F.P. Jeffrey, published by the American Bantam Association in 1984, gave some details on their initial development in America. George Fitterer had been in contact with J.F. Entwisle about 1910, and tried a mating between an undersized large White Wyandotte cockerel and White Cochin Bantams, but unfortunately the resulting youngsters all died, and he never tried again.

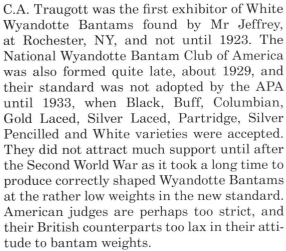

Buff Laced Wyandotte, bantam male. Photo: John Tarren

Columbian Wyandotte, bantam female. Photo: John Tarren

C.A. Traugott was the first exhibitor of White Wyandotte Bantams found by Mr Jeffrey, at Rochester, NY, and not until 1923. The National Wyandotte Bantam Club of America was also formed quite late, about 1929, and their standard was not adopted by the APA until 1933, when Black, Buff, Columbian, Gold Laced, Silver Laced, Partridge, Silver Pencilled and White varieties were accepted. They did not attract much support until after the Second World War as it took a long time to produce correctly shaped Wyandotte Bantams at the rather low weights in the new standard. American judges are perhaps too strict, and their British counterparts too lax in their attitude to bantam weights.

None of the UK Wyandotte Clubs were interested in the bantam version at first, so a United Wyandotte Bantam Club was formed at a meeting on 1 July 1916 at the Royal Show, held at Manchester that year. (The Royal Show moved about then, as this was before its permanent site at Stoneleigh.) The Columbian

Wyandotte Club was the first large fowl club to cater for bantams in 1917, with the Black and Partridge Clubs following in 1925. The Laced Club did not cover bantams until 1946, possibly because there were very few Laced Wyandotte Bantams before then. From 1916 until 1939 the most popular colours in bantams were White, Partridge, Columbian and Black, with modest numbers of Silver Pencilled and Blue. Even rarer, but seen from time to time, were all four Laced varieties, Barred/Cuckoo, Pile, Buff Columbian, Spangle (Black-Mottle), Pile and Duckwing.

Wyandotte Bantams rapidly became popular, as indicated by entries in the Wyandotte Bantam Club's Shows, in 1920 there were 271 at Ripley, and in 1921, at Bradford, 227. However, type remained poor, most being far too slender in general build, with oversized combs, white in lobes, long wings carried too low and low tail carriage. Exhibitors regularly bent wing and tail feathers to make them look better, or pulled out their main tail feathers to

Black Wyandotte, bantam male. Photo: John Tarren

Buff Wyandotte, bantam male. Photo: John Tarren

leave the tail coverts as 'the tail'. Perhaps the large fowl Wyandotte Clubs didn't want to be associated with such poor birds.

German fanciers seemed to make much more progress, as was shown to the British in a feature in the 1930 *Poultry World Annual*, which included photos of two beautiful Barred Bantam pullets bred by Richard Gunther of Leipzig which were decades ahead of any Wyandotte Bantams in the UK in their combination of large fowl type in bantam size. The lesson was not learnt here; Wyandotte Bantams changed from being nice and small, but of terrible type in the 1920s, to a range of types according to variety in the 1950s and 1960s. Whites were, and still are, too big and too fluffy; Laceds and Partridge/Pencilleds became beautifully marked, but too tall and narrow. Blacks and Columbians achieved a better balance.

British fanciers started to visit German and Dutch shows in the 1970s, which resulted in importations of Barreds, Blue Laced, Buff Laced, and eventually many more new colours, as well as fresh strains of varieties already established here – except Whites. Breeders of the patterned varieties recognized that they needed to improve body shape rather than just concentrate on markings all the time, and have made a lot of progress by crossing British, Dutch and German strains, followed by further selective breeding, but UK White Wyandotte fanciers seem convinced that they are right and everyone else is wrong, continuing with their big fluffy type. White Wyandottes in Germany and the Netherlands are the same shape as all other varieties, although one could reasonably argue that all German Wyandottes are rather too tall and narrow. However, they are extremely popular; it is not unusual to see over 300 large and 1,000 bantam Wyandottes at major German shows!

Several new colour varieties have been made since 1990, including Blue-Partridge,

Partridge Wyandotte Bantams, exhibition male and cock-breeder females. Photo: John Tarren

Blue-Silver Pencilled, Blue-Silver Laced, Blue-Columbian, Blue-Buff Columbian, Salmon (as Faverolles), Red and Red Spangled (Red-Millefleurs). The late Clive Carefoot made Chocolate Partridge Wyandotte Bantams, although there were only two cockerels, and they died. They were a sideline from a Chocolate Orpington project, one of which was passed on to Rob Boyd before ill health forced Clive to give up poultry breeding. Rob managed to build up a strain of Chocolate Orpingtons by crossing with Blacks, some of which were passed on to Wyandotte enthusiasts Grant Brereton and Richard Davies who started (in 2005?) to remake Chocolate Partridge Wyandottes and start self Chocolate and Chocolate/Gold Laced varieties.

Reds are excellent, but some of the others are still at the prototype stage. Blue-Partridge males are beautiful, at least those with solid blue breasts are. Blue-Partridge females are well behind normal Partridge females in precision of markings, so it might be best to concentrate on proper cock-breeder strains. Salmon females are a beautiful mixture of creamy shades, much prettier than males. The markings on Blue-Silver Laced and Blue-Silver Pencilled are rather faded and blurry at present (2008). It will be interesting to see how much improvement is possible.

It would take too much space to fully describe Wyandottes, partly because they vary so much between varieties and from country to country. Fanciers could learn a lot by comparing their own national Wyandotte standard with those of other countries.

Just to take comb shape as an example, all standards actually require a compact rose comb with the top surface covered in 'workings' (papillae in scientific terminology) and

Partridge Wyandotte Bantams, pullet-breeder male and exhibition females. Photo: John Tarren

the leader (rear spike) to follow the surface of the skull. Some strains, especially in the UK, are rather too large and coarse, whereas German Wyandottes have completely smooth combs, arguably too small as well. Some UK Black and White Wyandottes have excellent combs in their first show season (neat, but with workings) which get oversized and misshapen in subsequent years.

SPECIAL MANAGEMENT REQUIREMENTS

Wyandottes are easy to keep and show, so are ideal for beginners, but considerable expertise is needed to win at major shows. The special feeding, housing and breeding requirements are detailed in *Exhibition Poultry Keeping*, also by David Scrivener, and include feeding and housing Columbian, Silver Laced, Silver Pencilled and White varieties to keep shanks and feet bright yellow while avoiding any yellowish tinge in white plumage. It also describes the double mating of Blacks (for black plumage, including undercolour, with yellow shanks/feet); the double mating of Laceds (for well laced females or exhibition males with clear back/shoulders); and the double mating of Partridge, Blue-Partridge, Silver Pencilled or Blue-Silver Pencilled Wyandottes to produce solid (black or blue) breasted males or finely pencilled females.

Bibliography

All published in UK unless otherwise stated.

American Bantam Association, *Bantam Standard*, USA, 1979. There are other editions.

American Bantam Association, *Cornish Bantams*, USA, 1981

American Bantam Association, *Wyandotte Bantams*, USA, 1984

American Poultry Association, *The American Standard of Perfection*, USA, 1890, 1974, 1985

American Poultry Association, *The Rosecomb Bantam*, USA, 1992

American Poultry Journal Yearbook, USA, 1913

Atkinson, Herbert, *The Old English Game Fowl*, 1924, 1960

Atkinson, Herbert, *Cock-fighting and Game Fowl*, 1938, 1877

Baldwin, John P., *Modern and Old English Game Bantams*, USA, 1940

Banning-Vogelpoel, A.C., *Japanese Bantams*, USA, 1983

Batty, Dr J., *Understanding Old English Game*, 1973

Batty, Dr J. and Bleazard, J.P., *Understanding Modern Game*, 1976

Bennett, Dr John C., *The Poultry Book*, USA, 1850

Broomhead, William W., *Poultry Breeding and Management*, circa 1930

Brown, Edward, *Races of Domestic Poultry*, 1906, 1985

Brown, Edward, *Poultry Breeding and Production*, 1929

Brown, J.T., *The Encyclopedia of Poultry*, 2 vols, 1909 and revised by J.S. Hicks edition, 1921

Campbell, E., *The Orpington and Its Varieties*, 1922, 1995, 2008

Crellin, William, *The Story of Old English Game Large and Small*, 1986

Der Grosse Geflügelstandard, Vols 1 and 2, Germany, *circa* 1980

Doyle, Martin, *The Illustrated Book of Domestic Poultry*, 1857

Easom Smith, Harold, articles in *Poultry World* magazine, 1968 to 1974

Easom Smith, Harold, *Bantams for Everyone*, 1967

Easom Smith, Harold, *Modern Poultry Development*, 1976

Ellett, Arthur E., *Modern Wyandottes*, 1908

Entwisle, William Flamank, *Bantams*, 1894, 1981

Fancy Fowl magazine, Vol. 1 , No.1. October 1981 to 2008

Feathered World magazine, various issues, 1892 to 2008

Feathered World Yearbooks, 1910 to 1938

Finsterbusch, C.A., *Cockfighting All Over the World*, USA 1929, UK 1980

Harris, Rod, *The Silkie*, Australia, 1980

Hawkey, K.J.G., *Understanding Indian Game*, 1978

Hewes, Theo., *The Book of the Hamburgs*, USA, 1905

Hewes, Theo., *Wyandottes in Colors*, USA, 1908

House, Charles Arthur, *Leghorn Fowls, Exhibition and Utility*, 1927

House, Charles Arthur, *Bantams and How to \ Keep Them, circa* 1930

Indian Game Club Centenary Year Book, 1986

Jeffrey, Fred P., *Bantam Breeding and Genetics*, 1977

Jeffrey, F.P. and Richardson, W., *Old English Game Bantams in the United States*, USA, 1991

Kay, Ian, *Stairway to the Breeds*, 1997

Keeling, Julia, *The Spirit of Japanese Game*, 2003

Kraft, John, *The British Faverolles Society Breed Book*, 1995

Lamon, Harry M. and Slocum, Rob R., *The Mating and Breeding of Poultry*, USA, 1927

Lind, L.R., *Aldrovandi on Chickens*, USA, 1963 (trans. from Latin of book published 1600)

Long, James, *Poultry for Prizes and Profit, circa* 1890

McGrew, T.F., *The Bantam Fowl*, USA, 1899, 1991

Moubray, Bonington, *Domestic Poultry*, 1842

Nederlandse Bond van Hoender-, Dwerghoender, Sier-, Watervogel, Hoenderstandaard, 1986

Outram, L.F., *Sussex Poultry*, 1934

Palin, John K., *Understanding Japanese Bantams*, 1980

Pigeons and Bantams magazine, Vol. 1, May 1947–April 1948

Plant, W.J., *Australorp History*, Australia, 1994

Poultry Club of Great Britain, *The Poultry Club Standards*, editions from 1886 to 1926

Poultry Club of Great Britain, *British Poultry Standards*, 1954, 1960, 1971, 1982, 1997

Poultry Club of Great Britain, *Yearbooks*, 1927 and 1985 to 2008

Poultry magazine, bound volume of 1901 issues

Poultry magazine, 1923 and 1924 Yearbooks

Poultry Press magazine, USA, 1980–2000

Poultry World magazine, various issues 1918 to 2005

Poultry World Yearbooks, 1913 to 1932

Powell-Owen, W., *The Welsummer*, 1932, 2004

Proud, Pringle, *Bantams as a Hobby*, 4th edition, 1912

Raines, H.P. and Marx, J.P.W., *The Wyandotte*, 1907, 2004

Robinson, John H., *Popular Breeds of Domestic Poultry*, USA, 1924

Schmidt, Horst, *Handbuch der Nutz- und Rassehühner*, Germany, 1985

Schmudde, Horst W., *Oriental Gamefowl*, USA, 2005

Scott, G.R., *The Rhode Island Red*, 1939

Scott, George Ryley, *The History of Cockfighting*, 1960, 1975

Shakespeare, Joseph, *The Bantams Down-to-Date*, USA, 1925

Silk, W.H., *Bantams and Miniature Fowl*, 1951, 1974

Sussex Poultry Club Year Book, 1952

Toothill, Fred, *The Modern Minorca Fowl*, 1925

Verhoff, Esther, and Rijs, Aad, *The Complete Encyclopedia of Chickens*, The Netherlands, 2003

Wandelt, Rüdiger and Wolters, Josef, *Handbuch der Hühnerrassen*, Germany, 1996

Wandelt, Rüdiger and Wolters, Josef, *Handbuch der Zwerghuhnrassen*, Germany, 1998

Weir, Harrison William, *The Poultry Book*, USA edition, 1905 (1st UK edition, 1902)

Williams, Rev. J.N., *Hamburghs in a Nutshell*, 1910

Wingfield, Rev. W.W. and Johnson, George, *The Poultry Book*, 1853

Wingfield, Rev. W.W. and Johnson, George, *The Cottage Gardener* magazine, 1855–56

Wiseman-Cunningham, R., *Gold and Silver Sebright Bantams*, 1905

Wright, Lewis, *The Book of Poultry*, Popular Edition, 1888

Wright, Lewis, *The New Book of Poultry*, 1902

Wright's Book of Poultry, revised by S.H. Lewer *et al.*, 1919 (after Wright's death)

Wulfften Palthe, A.W., *C.S.Th. van Gink's Poultry Paintings*, The Netherlands, 1992

Wulfften Palthe, A.W., *Ornithophilia*, The Netherlands, 1994

White Japanese and Sebright Bantams. Artist: F.J.S. Chatterton

Dark and Light Brahmas. Postcards given as a free gift with Feathered World *magazine, 5 April 1912. Artist: A.F. Lydon*

Index